Environmental Ethics for a Postcolonial World

Nature's Meaning

Series Editor: Roger S. Gottlieb, Professor of Philosophy, Worcester Polytechnic Institute

Each title in Nature's Meaning is created to have the personal stamp of a passionate and articulate spokesperson for environmental sanity. Intended to be engagingly written by experienced thinkers in their field, these books express the comprehensive and personal vision of the topic by an author who has devoted years to studying, teaching, writing about, and often being actively involved with the environmental movement. The books will be intended primarily as college texts, and as beautifully produced volumes, they will also appeal to a wide audience of environmentally concerned readers.

Integrating Ecofeminism, Globalization, and World Religions, by Rosemary Radford Ruether

Environmental Ethics for a Postcolonial World, by Deane Curtin

Environmental Ethics for a Postcolonial World

Deane Curtin

Rowman & Littlefield Publishers, Inc.
Lanham • Boulder • New York • Toronto • Oxford

ROWMAN & LITTLEFIELD PUBLISHERS, INC.

Published in the United States of America
by Rowman & Littlefield Publishers, Inc.
A wholly owned subsidiary of The Rowman & Littlefield Publishing Group, Inc.
4501 Forbes Boulevard, Suite 200, Lanham, Maryland 20706
www.rowmanlittlefield.com

PO Box 317
Oxford
OX2 9RU, UK

British Library Cataloguing in Publication Information Available

Library of Congress Cataloging-in-Publication Data

Curtin, Deane W.
  Environmental ethics for a postcolonial world / Deane Curtin.
    p. cm. — (Nature's meaning)
  Includes bibliographical references and index.
  ISBN 0-7425-2578-3 (alk. paper) — ISBN 0-7425-2579-1 (alk. paper)
  1. Environmental ethics. I. Title. II. Series. GE42.C89 2005
  179'.1—dc22   2004017642

Printed in the United States of America

♾™ The paper used in this publication meets the minimum requirements of American
National Standard for Information Sciences—Permanence of Paper for Printed Library
Materials, ANSI/NISO Z39.48-1992.

To the memory of my father, John L. Curtin, and
to my sons, Evan Curtin and Ian Curtin

CONTENTS

"Tarzan . . . was the name they had given to tiny Lord Greystoke, and which meant 'White-Skin.'"

—Edgar Rice Burroughs, *Tarzan of the Apes*

"Now . . . in what manner was this wonderful thing done?" And the officer answered: "An order was given, and they obeyed."

"But are the beasts as wise as the men?" said the chief.

"They obey, as the men do. Mule, horse, elephant, or bullock, he obeys his driver, and the driver his sergeant, and the sergeant his lieutenant, and the lieutenant his captain, and the captain his major, and the major his colonel, and the colonel his brigadier commanding three regiments, and the brigadier his general, who obeys the Viceroy, who is the servant of the Empress. Thus it is done."

"Would it were so in Afghanistan!" said the chief, "for there we obey only our wills."

"And for that reason," said the native officer, twirling his moustache, "your Amir whom you do not obey must come here and take orders from our Viceroy."

—Rudyard Kipling, *Servants of the Queen*

* * *

"Growth for the sake of growth is the ideology of the cancer cell."

—Edward Abbey, *A Voice Crying in the Wilderness*

"There is a sense in which the 'Nigerian' oil which the Americans, Europeans and Japanese buy is stolen property: it has been seized from its owners by force of arms and has not been paid for."

—Ken Saro-Wiwa, Nigerian writer, before his execution by the government of Nigeria because of his defense of the Ogoni homeland

PREFACE

If you are young, and fortunate enough to live in a country with good health care, it's very likely that by the time you retire you will live in a world of more than nine billion people, three billion more than inhabit this planet today. You will have lived through a half century of "globalization," the ever more intense search for finite resources to support a rapidly growing population. More people in pursuit of finite resources. . . . It's easy to imagine the demands—moral and economic—of the next fifty years. How do you plan to react to these profound changes that will unfold during your lifetime?

Today, more than ever before in history, we need to think about the ways social and environmental justice intersect, and we need to think about these issues in a truly integrated, global fashion. The arguments in this book center on the compelling need for those of us in the first world to think about the relationships of people to place outside of our normal comfort zones. More than three out of four people today live outside the so-called first world. Most of the world's biological diversity, as well as most of the world's human biological and cultural diversity, exist outside the first world. Clearly, one of the great dangers of an environmental ethic is that it will reflect only those voices that are easily heard, our own. Justice, not to mention pragmatism, requires that a new environmental ethic be plural-voiced. At a deep level, it needs to reflect the world of diverse places and peoples.

I have taught environmental ethics to college students for more than two decades. A question I wrestle with every semester is, "How is it possible to develop an awareness of third world issues in a classroom when we are so geographically and conceptually distant from the third world?" This book is designed to provide part of a response to that question. Part of the answer, of course, is to remember that there is a "third world in the first world." Many of the same conflicts that are making lives difficult for women in India are also affecting the lives of citizens of the United States. The question we raise can no longer be, "What can we do to help *them?*" The reality of economic and cultural globalization means that we must face the same issues that "others" are facing. If only out of self-interest, Americans need to be informed about globalization.

Furthermore, after decades of teaching, writing, and speaking across the United States, and in locations as diverse as India, Central America, North Africa, Italy, and Japan, I have developed approaches to these issues that allow American students to connect with a broader world. The Internet, for example, has fundamentally changed the ways students learn. Through much of the text, and through the appendix listing important websites, I open up some of this world to students so people who are affected by globalization can speak for themselves.

Unlike much writing on globalization, this book is deliberately written in a style that is concrete and empirically nuanced. It puts contemporary issues into their historical, political, and philosophical contexts. Thinking responsibly in a world of globalization requires us to practice the art of thinking "in context." To reach responsible conclusions we need to understand and appreciate "how we got here."

The book is intended for a broad reading audience including students like mine: intelligent, curious students at reasonably good undergraduate institutions who want to know "how the world works." It emphasizes narrative flow with a minimum of academic jargon.

Writing "in context," using appropriate sources of information such as the Internet, arguing that "their" issues are also "our" issues—these approaches are all important. However, they are not enough. Truly engaging questions of environmental justice over the next half century is really a project of the *moral imagination*. Right thinking needs to be complemented by moral empathy. This is why I frequently have recourse to works of literature.

While writing this book I was motivated by a rereading of Edgar Rice Burroughs's 1914 novel *Tarzan of the Apes*. The book spawned twenty-two sequels that sold more than thirty million copies. With its profits Burroughs purchased a California farm that was later subdivided into the contemporary city of Tarzana. What made this book so successful, and what can we learn from its success today?

Tarzan is an unveiled and unsubtle polemic for the evolutionary aristocracy of white people over Africans. Its corollaries include the superiority of men over women, and the power of technology over nature and those who live in nature, as well as the inherent caste superiority of some animals over others in the "animal kingdom." (Tarzan is "of the apes," not the gorillas.)

In opposition to *Tarzan*, I ask readers to consider an alternative: Mary Shelley's classic book, *Frankenstein*. Like Burroughs, Shelley imagined a Creature living on the border between culture and nature. But, unlike Tarzan, Shelley's Creature looks back on human culture's violent attempt to gain godlike control over nature with horror and foreboding. In sharp contrast to human culture, the Creature is peaceful. Shelley notes that he is a vegetarian, for example, in order not to conflict with the ecological niche occupied by humans. Burroughs's bloodthirsty aristocratic gentleman, by contrast, enjoys killing just for the sake of killing. Senseless killing is one of his aristocratic privileges.

These works of the literary imagination, then, pose similar questions of continuing relevance about the relationships of people to place. They do it through imagining a creature who occupies a sort of hybrid space between nature and human culture. Their sharply different moral conclusions frame many of the questions readers of this book will need to answer over the next half century.

Philosophically, this book centers on an analysis of the puzzling legacy of the British Utilitarians: Jeremy Bentham, James Mill, and John Stuart Mill. The voice of liberal reform and egalitarianism in Europe, Bentham wrote a complete set of laws for Great Britain's most important colony, India, hoping to be named its colonial governor. The Mills spent their professional lives working for the East India Company, each as Examiner of Indian Correspondence. The Utilitarian experiment in India was perhaps the only case of truly great philosophers actually writing the social, economic, and environmental legislation for millions of people.

In retrospect, we can see that the Utilitarians decided to embrace *both* Burroughs's Tarzan and Shelley's Creature. The jungle laws of Tarzan applied to the colonies while the humanistic vision of the Creature applied to "civilization." In the words of John Stuart Mill, "Exactly in proportion as *Utility* is the object of every pursuit, may we regard a nation as civilized."

Chapter 4, then, examines a concrete, contemporary example of the Utilitarian legacy: the population crisis. The Utilitarians were closely allied to Reverend Thomas Malthus, who taught at the East India Company's university, Haileybury. Malthus famously argued that, in the long run, population growth must outpace food production. The result of this inevitable "law" is tragedy. Population does not admit of an ethical or democratic solution; only "war, pestilence, and famine" can stem the tide of population growth.

One of Malthus's critics was William Godwin, Mary Shelley's father. Godwin believed in the ability of human beings to control their own fate. He made this argument explicitly with reference to the population issue. Malthus responded to Godwin in language that is curiously similar to contemporary dismissal of the possibility of ethics in public affairs. Godwin, according to Malthus, was a utopian dreamer who thought more about the way he wished the world might be, instead of how it really is.

Following the Malthusian legacy, some contemporary first world environmentalists have argued that the critical environmental problem is "the population bomb," in Paul Ehrlich's words. Malthusian theorists, like Ehrlich and Garrett Hardin, have concluded that third world population problems defy democratic and ethical solutions. Our only solution is to close our borders and "let them drown" until their populations fall below the land's carrying capacity.

Chapter 4 argues in detail that the Malthusian approach is wrong in both theory and in application. In fact, ethical community development based on the democratic reconciliation of people with place is better informed about the dynamics of population growth, and far more effective in actually addressing population issues, than the Malthusian approach.

These Malthusian conclusions are often combined today with a call to stop immigration—legal and illegal—in order to prevent damage to America's natural resources: wilderness areas and National Parks. However, the American concept of "wilderness" was a colonial construction that conveniently ignored the presence of indigenous peoples. Further-more, most of the "wilderness areas" in third world countries have long been inhabited. In pursuit of tourist dollars local governments have often divided people from place by forcibly "creating wilderness."

Chapters 6 and 7 follow up the philosophical, historical, and eco-nomic conclusions of the previous chapters by examining concrete, con-temporary issues that are the result of cross-cultural conflict over people in relation to place. One such issue is the controversy in the Pacific North-west over the Makah tribe's reassertion of their right to hunt whales. Sev-eral "radical" American environmental groups, such as the Sea Shepherds, opposed the Makah. This conflict provides a classic case through which we can examine the rights of indigenous peoples as they respond to out-side protest.

Other concrete issues examined in these chapters are the threat of ge-netically modified seeds to indigenous agriculture, such as corn produc-tion in Mexico as well as the new soybean industry in the Brazilian Amazon to produce food for cattle production. These practices have in-troduced both genetically modified seeds and industrial pesticides in areas that have been remote from industrialized agriculture. The social and en-vironmental consequences of such practices can be devastating. In Mex-ico, for example, GMO seeds are cross-pollinating with traditional Mexican corn. In the near future, indigenous corn, the foundation of food security, may no longer exist.

The positive ethical position that emerges from examination of such cases holds that ethical development in ecological communities must be based on augmenting the actual capability to function within a commu-nity context. The solution to the population problem, for example, lies in a cluster of capabilities typically exercised by women: the ability to secure appropriate healthcare, safe water, and a secure source of basic foods grown at the local level.

In conclusion, I suggest, cautiously, that social and environmental jus-tice are, or at least can be, compatible, even in a world of more than nine billion people. Of course, nothing so important can happen by accident. It is not too late to plan for a just future.

My appreciation to three talented research assistants who helped with this book: Anne Kautzer, Bethany Mueller, and Emily Wenzel. Sara Bergan, Executive Director of the Great Plains Institute for Sustainable

Development, provided invaluable help with chapter 1. Thanks also to Roger Gottlieb, academic editor of this series, as well as Brian Romer of Rowman & Littlefield.

* * *

Parts of chapter 3 concerning the green revolution were adapted from "Making Peace with the Earth: Indigenous Agriculture and the Peace Politics of the Green Revolution," *Environmental Ethics*, vol. 17 (spring 1995): 59–73.

CHAPTER ONE

ONE WORLD UNDER GOD

AWilderness, in contrast with those areas where man and his works dominate the landscape, is hereby recognized as an area where the earth and its community of life are untrammeled by man, where man himself is a visitor who does not remain" (U.S. Congress, 1). Thus reads the landmark piece of environmental legislation that established the legal definition of wilderness in the United States, the Wilderness Act of 1964. Those of us who care deeply about the preservation of nature can rightly look to this legislation as the consummation of a century of environmental activism aimed at saving the country's remaining wild places.

Perhaps the greatest saint of the American environmental movement was John Muir (1834–1914), founder of the Sierra Club and influential advisor to President Teddy Roosevelt. Muir was the author of *My First Summer in the Sierra*, an account of his experiences in the High Sierras of California in the place that would later become Yosemite National Park. He left civilization behind in the hope that "I might learn to live like the wild animals. . . ." (Muir [1911] 1987, 3). In his book he described how he disdained the elements of human culture that were changing the Yosemite Valley: the domesticated sheep that grazed there were nothing more than "locusts." Untamed wilderness, for Muir, was sacred. He described the High Sierras as "temple wilderness." The sacredness of nature could only be experienced in places untouched by the human hand.

Reading the text of the Wilderness Act today, we can easily detect Muir's influence on the ways we think about the relationship of people to place. Wilderness and human culture must be held apart, according to this American tradition. Wilderness is "untrammeled by man," a place "where man himself is a visitor who does not remain." This definition of wilderness implies that there are also parts of nature that *are* suited to human use. It divides nature into two zones: those suitable for human habitation, and those that are set apart from civilization.

The Wilderness Act explains why this division of nature into zones is necessary, given the dynamics of American culture: wilderness is needed "In order to assure that an increasing population, accompanied by expanding settlement and growing mechanization, does not occupy and modify all areas within the United States. . . ." (U.S. Congress, 1). In typical American fashion, we decided to conquer by division. Land either has value in itself (intrinsic value), which places it beyond human use, or it exists as a resource for human beings (extrinsic value).

Those who spend time in America's wilderness areas are familiar with the trail signs that read, "You Are Now Entering the Wilderness." These signs always make me want to encourage my hiking companions to take a photograph at these spots: one foot in the wilderness, the other in civilization. Although both sides may look the same, the legal difference can be momentous. On one side, for example, logging and mining are allowed. On the other side nature is to remain undisturbed.

Looking back from the perspective of the twenty-first century, we can understand why Muir regarded human culture as a sea of locusts, bent on destroying everything in its path. Ours is a culture defined by the ideology of "progress" and faith in "Manifest Destiny." As Euro-Americans swept over the grasslands of Kentucky, through the endless plains of the Midwest, across the Rocky Mountains, and arrived finally at the Pacific Ocean, we fundamentally changed the land we "conquered." We brought a kind of agriculture that required the horse and plow; it fundamentally disrupted the ecology of prairie grasslands. We built cities as hubs for commerce, with spokes reaching north to the traplines of the Canadian wilderness and south to the place where the Mississippi River empties into the Gulf of Mexico. To those, such as Muir, who were anguished over this confident faith in industrial progress, it seemed clear that these increasingly rare tracts of unaltered land would soon be lost without a national system to protect wild places.

We should all be grateful to Muir and the other saints of the American environmental movement. The successes of this movement stand alongside those of the civil rights movement, the trade union movement, and the women's rights movement as great achievements of American liberalism. Despite being the most powerful industrial machine in the history of humankind, the United States has also succeeded in securing a large measure of social justice for women and racial minorities, as well as environmental justice for some parts of nature.

However, I believe that in an increasingly interconnected world, we need to recognize that this popular understanding of nature's zones is distinctively American, and it rests on a kind of cultural amnesia. This cognitive and emotional lapse in the ways we think of people in relation to place continues to affect our conceptions of the American past, as well as the ways we think of ourselves today and into the future. The concept of wilderness, after all, is much more a social concept than a natural category. It is a tool through which we depict aspects of our common past to ourselves.

If we look carefully at Muir's *My First Summer in the Sierra*, for example, we note that he not only encountered sheep and their shepherds in the Yosemite Valley. He also met members of local tribal groups who had used and occupied the valley long before the arrival of white settlers in California. A member of the Digger tribe who accompanied Muir through the lower valleys is described in these words: "The Indian kept in the background, saying never a word, as if he belonged to another species" ([1911] 1987, 10). Muir's irritation with human civilization may have caused him to look past the fact that the Yosemite Valley was inhabited before he arrived. The place by which the American wilderness is defined was not really a wilderness.

If we broaden our view to include all of North America, we recognize that almost the entire "wilderness" was already inhabited by a vast array of tribal groups speaking different languages and practicing widely varying connections to place. The land colonists first encountered was not "untrammeled by man." North America was already thoroughly inhabited.

So, how could anyone have thought they were encountering a "wilderness" as they moved west across North America? The answer has more to do with the minds of the colonists than with the reality of the place. As white colonists moved west they imported a European philosophical idea with them, the doctrine of *terra nullius*. This was the philosophical key used to answer the question, "How can public land, owned by no one, be

3

transformed morally into private property?" North America somehow needed to be thought of as uninhabited to provide colonists with a moral and legal claim to land.

Literally, *terra nullius* means "vacant land." "Indians"—those vastly different tribal groups whose differences were subsumed under a single, geographically ignorant name—may have *used* the land, according to this doctrine. That much was impossible to deny. But, according to the doctrine of *terra nullius*, they did not *own* it. Euro-American colonists classified all Indians as nomadic. They inhabited no place permanently. Rather, they traveled constantly in pursuit of game. According to European ideas, nomadic people may *occupy* the land, but they do not *own* it.

We now know that this gross simplification of tribal cultures under the name "Indian" was untrue. Some tribes practiced farming rather than hunting and gathering. Coastal tribes often fished. Nevertheless, this stereotype of the nomadic hunter-gatherer was enough to justify colonial claims to ownership. Hunter-gatherers *use* the land without transforming it into private property.

Colonists used the doctrine of *terra nullius*, then, to claim that the vast expanse of North America was there for the taking. It was not owned by anyone. In European terms, only *work* transformed wild nature into private property: to establish a moral and legal claim to ownership a man had to *alter* the land. Agriculture gave the new Americans a moral claim to ownership of the land that had previously been occupied by Indians. Fifteen thousand years of hunting and gathering provided no moral claim at all.

If the doctrine of *terra nullius* cleared men's minds for western expansion, other colonial policies literally cleared people out of the way. We still like to forget that history's most extensive and complete genocide occurred in the Americas: within two hundred years of Columbus's landing, 98 percent of the original population of the hemisphere had been eradicated (Churchill 1997, 97). Our cultural amnesia allows us to neglect the fact that the American "wilderness" was not uninhabited. It was *created* through the extermination—by means both intentional and unintentional—of those who had *stayed* and made homes in the "wilderness" over a period of perhaps 15,000 years. From this perspective, the definition of wilderness in the Wilderness Act can be viewed as an astonishing act of cultural imperialism.

Traveling in federally designated wilderness areas today, we can witness the effects of these imported European ideas. One of the actual wilderness areas the authors of the Wilderness Act had in mind was the border country between Minnesota and Canada. This is a vast region of interconnected lakes with a rich history of interaction between the tribes and French traders who transported their skins across these waters to Lake Superior for sale in the East and in Europe. After passage of the Wilderness Act, the United States side was named the Boundary Waters Canoe Area Wilderness (BWCAW). Under the influence of the American definition of wilderness, all human residents were removed when the BWCAW was created. American policy *created* a wilderness by removing human inhabitants. On the Canadian side, however, a similar wilderness was created called the Quetico. There, tribes were allowed to stay after the creation of wilderness. Across the border, real wilderness does not require the expulsion of human beings.

Recently, scholars have vigorously challenged the "sacred wilderness" theme in American culture. They insist that a more accurate reading of our history requires us to admit far greater interconnectedness of people and "wilderness" than we would like to allow. William Cronon, an environmental historian, has written, "the way we describe and understand [the] world is so entangled with our own values and assumptions that the two can never be fully separated. What we mean when we use the word 'nature' says as much about ourselves as about the things we label with that word" (Cronon 1995a, 25). Cronon is not suggesting that nature is just a figment of the human imagination. There is something "out there," as we like to say. His point is that the only access we have to that reality is through our cultural concepts. Concretely, wilderness policy in this country is a reflection of our *mental image* of wilderness. To a large extent, in Cronon's terms, we still view our alternative relationships to nature through two categories: the sublime and the frontier (Cronon 1995b, 72).

Cronon pushes the cultural specificity of the wilderness idea even further: "Ever since the nineteenth century, celebrating wilderness has been an activity mainly for well-to-do city folks. Country people generally know far too much about working the land to regard *un*worked land as their ideal. In contrast, elite urban tourists and wealthy sportsmen projected their leisure-time frontier fantasies onto the American landscape and so created wilderness in their own image" (1995b, 79). The concept of untrammeled wilderness is an artifact of the urban elite moral imagination.

It would be unfortunate enough if our cultural amnesia caused us not to recognize the truth about our past. However, I think the categories that were developed through our colonial history continue to distort the ways we view ourselves in relation to people and place. Because of our idea that wilderness is not occupied by human beings, even the most progressive among us have tended to see problems of environmental justice as distinct from issues in social and economic justice. The radical environmental philosopher George Sessions has complained that integrating the social justice movement with the environmental movement weakens both. An environmental ethic, for Sessions, is ecocentric. It is centered on place, not people. The social justice movement, on the contrary, is human-centered (anthropocentric). Therefore, from Sessions's ecocentric perspective, the environmental movement competes with the social justice movement to the detriment of the environment. Sessions concludes, "anthropocentric urban-pollution and social justice concerns cannot be allowed to take precedence over the issue of dealing realistically with the urgency of the global ecological crisis" (Sessions 1993, 163).

One consequence of this radical ecocentrism, as we will see in chapter 4, is that the increasing population of the third world is depicted as the major threat to environmental preservation. There are simply too many of "them" to save the planet. Some extremists, such as the ecologist Garrett Hardin, have even suggested that people in the third world are in such utter contradiction to environmental preservation that we need to dispense with ethical treatment of people if we hope to save the environment. In the face of the crisis in environmental justice, the extremists say, human justice then becomes a luxury we can no longer afford.

Paradoxically, many radical environmentalists—those who assume that environmental and social justice necessarily conflict—seem to assume that human beings are unnatural; we may be *in* nature, but we are not part of it. This, too, is part of the Euro-American environmental legacy. Many cultures, including those that were destroyed by American colonialism, see human beings as distinctive parts of nature, not beings whose nature sets them apart from, and outside of, nature.

Cronon also recognizes this unfortunate consequence of the wilderness idea. He writes, "This, then, is the central paradox: wilderness embodies a dualistic vision in which the human is entirely outside the natural. If we allow ourselves to believe that nature, to be true, must also be wild, then our very presence in nature represents its fall" (1995b, 80–81). The American wilderness idea resonates with the Christian myth of Adam and Eve.

A fundamental question we need to address in this book, therefore, is, "What is an environmental ethic?" Should we base an environmental ethic on the assumption that people and place are categorically distinct, or should an environmental ethic help us to understand the ways in which human beings are one kind of natural being, an intelligent animal in a place that is more-than-human?

This book is an extended argument for the idea that human beings are one part of the community of nature. We may differ from other coinhabitants of the earth, but fundamentally we are part of one community, the ecological community. An environmental ethic should see environmental justice, social justice, and economic justice as parts of the same whole, not as dissonant competitors. No adequate account of "wilderness" is possible, for example, without full recognition of the fact that the concept of wilderness is partly a question of social justice.

The fundamental commitment to environmental ethics as an ethic of the whole community is important, furthermore, not just because it corrects American conceptions of the relationship of people to place. A second basic argument advanced in this book is the claim that the Euro-American ideas of place continue to function as a lens for viewing the rest of the world. This lens systematically distorts what it seeks to understand. All people and all places are *not* the same, despite the comforting aphorism to the contrary. When we project comfortable Euro-American ideas onto the rest of the world, we often create problems instead of solutions.

Candace Slater has argued, for example, that our views of the Amazonian rain forest embody exactly the distorting lens about the wilderness that we have been examining in relation to American culture. She calls this the "Edenic Narrative." Almost as if it were the "jungle" of countless Disney narratives, we unconsciously project a false image onto the real rain forest as a kind of perfect Garden of Eden before the fall. Indigenous peoples are residents of this fantasyland, despite the fact that they make up less than 2 percent of the population (Slater 1995, 114).

Our image of the Brazilian rain forest is contradicted by reality. The idealized environmental "purity" of these tribes is undermined by the reality that some tribes have actively collaborated with miners and loggers.

7

Some carry cell phones and communicate regularly with the media in the United States. Slater remarks, "The real difficulty with Edenic representations is not even that they are partially untrue, if not downright false. Romanticizations of a particular place and people, they dehumanize through idealization" (1995, 129). This process through which people we claim to care about are dehumanized through our cultural/environmental categories is an example of the way our conceptual lens causes problems rather than provides solutions.

I will come back to this fantasy aspect of the wilderness idea in chapter 8, where I examine the ways American consumerism uses images of wilderness. For now, let us stick with the real impact these fantasies have on people when they are exported to cultures that are profoundly different from our own. Under American influence, many countries created their own natural parks, places where people are only "visitors." But these countries are not like the United States. Unlike in the United States, where genocide created the impression of a vast, uninhabited wilderness, in Asia, no such genocide occurred. Rich soils and diverse agriculture led to high levels of population density thousands of years ago, long before the quick acceleration in population over the past two hundred years. American ideas of the wilderness were, therefore, exported to countries like India and Nepal, which lacked the open space that was created in North America. When people are removed to create a "wilderness" in these places there is no simple solution to the question of where to put them. In most cases, all arable land has long been settled. The social creation of wilderness displaces people who have no place to go.

In the jungle of southern Nepal, Chitwan National Park was created when the people who were indigenous to the land were removed to create a wilderness experience for tourists who pay hundreds of dollars a night to sleep in tree houses and experience "wild" nature outside their windows. Seen from the air, however, Chitwan looks like a giant donut. In the center is what remains of the jungle, now the National Park. Around the periphery of the park there is a circle of deforestation where people have been resettled. Wilderness caused problems with population density that did not exist before. These people's lives have been made even worse by a corrupt royal family that extracts elephants and other large mammals for sale to zoos around the world. Those in power are urban elites who profit from tourists and the commodification of nature, not from helping the poor.

Nepal is not alone in causing conflict between social and environmental priorities. The same situation occurred in Indira Gandhi National Park in India, where people were removed to create a wilderness for large mammals such as tigers and elephants. In many parts of Africa, and in Malaysia and Thailand, similar social injustices are caused by "sustainable development." Often, as happens in Nepal, the new global economic elite joins with old, local sources of corrupt power to further disenfranchise the most vulnerable people in poor countries. The export of the wilderness idea usually benefits the elite at the expense of both the environment and the poor.

When we export our conceptions of nature, culture, and the economy to the rest of the world, the mixture is unpredictable, and sometimes explosive. Ideas that we connect with responsible nature preservation can cause deep social injustice in other contexts: people are dislodged from their longstanding places in nature with disastrous consequences. If we wish to arrive at a better environmental ethic we need to become good listeners to cultures that are different from our own. We need to decenter ourselves from self-understandings as "the experts" and admit that other cultures could have something to teach us.

Problems similar to these arise when we export American ideas of economic progress. Americans are generous people. However, many times when we attempt to help others economically we fail. What works in one context may not work in another. The attempt to help actually worsens the lives of those we care about. Not surprisingly, this disconnect between our intentions and their consequences leads to what might be called "compassion fatigue": "Didn't we give money last year to alleviate starvation in Africa? Why are they starving again this year?" We give up the attempt to help when good intentions go awry.

This disconnect between good intentions and consequences should not be surprising, however, if we consider the enormous differences between the situation early in our history and the contemporary situation in the so-called third world. The United States became phenomenally wealthy by exploiting its "frontier" as well as the wealth of other countries to jump-start its economy. In a crowded world, this unfettered access to natural wealth no longer exists.

International lending agencies, such as the World Bank, often counsel "developing" countries to exploit their natural wealth as a way of catching up to the "developed" world. Often, the natural resources that built the American economy were extracted from colonized countries long ago by distant powers bent on profiting from their colonies. And in most situations, the smaller pie of environmental riches left over after colonization must be split among a far greater number of people than in the United States.

The term "sustainable development," for example, was coined originally to refer to forms of community development that strengthen the community from the bottom up, while also respecting the impact the community has on the environment. In the hands of many banks, corporations, and international development agencies, however, the term has come to mean just the opposite of what it originally meant. Frequently, sustainable development is nothing more than a euphemism for top-down economic development from wealthy countries and banks to other, less developed, countries and banks. The wealthy add to their riches, while the poor are left to suffer.

What counts as development amounts to rapid funding for the industrialization of cities and the mechanization of farming. The combined result is that human work is less valuable. People in countries that are already densely populated then migrate to the cities in search of jobs. When new jobs are not created the newly landless poor move to vast urban slums. In large part, the slums of the third world are caused by misguided first world development policies. Urban problems are often caused by rural failures.

One clear model of sustainable development in its original meaning is Mahatma Gandhi's concept of village *swaraj*. Gandhi used the spinning wheel every day to make his own clothing. More importantly, the spinning wheel symbolized to Indians and British colonists the need for development to empower people at the village level. Gandhi showed that there was no need for Indians to export raw cloth to England to be tailored and then reexported to India at exorbitant prices. Indians were capable of making their own clothing, without the added cost of colonialism.

Still today, one of the most successful sustainable development programs in India trains poor village girls to sew. These girls are offered six months of training to be a seamstress. Upon successful completion of the course, each is given a sewing machine, which allows her to return to her village and set up a business. The poorest of the poor then become business owners who provide valuable services to their communities: good clothing at a reasonable price where the profits are reinvested in the community. Still today, many real solutions to the world's social and environmental problems are like those imagined by Gandhi: low-tech, simple approaches that employ local people and resources, and that keep power at the village level. In India, for example, the production of biogas is far more sustainable and culturally appropriate than nuclear or hydroelectric power. Cow dung is abundantly available. Often the so-called Untouchables (Dalits) earn an income by being paid to collect the refuse. Cow dung can easily be converted into methane gas for cooking. Villagers dig a hole and line it with bricks. A piece of PVC pipe is inserted, the hole is covered, and within hours after shoveling in the cow dung methane gas flows through the pipe.

Methane is not a perfect fuel. It contributes to global warming. However, comparison of methane by traditional people to industrialized countries' contribution to global warming is misguided. Survival should not be equated with the production of luxuries for a consumer society. Methane also helps maintain women's health since it burns cleaner than the other alternatives: coal and wood. When these less sustainable fuels are used in unventilated houses women suffer from severe respiratory problems. Methane stoves relieve these problems. Furthermore, methane, unlike nuclear power or the megadams required to create hydroelectric power, keeps political power at the local level. Village people control their own energy resources, not powerful urban industrialists and politicians.

In stark contrast to this Gandhian approach to sustainable development, much of what is called sustainable development uses diametrically opposed methods. Sustainable development often means top-down, high-tech development designed to transfer large-scale industrial economic development to the "developing world." Far from empowering the world's poor and vulnerable populations, this kind of unquestioned faith in first world economic progress has disenfranchised billions, contributed to environmental destruction, and caused urban slums as people migrate to the cities in hope of finding work that does not exist. Chapter 5 considers these issues in detail by considering the Gandhian approach to ecodevelopment, environmental resistance movements around the world that are localized defenses of human relationships to place, and, finally, the philosophy of development that is consistent with this model.

I am insisting that those who care about environmental justice in a globalized world need to move past the American idea that social and environmental justice are categorically different. Technology has largely split Americans from nature. Very few of us grow our own food anymore. We visit "nature" while on two-week vacations during the summer.

In contrast, around the world, many people are connected to nature in ways that Americans can barely imagine. They grow diverse crops to meet the nutritional needs of their families. They access the forests for building materials. They also depend on what remains of the biological commons for natural medicines. To cut off access to the environment for these people is like suddenly closing all the pharmacies, lumberyards, and grocery stores to Americans. The disruption to our culture would be disastrous. We would not be able to adapt.

The same is true when subtle, intricate cultural relationships to nature are suddenly disrupted in traditional societies. These relationships between human cultures and nature have worked throughout the centuries. They depend on local wisdom that manages the mutual adaptation of culture and nature. To disrupt these local arrangements—even with good intentions—without knowing what is at stake amounts to cultural imperialism. It assumes the magisterial voice of the colonist who "knows" what is good for distant cultures. To avoid this, it is imperative that we see how an environmental ethic requires and includes social justice. In the words of the great American ecologist Aldo Leopold, "a land ethic changes the role of *Homo sapiens* from conqueror of the land-community to plain member and citizen of it" (Leopold [1949] 1970, 240).

When we begin to connect environmental and social justice, and see them in a deeper historical context, I believe a further insight emerges. Many of the arguments for the export of American ideas about the economy, culture, and nature—ideas that sound good if they are taken out of context—are really just updated versions of the old arguments that were made for colonialism. This does not mean that Americans wish misfortune on the rest of the world. But we need to know enough history to appreciate the fact that the people who colonized much of Africa, Asia, and the Western Hemisphere thought of themselves as performing a moral good. Most of us would now agree that they were mistaken. Unless we wish to exempt ourselves from history, we must consider the possibility that what we now consider to be a moral good when we attempt to help others is a form of cultural amnesia.

As I develop the case for an alternative environmental ethic, then, one that is coherent, but also diverse enough to include the world's diverse people and places, I will need to examine a wide variety of issues that are not often thought of as parts of an environmental ethic. When we see environmental justice and social justice as connected, then issues of rural migration to cities become environmental issues. Questions of the urban environment are just as important as the preservation of wilderness. The same is true of population pressures. A simple view of the world's environmental problems has it that there are simply too many people in the third world. Their very lives are sometimes regarded as an unsustainable luxury that the world can no longer afford. However, this view of the relationship between human population and the environment is tragic because it projects inappropriate Euro-American attitudes onto contexts where they do not belong. As we will see in chapter 4, the most common "solutions" for population problems are among the *causes* of the population crisis.

Finally, in focusing on the kinds of damage that occur to traditional cultures when inappropriate ideas of development are exported, we might easily depict these cultures simply as victims. This, too, would be an unfortunate stereotype. The other half of the story is that these cultures often do not need an imported environmental ethic. Because of longstanding connections to place, these cultures have evolved exquisitely subtle and complex relationships to nature. They include food gathering and cultivation, the production of medicines for local diseases, and cultural stories that connect people with place.

Once we see that these cultures that are defined as needing development are already developed in ways that we can scarcely imagine, we are also in a position to understand the indigenous environmental resistance movements that are emerging around the globe. From tribal groups in the United States asserting their cultural and environmental rights as spelled out in treaties to the Ogoni people in Nigeria who are fighting to save their homeland from Shell Oil, from the Chipko Movement in India whose defense of the Himalayan foothills gave rise to the term "tree hugger" to the Huarani in the rain forests of Ecuador, people are not just standing still, allowing unsustainable and culturally inappropriate development to wash over them. These people are not just victims. They represent cultures with an indigenous environmental ethic, and they want to world to know what they stand for. In short, the most important environmental activists today are not the Sierra Club and similar organizations, as important as their work might be. The leading edge of a new environmental ethic emerges from the voices of those diverse people around the globe who are determined to defend their homes, now and for generations to come.

I have said it is important that we discuss the connected issues of social and environmental justice in a way that is concrete, and that reveals the diversity of people and places. So, let me turn to a concrete example to illustrate the hidden connections between the first world and the third world that I am attempting to highlight.

In the 1960s Manitoba Hydro, a corporation owned by the Province of Manitoba, Canada, embarked on a plan to control the Nelson River Drainage Basin in central Canada to produce electrical energy. The Nelson Drainage Basin is so vast that it covers much of the provinces of Alberta, Saskatchewan, Manitoba, and Ontario in Canada, as well as smaller regions of the states of Montana, North Dakota, South Dakota, and Minnesota in the United States.

The first dam on the Nelson River provided power to the International Nickel Company's mining and smelting operations in Canada. However, as technology improved for long-distance transmission of electrical power, thirteen additional power generation plants were added. By the middle 1970s the once mighty Churchill River had been drained and diverted into the Nelson River, relieving Manitoba Hydro of the need to build separate power generation plants on the Churchill. This diversion saved the company in excess of $600 million.

Manitoba Hydro has represented the Nelson River project as a case of ecologically sustainable development. Water, after all, is a renewable resource. However, the diversion project was undertaken without a careful study of its environmental impact. Only in recent decades has the true cost of the project become clear. Flooding of the combined rivers has caused extensive erosion of shoreline. One study found that forty to fifty meters of shoreline are being lost every year (Krotz 1991, 42). The erosion felled trees, contributing to greenhouse gases, and it caused the river to become murky with sediment. The flooding also disrupted the permafrost, which, in turn, caused mercury to leach into the water. Mercury poisoning harmed the fish and wildlife.

Fishing and trapping were the two main forms of subsistence for the five villages of Cree people who live along the Nelson and Churchill rivers. The diversion project destroyed their economy as well as their health. Suicide rates and alcoholism have worsened dramatically since the 1960s. The destruction of permafrost has caused severe problems with mobility. Trappers, who used to be able to count on solid ground, can no longer find access to their trap lines. Hazardous currents have caused deaths among fisherfolk despite generations of experience with northern rivers.

After more than a decade of unregulated change to the northern environment and indigenous peoples, the Manitoba government and Hydro Manitoba negotiated a Northern Flood Agreement in 1977. It provided land in exchange for every acre that was destroyed, protection for wildlife, community infrastructure, and eradication of poverty and unemployment. In the years following the agreement, none of these treaty provisions was met.

Finally, the Manitoba government sought to abrogate the 1977 treaty with a set of "Comprehensive Implementation Agreements" with each of the five Cree communities. Unlike the 1977 agreement, which promised restitution for all damage into the future, the Comprehensive Implementation Agreements proposed a one-time payment in exchange for all future claims. As is often the case where tribal groups face this kind of outside pressure, the Comprehensive Implementation Agreements split the Cree communities. Four of the five communities accepted the Agreement. Chief Norman Flett, speaking for the Split Lake Cree First Nation, reported that "Our traditional lands and way of life have been devastated and desecrated by the adverse impacts of the Hydro Project." He then explained the reasons for accepting the Comprehensive Implementation Agreement:

> Over the past ten years the Split Lake Cree leadership, in concert with our Elders and our people, have accepted the fact that we cannot change the past. Nevertheless, we continue to grieve for a way of life that has passed. In the manner of our forefathers, the present generation are searching for a way to adapt our total physical, social, and economic environment for the benefit of all our people. We are keenly aware of all the social and economic challenges we are facing. We are moving to deal with these challenges within the context of the existing environment and our traditional culture. (Flett n.d., 2)

When this agreement was put to a vote in 1993, 93 percent of the Split Lake community approved it. Eventually, all but the Cross Lake community voted to give up their claims against Hydro Manitoba.

Speaking in 1999, Vice-Chief John Miswagon expressed a conflicting view, which represented the continuing determination of the Cross Lake community to enforce the terms of the original Northern Flood Agreement. Miswagon, whose thirteen-year-old brother had died in the floodwaters, reported the remarks of the president of Manitoba Hydro about such incidents: "we'll sit down and work this out, but it's just the cost of doing business" (Miswagon 1999, 4). Miswagon responded, "I ask myself what kind of society permits this kind of mentality? A corporate society—that's what! I strongly believe that in Canada it is still illegal to kill someone, but the message we get in Cross Lake is that it is okay to do this if you are going to make money as a result" (1999, 4).

Miswagon's fundamental point was that the problems Manitoba Hydro had created were *ethical*, not simply economic: "The governments must realize that once you've KILLED THE WATER, KILLED THE FISH, KILLED THE FORESTS AND ANIMALS—THAT MONEY *CANNOT* BE EATEN" (1999, 8).

Unfortunately, the events briefly recounted here among the Cree are hauntingly familiar to anyone who follows the practices of private energy corporations and national governments in the "third world": Texaco in the Brazilian rainforests, Shell Oil in Nigeria, the Narmada Dam in India, the Three Gorges project in China. The events played out among the Cree are part of a global pattern. Progress for industrialized cultures causes displacement for relatively small, sometimes indigenous cultures that are dismissed as being inconsequential to the future of "civilization." These projects are part of a pervasive faith in economic development as an ultimate good, a faith so devout that it apparently doesn't invoke the basic moral principle of informed consent for those who are affected most directly.

Because these small cultures are often so closely tied to nature—through their material cultures as well as their cultural stories—it is difficult to distinguish violations of human rights from questions of environmental justice. People and places are just part of the cost of "doing business."

We need to ask, "Why are these conflicts so common today?" One answer, surely, is that the people who are most directly affected are "remote" from those who benefit. The very term "third world" suggests a world twice *removed* from ours. According to common ways of thinking, the third world is also two steps *below* us in terms of development, both cultural and economic. Surely there is also a utilitarian calculus at work here: a few are harmed for the benefit of many.

Remoteness, however, needs to be understood in two ways. The Cree people are geographically remote, but they are often cognitively remote as well. Disastrous events can befall them, and most of us remain ignorant. We might be upset by the policies of Manitoba Hydro, if we only knew about them, but for some reason we don't.

Actually, there is more to the story of Manitoba Hydro. The power generated by Manitoba Hydro far exceeds what can be used in Canada. Forty percent of all its power is now exported to the United States. States as far away as Texas benefit from the Crees's misfortune. However, most of the exported power, more than 90 percent, is used in my own state, Minnesota, by Xcel Energy and its customers. By one way of accounting, this energy is cheap: the rate for Manitoba's "sustainable" energy is roughly half what we pay for energy generated within the state of Minnesota through a combination of coal, nuclear, and other fuels. However, the energy bills we pay don't take into account what economists call "externalities": death, depression, alcoholism, and the utter destruction of one of the world's great ecosystems.

In a world of pervasive globalization, it is hazardous business to dismiss conflicts of the sort we are discussing just because they are thought of as geographically remote. The world is now intricately connected in ways that often escape our notice. More importantly, the sense of cognitive remoteness that characterizes our relationships to much of the world is surely a case of what psychologists call "denial." We may be dimly aware that we don't *want* to discover more. What difference would knowledge make? Perhaps sensing the enormity of the task we don't want to reverse the question and ask: What would our economic life be like if *all* products—the energy that heats and cools our homes, the wood, stone, and brick we use to build them, our clothing and our food—were labeled with the true cost of production? What changes might we make in our lives if we only knew? Would knowing lead to caring?

When I tell the story of the Crees's misfortune, and the energy that runs through our electrical lines, it may appear that I want to cultivate a sense of guilt. However, this book emphatically is not about guilt. Guilt, which follows denial, is often an excuse for inaction. Perhaps we prefer denial to knowledge because we think knowledge may reveal that our problems are hopeless. Knowledge then might give way to despair. However, the billions of people who suffer from contemporary environmental and economic policies, as well as the diverse places they inhabit, are not benefited simply by whether we *feel* guilty.

I am convinced that with clear understanding of the causes of our present condition a new consensus can arise among people with similar interests, an informed moral commitment to caring about the world's diverse ecological communities. There are identifiable *reasons* for the fact that we are largely unaware of either the problems or possible responses to them. One of the major reasons is that we are trapped within a set of ideas that have been contributing causes of our present condition. Attempting to implement these causes as if they were solutions has led us to confusion, and then to denial.

There are real alternatives available to us that get to the causes of the problems we face. We need not simply accept the "real world." The "real world" is a mental construct that benefits only cynicism. Once we become aware of the true causes of the social and environmental problems we face, we can work toward solutions that are meaningful and transformative for all of us. The majority of the world's people do sustain lives of bare necessity. Some believe the present situation is so desperate that we can no longer afford the luxury of ethics. They counsel us to bar the door and save what is ours. I think it is time we get past denial and open our doors to the world as it really is. A meaningful and moral public life is still possible. A real ecological community can be secured.

In order to understand the dynamics of people and place in the contemporary world we need to acknowledge that contemporary economic and cultural globalization—the spreading of Western culture throughout the world—is an extension of traditional colonialism. Granted, globalization operates on new levels—at the level of the individual gene and on the biosphere as a whole—but these new domains are extensions of the economic system that has prevailed over the last five hundred years. Contemporary globalization is a form of neocolonialism.

This is a serious charge. In order to evaluate it fairly, we need to know some of the details of the ways colonialism and globalization work. In each case, when I use the words "colonialism," "neocolonialism," and "globalization" I intend to refer to a specific time period, and to specific places, as well as to the general patterns of thought and action that govern(ed) these times and places. When I speak of colonialism in a historical sense, for example, I am referring to the European conquest of parts of Asia, Africa, the Americas, and to parts of Europe itself that were defined as peripheral, such as Ireland. Roughly, this period began in the late 1400s when England, Spain, and other European countries began to explore new political and economic relationships with distant cultures, India in the case of England, and the Americas in the case of Spain. The period ended roughly in the late 1940s through the 1960s when colonized countries succeeded in throwing off the direct rule of colonial masters, first in China and India, later throughout Africa, Asia, and the Americas.

Of course, this specific period is not unique in the way a self-perceived "center" of power and civilization exploited "distant" places and peoples for its economic benefit. The ancient Greeks are well known for their use of colonies to control the coast of what is now Turkey on the east, and west in what is now Italy. Roman colonies extended all the way to what is now Morocco in the northwest corner of Africa, and to Great Britain.

Nor was modern European colonialism uniquely violent in the ways it exploited people and nature. The Greeks and Romans both held slaves. Much of North Africa's native ecology was destroyed by the avarice of the Roman Empire. It is said that contemporary Morocco lost all its large mammals when tens of thousands of tigers and other predators were removed and sacrificed each day to celebrate the opening of the Coliseum in Rome.

In the next chapter, however, I will focus on European colonialism, and especially on an ideology that *combined* rationales for exploiting people and nature. One of the ways "civilized" cultures provided a moral self-justification for exploiting colonized places was to describe native people as "animals." Was there a more common term for Native American peoples than "wild"?

If colonialism largely ended with the disruption of direct control in the 1950s and 1960s, neocolonialism carried forth the agenda of colonialism in a more subtle way. When I speak of neocolonialism I refer to a period that began immediately after World War II as the United States and its allies—the newly termed "first world"—began to respond to Russian and Chinese Marxism. In this newly emerging Cold War reality, the Soviet Union and its satellite counties became the "second world." The countries where the battle was fought between the first and second worlds were termed the "third" world, despite being vastly different from one another. Eventually tribal groups were added to the hierarchy. They were the "fourth" world. If possible, they were even farther from the center.

The moral, political, and economic hierarchies evident in this numerical ranking of people and places are so obvious they hardly need mentioning. But the agenda behind the ranking is complex. In his inaugural address, delivered on January 20, 1949, President Harry S. Truman announced a new American vision for the postwar world. America was being called to bring about "a major turning point in the long history of the human race." The first half of the century had been marked by unprecedented attacks on "the rights of man" in two world wars. "The supreme need of our time," Truman announced, "is for men to learn to live together in peace and harmony." Based on a conception of inalienable human rights granted by God, the new American vision offered peace and justice originating in "genuine agreement freely arrived at by equals." Truman asserted, "We have sought no territory and we have imposed our will on none." The chief threat to Truman's vision was communism, which opposed inalienable human dignity, and was based "on the belief that man is so weak and inadequate that he is unable to govern himself, and therefore requires the rule of strong masters" (Truman, 286–87).

Announcing the birth of the project to "develop" the third world, Truman continued:

> we must embark on a bold new program for making the benefits of our scientific advances and industrial progress available for the improvement and growth of underdeveloped areas.
>
> More than half the people of the world are living in conditions approaching misery. Their food is inadequate. They are victims of disease. Their economic life is primitive and stagnant. Their poverty is a handicap and a threat both to them and to more prosperous areas.
>
> For the first time in history, humanity possesses the knowledge and the skill to relieve the suffering of these people. (289)

President Truman equated political freedom with economic freedom. Being a citizen was at least deeply connected to being a consumer. Furthermore, as both Truman and Marx noted, capitalism is a dynamic system. Its health requires constant expansion to include new markets and new access to resources. A fire without fuel quickly dies.

The sequence of events I will trace in chapter 3 begins with one of the initial responses to the postwar world of political tension, the green revolution. The green revolution was an attempt to radically transform the third world's agriculture from subsistence farming to mechanized agriculture that focuses on export crops. In short, it sought to globalize world agriculture into a capitalist model of food production. Very often, local subsistence was sacrificed for corporate profit. In turn, the disruption of the agricultural economy caused migration to the cities, which was the beginning of vast slums in the third world.

Recently we have witnessed a second response to global agriculture, the gene revolution in which seed genetics are controlled directly by the manipulation of DNA. I want to be clear that the arguments presented here are not against innovation in agriculture, or against medical research at the level of DNA. They are against the ways these kinds of research function in a world of globalization. Seeds are privatized as intellectual property, and can only be used in packages with pesticides and herbicides from the same corporation. As a result, countries no longer control their food security; private corporations do. These changes are not in the public interest. Millions of people starve while the world produces an oversupply of food.

These revolutions for "peace and profit" needed support from new, global institutions, such as the World Bank and the International Monetary Fund (IMF) in the case of the green revolution, and the General Agreement on Tariffs and Trade (GATT) in the case of the gene revolution. Mechanized farming requires expensive inputs: farm machinery, pesticides, herbicides, and irrigation. These, in turn, require energy, which has usually been provided by damming the world's rivers. Likewise, advanced scientific research at the level of DNA is an expensive proposition. Its benefits may lead to a division of the world into two classes: those who can afford gene therapy to live longer and look better, and those who cannot.

Some may wonder why I continue to use the terms "third world" and "first world" in describing the contemporary conflict over the relationship of people to place. After all, they mark a kind of moral, economic, and political hierarchy that is being challenged here. There are alternative terms that seem less prejudicial: the "developing" world, and the "two-thirds world."

All terms are problematic, however the term "developing" begs most of the important questions I want to raise. "Developing into what?" we might ask. Economist Herman Daly has calculated that to give everyone in the world a per capita use of resources comparable to the average American would require an increase in the use of resources by a factor of seven (Daly 1996, 192–93). This kind of "development" is simply unthinkable. It makes a mockery of the euphemism "sustainable development." The term "developing" also has a mirror image that is equally complex: "developed." This term signifies that some countries have reached the end of this road. A developed country is at the center; it is the model by which other places are measured.

The term "two-thirds world" is probably more accurate, but it reads like a simple demographic fact: two out of every three people don't live in the "first world." This should make us cautious about generalizing on the basis of our own narrow experience, but in seeking to raise ethical issues, I prefer a term that is more contentious.

The term "third world" was apparently coined by a French demographer, Alfred Sauvy, who sought to draw a parallel between the *tiers monde*, the world of poor countries, and the *tiers état*, the French third estate consisting of the poor during the French Revolution (Ellwood 2001, 23). Although the term "third world" may appear prejudicial, it has, in fact, been adopted widely as a term that expresses much about contemporary hierarchies. Some important nongovernmental organizations that monitor contemporary trade, environmental, gender, and social justice issues have adopted the term, for example, the Third World Network (TWN). I will continue to use "third world" as a way of putting issues into the spotlight.

Enough definitions. To *feel* the connections between colonialism and globalization, we need to employ the moral imagination. Literature is far better at evoking the moral imagination than philosophy. Consider, for example, one of the great literary voices of British colonialism, Rudyard Kipling. By the time Kipling sat down in his lodge in Vermont to write *The Jungle Book* the period of overt military hostility in India had long since passed. Great Britain had won the battle of the sword; it had settled into a period of mostly quiet institutional control. Bodies had been disciplined; this was the period of mind control.

The principal weapons were an educational system imported from Britain to regulate what could be known, and a civil service that privileged an elite minority of Indian citizens who could be counted on for loyalty to Great Britain should the need arise. This institutional period also required a literary voice; it found this voice in Rudyard Kipling.

One of the most striking stories in *The Jungle Book* is "Servants of the Queen." It involves the spare landscape of Afghanistan, not Mowgli and his jungle friends. In this story, the Viceroy of India is to receive the Amir of Afghanistan, a "wild king of a very wild country," at Rawalpindi. Thirty thousand men and thirty thousand "camels, elephants, horses, bullocks, and mules" are all gathered in the mud; it has been raining for a month. Billy the Mule, Two Tails the Elephant, the troop-horse, and others converse in their common "camp-beast language" about what they contribute to the Viceroy's military power. Their unique strengths and particular fears complement each other. "It is very lucky for us that we haven't all got to fight in the same way," says the troop-horse (Kipling 1961, 142). It is as if they are different parts in a single, seamless colonial organism.

Then, a young mule asks,

"what I want to know is, why we have to fight at all."
"Because we're told to," said the troop-horse, with a snort of contempt.
"Orders," said Billy the mule, and his teeth snapped. . . .
"Yes, but who gives the orders?" said the recruit-mule.
"The man who walks at your head—or sits on your back—or holds the nose rope—or twists your tail," said Billy.
"But who gives them the orders?"
"Now you want to know too much, young 'un," said Billy.

Out of this lesson on colonial loyalty evolves a corollary on white power. Colonialism used racism to support its economic agenda. Vixen the dog enters the conversation, and where there is a dog there must be a man because the dog, unlike other animals, is man's best friend.

"Yes," Vixen says, "and my man is angry with the camels for upsetting his tent."
"*Phew!*" said the bullocks. "He must be white!"

"Of course he is," said Vixen. "Do you suppose I'm looked after by a black bullock driver?"

Hearing a white man is in the vicinity, the bullocks rise and try to pull away out of fear for their treatment at the hands of a white man, only to get stuck in the mud. They are asked why they want to get away from the white men.

"They—eat us! Pull!" said the near bullock.

"I never knew before what made Indian cattle so scared of Englishmen" (1961, 142–43).

Within two pages, the same moral lesson is repeated, however, this time for a human being, the Amir of Afghanistan:

> The rain began to fall again, and for a while it was too misty to see what the troops were doing. They had made a big half circle across the plain, and were spreading out into a line. That line grew and grew and grew till it was three-quarters of a mile long from wing to wing—one solid wall of men, horses, and guns. Then it came on straight towards the Viceroy and the Amir. Up till then he had not shown the shadow of a sign of astonishment or anything else. But now his eyes began to get bigger and bigger, and he picked up the reins on his horse's neck and looked behind him. For a minute it seemed as though he were going to draw his sword and slash his way out though the English men and women in the carriages at the back. Then the advance stopped dead, the ground stood still, the whole line saluted, and thirty bands began to play all together. (1961, 145)

The Amir of Afghanistan has been trapped and humiliated, not so much by brute military force, as by subtle tones of colonial power. The mark of his submission is "thirty bands play[ing] all together."

A grizzled Central Asian chief has witnessed this and turns to a native officer inquiring, "Now . . . in what manner was this wonderful thing done?" And the officer answered:

> "An order was given, and they obeyed."
> "But are the beasts as wise as the men?" said the chief.
> "They obey, as the men do. Mule, horse, elephant, or bullock, he obeys his driver, and the driver his sergeant, and the sergeant his lieutenant, and the lieutenant his captain, and the captain his major, and the major

his colonel, and the colonel his brigadier commanding three regiments, and the brigadier his general, who obeys the Viceroy, who is the servant of the Empress. Thus it is done."

"Would it were so in Afghanistan!" said the chief, "for there we obey only our wills."

"And for that reason," said the native officer, twirling his moustache, "your Amir whom you do not obey must come here and take orders from our Viceroy" (1961, 145–46).

Stories such as Kipling's reveal far more than philosophical tracts ever could about the real dynamics of colonialism. Exploitation must be made to seem "natural," so there is no alternative. White men are "made" to rule over men of color, just as men in general are "made" to rule over nature. To question this natural line of authority would show the temerity of the soldier in the muddy trench questioning the wisdom of the Viceroy. The most fundamental line of control in colonialism occurred when people's identity could be connected with beings that "everyone knew" were subservient: mules, oxen, and dogs. Social injustice was tied to "common sense" attitudes about ecological injustice.

Throughout the examination of colonialism and neocolonialism in the coming chapters, I will return often to the two themes already announced: first, American ideas of the human relationship to nature as either the *sublime* or the *frontier* are based on a Disney-like fantasy. They are based on a historical, cultural, and economic amnesia, and they continue to affect the often tragic ways in which we interact with the rest of the world. Second, contemporary globalization is philosophically and economically an old phenomenon. It is colonialism dressed in new clothing. Globalization and colonialism oppress people and damage the environment through a philosophy that combines a rationale for exploiting nature with people who are defined as "natural": the Amir of Afghanistan is defeated when he can be portrayed as a trapped *animal*. Third, if we want to fully respond to colonialism and globalization as they have unfolded over the last five centuries, we need an environmental ethic that connects social justice with environmental justice.

LORD GREYSTOKE'S LEGACY

I recall a seventh-grade World History class that devoted a year to studying "foreign" cultures and their histories. When the teacher spun the classroom's globe and we arrived at the continent of Africa he announced, "Africa is the 'Dark Continent.' Nothing ever happened there that is worthy of being recorded by history." We skipped over Africa and went on to something else.

To come to terms with this moral and historical amnesia, we might look at a popular novel that is expressive of these ideas about Africa. It was also a rich source of fantasy for Walt Disney. In his novel *Tarzan of the Apes*, Edgar Rice Burroughs's Tarzan does not marry Jane, and there is no "Boy." He speaks English well and is fluent in French. In approaching the first Tarzan, it is probably best to set aside childhood memories of Johnny Weismuller movies, or, depending on your generation, Bo Derek as Jane, or Disney's sanitized cartoon, *Tarzan*. Burroughs's original Tarzan had other issues in mind.

Burroughs published *Tarzan* as a newspaper serial, hoping it would make him rich and famous. He succeeded: the city of Tarzana, California, was once Burroughs's private ranch, bought with the profits from *Tarzan*, and later subdivided as a real estate development. What was it in Burroughs's tale that so resonated with his public?

This is some of the cultural context for *Tarzan:* the 1897 World's Fair was held in Brussels, Belgium to celebrate King Leopold's African colony, Congo, just down the coast from where *Tarzan* takes place. The main exhibit was 267 Congolese men, women, and children. They were installed, for the public's edification, in three "villages": a river village, a forest village, and a "civilized" village. Even those villagers in the "uncivilized" villages wore clothing, however, since "clothing is the first sign of civilization" (Hochschield 1998, 176). When some fairgoers fed the exhibited people food that made them sick, the organizing committee posted a sign. It read: "The Blacks are Fed by the Organizing Committee." They were fed, and housed, in Leopold's royal stables.

This sort of degradation of people by identification with nature also occurred in the United States. In 1906, a man named Ota Benga, a Congolese Pygmy, was displayed in the monkey house of the Bronx Zoo in the same cage as an orangutan. People speculated that his sharpened teeth were for cutting through human flesh. The zookeepers fostered this image of cannibalism by leaving bones around the floor of the cage.

Published only eight years after Ota Benga was exhibited in the Bronx Zoo, *Tarzan* posited the contrary hypothesis. Burroughs asked not what would happen when a black man was wrenched from the jungle and displayed before "civilized" eyes but what would happen if an aristocratic white man were torn from civilization and abandoned in the jungle. Deprived of his cultural setting, what would such a tale show about a man's innate, genetic character?

Burroughs's answer tells us much about how our culture has dealt with the Industrial Revolution and the rise of new technologies, with evolution, race, and gender, with economic and social status, and, most of all, with that quickly receding "memory" of our ancestral home in nature. Burroughs is also a good place to begin because he, like a rogue elephant, is not subtle. Perhaps because this was newspaper fiction, he often tells us straight out what a passage means—just in case you've forgotten something from last week's installment. Moreover, *Tarzan of the Apes* is a thoroughly American take on European royalty—Tarzan ends up in Wisconsin of all places.

The year is 1888. John Clayton, Lord Greystoke, has arranged a transfer from the army to the colonial office, thinking this will further his political ambitions. He makes an investigation of a British colony on the west coast of Africa where "another European power" is recruiting "simple native inhabitants" for the army in the Congo, conscripts who will become de facto slaves.

Clayton is a fine moral and physical specimen, whose superior constitution becomes evident in contrast to the exploits of the morally bankrupt

Belgians who are at work next door in the Congo. (The British and French are high-minded in their colonialism.) Clayton is also a different moral type from the captain and crew who transport Clayton and his wife, Lady Alice, to Africa. The captain treats his men brutally, and Clayton soon catches wind of the crew's plan to mutiny. Alice lectures him, "You have but one duty, John, and that lies in the interest of vested authority" (Burroughs 1990, 8). No matter how morally repugnant the captain may be, Clayton's duty is to the captain's *rank*. He must inform the captain of the plot.

The captain, however, is too dense to take Clayton's warning seriously. Having done his duty, Clayton has no further responsibility for whatever the consequences may be. He stands aside, morally above it all, as "Black Michael" leads a group of "bloodthirsty ruffians" against the officers. Finally, a "burly negro" dispatches the captain with an axe to the head.

Contrary to Burroughs's racist thesis, there must be some honor among "ignorant half-brutes," because Black Michael intervenes to save the lives of John and Alice when the crew intends to throw them overboard. Though he saves their lives, he cannot return them to civilization, knowing that Clayton will feel duty-bound to report their mutiny to the authorities. So they are abandoned on the coast of Africa at the edge of a "primeval forest." Trembling with racial and sexual anxiety, Lady Alice shrinks from the "terror-stricken anticipation of the horrors lying in wait for them in the awful blackness of the nights to come" (1990, 15).

All this is only the prelude to the real story Burroughs wants to tell. In fact, the royal parents, building their hut on the beach in anticipation of the birth of their first child, are something of a narrative inconvenience. This is a tale about evolution. As Clayton describes their mission soon after having been deposited on the beach, "Hundreds of thousands of years ago our ancestors of the dim and distant past faced the same problems which we must face, possibly in these same primeval forests. That we are here today evidences their victory" (Burroughs 1990, 18–19). If anything, their chances seem to be better than primeval man's since they are "armed with ages of superior knowledge" and sustained by modern science (1990, 19). Seductively, Lady Alice vows that she will do her best to be a "brave primeval woman, a fit mate for a primeval man" (1990, 19).

A few pages later, however, they are both dead, and little Lord Greystoke lies abandoned in his cradle. (So much for the parents' genetic superiority.) This is as it must be, however, if Tarzan is to prove *his* genetic superiority. Burroughs believes, oddly, both in radical free will for aristocratic whites, and in genetic determination of character. The little lord of the jungle must go it alone. The novel is a thought experiment in which Burroughs thinks to himself: "let's control the variables and put little Lord Greystoke to a clean test of his genetic aristocracy."

We have already met with Burroughs's views on class and race. Aboard the ship the ranking runs from Clayton, through his wife, to lower-class whites, and finally to blacks, who obey no moral imperative, recognize no constraints of duty, and savagely kill the captain. But for Burroughs, nature is a mirror of human culture, and the animals of the forest must have their own class rankings. Little Tarzan—his name means "white skin"—is adopted by Kala the ape, who has lost her own child. The title of the book is important. Tarzan is "of the apes," not the gorillas, just as he is "of the whites," not the blacks.

Kala has a "round, high forehead, which denoted more intelligence that most of her kind possessed. So, also, she had a greater capacity for mother love and mother sorrow." Apes in general are more intelligent than gorillas. They, not gorillas, are "awe-inspiring progenitors of man" (1990, 31). In good Social Darwinian fashion Burroughs links European aristocracy to the apes. It is not so clear whether Greystoke descends from gorillas, however, and it is even less clear whether his genetic heritage runs through the black men of the jungle. Aristocracy begets aristocracy; it would be hard to explain how evil could generate the good, or light come from dark.

From the time Tarzan is adopted by Kala to the point that Jane Porter, a woman of his "race and kind" appears, we witness Tarzan pulling himself up by his evolutionary bootstraps. He breaks into his parents' cabin and teaches himself to read from baby books his parents had taken with them. Tarzan laboriously correlates letters with pictures in a primer and discovers that he is a "B-O-Y." This method of self-tutelage, which correlates words with things, leaves him strong on nouns but weak on the verbs.

In a chapter titled "The Light of Knowledge," Burroughs almost clubs his reader between the eyes with the meaning of this great event:

> Squatting upon his haunches on the table top in the cabin his father had built—his smooth, brown, naked little body bent over the book which

rested in his strong slender hands, and his great shock of long, black hair falling about his well-shaped head and bright, intelligent eyes—Tarzan of the apes, little primitive man, presented a picture filled, at once, with pathos and with promise—an allegorical figure of the primordial groping through the black night of ignorance toward the light of learning. (1990, 53)

Enough! We get the picture.

Reason and language are not the only marks of civilization. When Tarzan finally discovers, at age ten, that he is different from the apes by seeing himself reflected in a river, he realizes that he must be clothed. Clothing in these novels signifies the cultural and species difference between "Man" and those whose place is in the jungle. Later he begins to shave, and gives himself a haircut, because he is coming to see that he is not a hairy ape.

He also discovers technology: the noose, and a knife, which he found among his father's belongings. But it is the bow and arrow that is especially interesting because he captures it from a tribe of black men. Tarzan, the "superior being" (Burroughs 1990, 41), takes a symbol of progress and civilization from people who have not risen above the level of "bestial brutishness" (1990, 71), people with "bestial faces," "flabby lips," and "yellow teeth" (1990, 198). Not very seemly for the lord of the manor to admit his dependence on the slaves.

Though *Tarzan of the Apes* is the narrative of evolutionary progress toward civilization, Burroughs also criticizes what passes for civilization for having lost ancestral skills of the jungle. Technology, the material symbol of reason, allows Tarzan to realize his true nature as a killer: "Tarzan, more than the apes, craved and needed flesh. Descended from a race of meat eaters, never in his life, he thought, had he once satisfied his appetite for animal food. . . ." (1990, 61). Though he killed for food, he also killed for pleasure because "man alone among all creatures (kills) senselessly and wantonly for the mere pleasure of inflicting suffering and death" (1990, 82). Somehow, white savagery is a sign of true aristocracy; black savagery is bestial.

Blacks, it turns out, do not even belong in the jungle, much less in civilization. They have not yet invaded the primeval forest when the book begins. But they come closer and closer to the beach where his parents' cabin is until they are polluting the water at the animals' watering hole. So Tarzan reluctantly abandons his ancestral home and leads the animals "to a spot as yet undefiled by human beings" (1990, 100). Tarzan apparently does not count as a human being—the jungle remains pure and wild after his arrival—though he is also the highest expression of human development.

Could there be a clearer example of what Candace Slater called "The Edenic Narrative"? *Tarzan* turns the story of human relationships to nature into a fantasy where "polluted" human beings "pollute" the Garden of Eden. Marginalized human beings are the equivalent of John Muir's sheep as locusts.

Tarzan's lordship over the animals becomes burdensome, however, and he retreats ever more frequently to the solitude of his cabin. No longer feeling kinship with the apes, never having felt kinship with the tribes, he resolves to meet his true equal. Jane Porter arrives just in time. Accompanying her are her father, a harebrained professor, and, miraculously, Tarzan's cousin, who has taken Tarzan's rightful title, Lord Greystoke, in Tarzan's absence. Also accompanying them is Esmeralda—no last name—a "huge negress" who serves Jane.

Tarzan is a black-haired "forest god" (1990, 137). Jane is a "golden haired divinity" (159). Tarzan and Jane are meant for each other. (No surprise, he is not attracted to Esmeralda, though he "likes" her because she serves Jane. Domestication apparently makes black people safe.) It appears for some time that Jane is going to play the primeval woman to Tarzan's primeval man. It is "the order of the jungle for the male to take his mate by force," after all, but in the end Tarzan's aristocratic genes overcome his squirming Id. In a gripping newspaper conclusion, Tarzan even pursues Jane to Wisconsin, but knowing that she cannot live with him in the jungle, or he in a cabin in Wisconsin, he walks away, leaving Jane and his royal title to his cousin.

What Burroughs works to establish is an American system of caste in which civilization and nature are neatly ordered by generations of selective breeding. I say "caste," not "class." The order invoked by Burroughs is not simply a matter of economic position. Were this the case, those on the bottom might have a chance to end up on the top. Burroughs's order functions like a system of caste; one has no control over one's fate, though Tarzan is clearly supposed to receive credit for his heroism. One's genes, dating back hundreds of thousands of years, determine one's present position in nature and human culture. A close reading of the text even suggests there are issues of purity and pollution associated with this American caste system. Tarzan has more in common with the apes, the aristocracy of the jungle, than he does with black men, who pollute the water and the jungle and seem to have been shunted aside onto some branch of the evolutionary tree that does not lead to Tarzan.

Tarzan of the Apes vividly illustrates several important themes:

- Colonialism and racism function by establishing a series of oppressive relationships between center and periphery: civilized/uncivilized, white/black, culture/nature, male/female, light/dark, reason/emotion.

- Nineteenth-century colonialism posited the innate genetic superiority of white men. White men *must* dominate, by nature, but in doing so, paradoxically, they exercise their free will. Whites are beings who are both natural and transcendent over nature. (Tarzan lusts after Jane, but resists his "natural" urge to rape her.)

- This aristocratic superiority of white men sets up, in turn, natural and moral hierarchies that put all other beings in their place. If transcendence is at one end of the hierarchy, then brute, savage wilderness is at the other end. To the extent that one can be associated with transcendence, one gains the natural right to dominate. To the extent that one can be associated with the savage, with blackness, with wilderness, one is meant to be dominated. Oppression works at a metaphorical level: to justify oppression requires only that a being be associated with brute nature.

- In the broadest terms, what follows from this is that the oppression of human beings is internally connected in colonialism to the oppression of nature. It may stretch the normal meaning of "oppression" to say that we oppress nature. Normally we think that only human beings can be oppressed. However, remember the point that the American idea of wilderness is more a cultural invention than a natural category. Although there is a real world "out there" that resists our intentions, our access to it is through human concepts. Since human biases are connected to a license to damage nature, we can at least describe our attitudes toward nature as oppressive. Put positively, human justice and environmental justice are connected. Completeness requires us to address both sets of issues in a connected fashion.

Let us now turn from fiction to reality and follow up these insights as seen in the actual workings of colonialism. One of the deep-seated ideas about European colonialism is that its expansion to "neo-Europes" (the United States, Australia, New Zealand, South Africa . . .) around the globe was natural and inevitable. This view holds that there is something unique, culturally and perhaps racially, about white people that predisposes them to "progress." After all, while many countries have expanded to include adjacent lands, only European countries in the modern era have exercised global control. One of the rationales for European colonialism, therefore, was that colonized countries *needed* intervention from Europe to break them out of the stranglehold of irrational traditions. European liberals, as we will see, were among the strongest advocates of these colonial policies.

The historian J. M. Blaut has confronted these ideas directly in his book *The Colonizer's Model of the World: Geographical Diffusionism and Eurocentric History*. By "diffusionism" he means a complex set of ideas—technological, agricultural, racial—that explain and justify the European expansion of capitalism following 1492. Eurocentrism is the view that the world has a permanent, natural "inside," Europe, with the rest of the world being a permanent "outside."

Critical to this Eurocentric view is that, prior to 1492, capitalism had been developing uniquely in Europe, due to its progressive nature, and that the colonial expansion of Europe after 1492 was simply the inevitable expansion of this progressive "inside" to the backward "outside." The loot that flowed into Europe after 1492, therefore, was not the *cause* of European dominance, but merely the *effect*.

In Blaut's words:

One of the core myths of Eurocentric diffusionism concerns the discovery (so-called) of America. Typically it goes something like this: Europeans, being more progressive, venturesome, achievement-oriented, and modern than Africans and Asians in the late Middle Ages, and with superior technology as well as a more advanced economy, went forth to explore and conquer the world. And so they set sail down the African coast in the middle of the fifteenth century and out across the Atlantic to America in 1492. This myth is crucial for diffusionist ideology for two reasons: it explains the modern expansion of Europe in terms of internal, immanent forces, and it permits one to acknowledge that the conquest and its aftermath (Mexican mines, West Indian plantations, North American settler colonies, and the rest) had profound significance for European history without at the same time requiring one to give any credit in that process to non-Europeans. (1993, 180)

Blaut counters, "In reality, the Europeans were doing what everyone else was doing across the hemisphere-wide network of protocapitalist, mercantile-maritime centers, and the Europeans had no special qualities or advantages, no peculiar venturesomeness, no peculiarly advanced maritime technology, and so on. What they did have was opportunity" (1993, 181).

If it is true that Europe was undergoing economic changes that were common across the world prior to 1492, and that the European plunder of the Americas was nothing more than good fortune, then Blaut needs to explain in detail (1) why Europeans *did* discover the Americas instead of any other similar culture, and (2) having discovered it, why they succeeded in defeating the cultures they encountered—often far greater in numbers than the invading Europeans—in a short period of time.

Concerning the first issue, Blaut points out that the late Middle Ages saw the advent of long-distance oceanic voyaging in many locations, not just from Europe: "In the fifteenth century Africans were sailing to Southeast Asia, Indians to Africa, Arabs to China, Chinese to Africa, and so on" (1993, 181). What was unique to Europe was its geographical location. The Canary Islands, Columbus's point of departure, are hundreds of miles closer to the Western Hemisphere than any other point of departure. Furthermore, departure from the Canary Islands allowed Columbus to catch the trade winds, which carried him swiftly to the West Indies. On his return voyage he was able to catch the westerlies, farther north, which returned him to Europe.

In his book *Ecological Imperialism* Alfred Crosby gives a fascinating account of the ecological legacy of colonialism. He devotes an entire chapter to the question of the winds that facilitate ship traffic in the central Atlantic. Crosby recounts, for example, the failed expedition of the Vivaldi brothers, who sailed past the Canaries in 1291 and never returned. In the two centuries that followed, however, the Canary Islands were colonized and sailors extended their journeys farther out into the Atlantic. The problem was not how to get from Spain to the Canaries; one simply followed the trade winds. The real issue was how to return to Europe. Tacking into the wind for this distance was exhausting. In fact, Crosby speculates that this is what caused the Vivaldis to disappear: their sails were not big enough to allow them to tack with any success.

Finally, "Sailors of the Mediterranean Atlantic pinned in the Canaries by the southward rush of air and water had to steer northwest into the open ocean and steadily sail farther and farther away from their last landfall, perhaps without gaining a centimeter toward home for many days, until they finally sailed far enough out of the tropics to tap the prevailing westerlies of the temperate zone. Then they could steer for home" (Crosby 1986, 113). This is exactly the strategy Columbus adopted, simply on a larger scale: out on the trade winds, back on the westerlies. Without knowing it, the Spanish and Portuguese had been using the perfect jumping-off point for the West Indies for centuries.

None of this diminishes the courage that Columbus and his crew demonstrated when they took off from the Canaries, but it does prove that the success of his voyage was largely due to the luck of the winds. If he had departed from farther north, or farther south, he surely would have failed. The Atlantic sailors had great skill, but so did many other sailors around the world. What they had that the East Africans and Chinese lacked was favorable winds and a perfect point of departure. The European "discovery" of the Western Hemisphere was mainly due to good luck; it offers no proof of the superiority of European culture.

Still, the second issue remains: what about the fact that Europeans triumphed so quickly over the indigenous peoples they encountered? The number of people inhabiting the Western Hemisphere in 1492 is a hotly debated subject. However, almost everyone agrees that there were between fifty and two hundred million people at the time of the conquest. On either estimate, the indigenous population of the Western Hemisphere vastly outnumbered the colonial invaders. Blaut also points out that, while the Spanish may have had the technological edge initially, the history of warfare shows that technology quickly diffuses from one side to the other in warfare. So, an initial technological advantage does not explain the continuing success of the Spanish.

The fundamental reason the Spanish and other colonial powers triumphed so quickly is illness:

> The point is that history went in a different direction because of the incredibly severe and incredibly rapid impact of introduced diseases. Resistance collapsed because the Americans were dying in epidemics even before the battle was joined. Probably 90% of the population of central Mexico was wiped out during the sixteenth century; the majority of these deaths occurred early enough to assist the political conquest. . . . Perhaps three-quarters of the entire population of America was killed during that century. (Blaut 1993, 184)

The Native population of the contemporary United States alone hit a low of 237,000 in the 1890s, a 98 percent extermination rate (Churchill 1997, 97).

When Pizarro confronted the Incas, and when Cortés attacked the Aztecs, both populations were already decimated by smallpox. Ward Churchill reports that when Hernán Cortés attacked the Aztec capital of Tenochtitlán he laid siege to the city and then paused while smallpox weakened the population. By the time he attacked in earnest, the Aztecs were defenseless: "he initiated the wholesale slaughter of those who surrendered, were captured, or who were simply trapped by his troops. Twelve thousand people, many of them noncombatants, were butchered in a single afternoon, another 40,000 the following day, before Cortés withdrew because he and his men 'could no longer endure the stench of the dead bodies' that lay in the streets" (1997, 98). By the time it was over perhaps two-thirds of the Tenochtitlán population of 350,000 lay dead.

After the initial conquest, the sick and dying were subjected to slave labor to extract the greatest amount of wealth at the lowest cost. One of the most infamous Spanish enterprises was the silver mines at Potosí in Bolivia. Being assigned to work in the mine was a death sentence. Even the conquistadors described them as the "mouth of hell" (Churchill 1997,103).

The extraction of gold began with Columbus's arrival. The tribute system, which was instituted in 1495, required every Taino Indian over the age of fourteen to deliver a hawk's bell of gold every three months. Those who succeeded were given a token to wear around their necks; those who failed were punished by having their hands severed, and they were left to bleed to death.

Before 1640 the official count of gold exports was at least 180 tons, and the unofficial tally must have been at least double that (Blaut 1993, 189). Similar statistics apply to agriculture. In 1600 Brazil exported thirty thousand tons of sugar, whose value *alone* exceeded the value of all of England's exports to the entire world (Blaut 1993, 191). This conquest, not natural superiority, gave Europe the edge over all other parts of the globe during the last five hundred years.

To understand the ethical dimensions of this slaughter we need to back up and ask about the ideologies of the colonizers. Since Europeans thought of themselves as a morally superior civilization, the genocide in the Western hemisphere needed to be attributed to a "higher cause."

One indication of the Spanish attitude toward their conquests was a debate carried on between Bartolomé de Las Casas, a witness to the slaughter, and a Spanish nobleman, Juan Ginés de Supúlveda. Supúlveda argued for the Spanish majority in claiming that American Indians and African blacks are "lower animals" that "lacked souls" (Churchill 1997, 88). In an oppressive moral hierarchy different kinds of beings are often harmed by being associated with one another. Here, the Spanish, who regarded gold, silver, and agricultural lands as morally inert resources, clearly lacking a soul, connect nature with those human beings they seek to oppress. Blacks and Indians are "naturalized," and thereby oppressed.

We should not be surprised, then, that the most gruesome instruments of exploitation were designed to remind the oppressed that they could be treated like "animals." During and after Columbus's reign on the island of Española colonists often hanged "Tainos en masse, roasting them on spits or burning them at the stake (often a dozen or more at a time), hacking their children into pieces to be used as dog food and so forth, all of it to instill in the natives a 'proper attitude of respect' toward their Spanish 'superiors'" (Churchill 1997, 87). They were not only made to suffer unspeakably, but their very instruments of torture were designed to humiliate them by symbolizing their "animal" nature.

The Spanish justification for genocide was shared by other colonial powers noted for their brutality: the Belgians and the Portuguese. Other colonial ideologies naturalized human beings through their connections with nature, but with a different rhetoric. The British, in particular, considered themselves to be a better class of colonizers. Some of their main advocates even went so far as to argue that Great Britain did not colonize India at all. This form of colonial rhetoric issued not from the conservative, royalist sectors of British society, but from the leading voices of liberalism and tolerance: the British utilitarians.

Jeremy Bentham, James Mill, and John Stuart Mill invented utilitarianism as a "modern," "progressive," and "rational" way of standardizing moral claims. One of their goals was to replace common law with statute law. Common law, which institutionalized traditional privileges, usually for the royalty or the church, did not capture a modern sense of what we mean by justice. When the utilitarians said, "Each man counts for one," this was a revolutionary idea. The king's interests were to count no more than the common man's. The utilitarians were also among the first to argue vociferously for the equality of women.

In the most general terms, the utilitarians were representatives of what we now call "political liberalism." I mean by this, not just the contemporary Democratic Party, but a deep set of beliefs that are common to almost all American political life today, Democrats and Republicans alike. The basic features of political liberalism are a commitment to the primacy of individual rights, including the rights spelled out in the American Bill of Rights: free speech, freedom of religion, freedom of the press.

Political liberals believe in a relatively minimal role for the State. A State exists fundamentally to preserve and protect individual rights. John Stuart Mill, for example, in his book *On Liberty*, argues that there is a principle that divides the minimal public life from the more extensive private life: "That principle is that the sole end for which mankind are warranted, individually or collectively, in interfering with the liberty of action of any of their number is self-protection. That the only purpose for which power can be rightfully exercised over any member of a civilized community, against his will, is to prevent harm to others" (Mill, J. S. [1859] 1978, 9). Freedom is the ability to choose goods for oneself without state interference.

Political liberalism expresses most of the intuitions we now find to be "common sense" about the proper relationship between an individual and the state. Women and racial minorities have the vote because of political liberalism. Jim Crow laws were abolished under the fierce criticism of liberals. Important environmental legislation, such as the Endangered Species Act, represented an extension of liberal concern for the welfare of sentient beings. The Universal Charter of Human Rights, adopted by the United Nations after World War II, is an expression of the liberal idea of individual sovereignty on a global scale (United Nations 1948).

It is all the more puzzling, therefore, that the voice of political liberalism was also the voice of colonialism in British India. The British utilitarians— James Mill and his son—governed India through the East India Company. They wrote its history and its governing legislation. This raises the issue of how the most liberal and progressive voices in Europe's political scene justified their roles as governors of Britain's most important colony.

Jeremy Bentham envisioned himself as the patriarch of India. He authored a complete set of laws for the colony and then used India as a testing ground for utilitarian ideas. James Mill published *The History of British India* in 1818, which he saw, not just as the first history of India, but as *giving* India a history (Mill, J. [1817] 1858). Certainly, this is one of history's most breathtaking examples of controlling a people's identity through the control of language. Mill was rewarded for his efforts: he became the Chief Examiner of Indian Correspondence in 1830.

James Mill's son, John Stuart Mill, worked for the East India Company for thirty-five years. He also rose to the rank of Examiner of Indian Correspondence. Together, father and son governed India's economy, politics, and cultural affairs for twenty-eight years. John Stuart Mill's attitude summarizes the British ruling class's attitude toward India and the other colonial holdings:

> hardly to be looked upon as countries, . . . but more properly as outlying agricultural or manufacturing estates belonging to a larger community. Our West Indian colonies, for example, cannot be regarded as countries with a productive capital of their own . . . (but are rather) the place where England finds it convenient to carry on the production of sugar, coffee and a few other tropical commodities. (Mill, J. S. 1965, 693)

We should note, once again, the deep connections in colonial ideology between people who are naturalized, and places that are defined as suited for exploitation. When Mill says a colony has no productive economy of its own he was defining it as a precapitalist, feudal economy that had not, yet, begun to convert from localized barter economies to a capitalist wage-labor economy. In turn, a wage-labor economy needed to develop in order to "modernize" the production of export crops: sugar, coffee, and a few other tropical commodities.

To "modernize" India and convert it to an efficient capitalist economy, Mill introduced the ryotwari system. The ryots were small peasant farmers. To Mill's way of thinking, the best chance to make colonialism pay was to convert these subsistence farmers into capitalist producers who work for the export market. The mechanism for this transformation was the "law of rent," first described by Thomas Malthus (Malthus [1798] 1965; Malthus [1798] 1970; Malthus [1815] 1969).

Malthus's famous idea is that, over time, a population outgrows its food. This means that ever-poorer soils will need to be exploited to sustain population growth. A growing society will, therefore, experience a disparity between the output of rich and poor soils as more soil is brought under cultivation. Better-quality soils yield a profit plus an additional surplus. When there is a surplus, Malthus reasoned, the landlord can lay claim to this surplus as "rent." Since rent is the return over and above profit, the British could claim this margin with moral justification. Even though Indian farmers created this value by working the land, they did not own it. Rent is what made British colonialism profitable. In fact, as happens with most systems of "rent," over time the demands of the empire grew, rent was increased, and small cultivators were systematically driven off their land.

Mill had an unusually clear definition of "progress" as it was embodied in the system of rent. A society progresses when it approaches the ideal utilitarian society. This is a society in which an economically rational class of capitalist producers work for their own individual goods, thereby producing a surplus, which, accidentally, benefits society as a whole: essentially, Adam Smith's "invisible hand." As Mill said, "Exactly in proportion as *Utility* is the object of every pursuit, may we regard a nation as civilized" (Mill, J. [1817] 1858, ii, 105). Since "backward" people are, by definition, not rational, Mill viewed the role of the colonial elite as being a kind of benevolent despot. People's identities must be transformed, though they cannot understand the process and therefore cannot assent to it. For Mill, the rule of law governed *civilized* people; rule by force was the governing principle for those at the periphery.

One of the distortions the "civilized" lens causes is the impression that separating people from nature is the only way to preserve nature. This is, of course, not true. Prior to colonialism there were a vast number of different cultural arrangements with nature. Some of them still function today, in spite of the damage inflicted by colonialism.

In his book *The Unquiet Woods: Ecological Change and Peasant Resistance in the Himalaya*, Ramachandra Guha provides a detailed account of the ecological and social changes that Mill's colonial policies inaugurated. There are two unique and important features of this book that make it especially relevant: first, it seeks to understand the relationships between colonialism and ecological decline, whereas most treatments of colonialism in India focus exclusively on the social, political, and economic features of colonialism; and second, it sees resistance to these changes as arising primarily from the *peasant* classes: "A sociological perspective significantly reveals that the most celebrated 'environmental' movement [the Chipko movement] in the third world is viewed by its participants as being above all a *peasant* movement in defense of traditional rights in the forest, and only secondarily, if at all, an 'environmental' or 'feminist' movement" (Guha 1990, xii). Guha's point is that these resistance movements should not be subsumed under Western conceptions of what an environmental movement is. They grow out of culturally specific responses to colonialism, especially from the peasants who defend their interests for reasons of survival.

Guha illustrates peasant connections to place with the example of Himalayan hill tribes' use of the deodar tree. These tribes cultivated the foothills of the Himalayas at an altitude of up to five thousand feet. They established villages on mountain ridges and cultivated the rich land along the rivers below. Agricultural production was a complex balance of factors. Animal agriculture required access to grass, which was near forested areas. Goats and sheep were taken to the pastures above the tree line. Nearby oak forests provided leaves for cattle litter, and the dried leaves were mixed with cow dung to provide fertilizer for the fields. The forests also provided medicinal herbs, firewood, and hunting grounds.

These complex social relationships to the ecology of the Himalayan foothills were institutionalized through religion and folklore. Hilltops often developed into sacred groves, where ecological patterns went undisturbed for generations. Sacred groves perform multiple functions, religious, medicinal, and ecological.

The deodar groves in the Himalayan foothills were particularly magnificent. Groves ranged from an acre to hundreds of acres in size. Under these conditions some trees grew to monumental proportions—spreads of eighty feet with trunks ten feet in diameter—and often gained distinctive features with age. Guha tells of a particular sacred tree that grew from a boulder and eventually split the rock in two. Such precious examples were decorated with colorful cloth, and gifts of deodar leaves were often given to Patna Devi, the goddess of the leaves (1990, 30).

Sacred groves were coveted targets of the British when they colonized the Himalayan foothills. Great Britain itself had been almost completely deforested centuries earlier. If Britain was to become a great colonial power it needed access to almost unlimited supplies of lumber to build ships. To extract resources from India, England also needed to build an extensive railroad system, and trees were required to build "sleepers" for the tracks.

One of the clearest ways to check colonial progress in India is through the history of forest legislation, which was designed to grant ever-greater access to lumber, thus displacing people from traditional connections to place. Guha reports that India's finest stands of deodar were in the Tehri Garwhal region's Yamuna River Valley. Beginning in 1865, peasant access to the trees was cut off through a series of leases, first with private parties, and then through the Imperial Forest Department. In the years from 1869 through 1885 the Yamuna Valley exported 6.5 million deodar sleepers.

This process destroyed delicately tuned, centuries-old relationships between people and place. Colonialism not only displaced people from their land, but it deprived them of pharmaceuticals and a source for food, and caused extensive erosion and landslides.

This example, replicated all over the colonial world, is typical of the expansion of capitalism through colonial policies. The process transformed communal access to the land for multiple uses into private use by select individuals at the expense of the peasants. Guha summarizes, "The erosion of the social bonds which had regulated the customary use of the forests thus led to what can be described as an alienation of humans from nature" (1990, 56). This process of alienation replaced localized forms of barter in a sustainable system of agriculture with industrialized agriculture and forestry designed for the accumulation of capital through export.

Guha emphasizes that in the colonies capitalism was imposed from the outside: "Unlike the paradigm case of Europe, in the third world capitalism has been imposed from without, accelerating, even if not originating out of, the consolidation of the European imperium" (1990, 194). We should also note, however, that this process was coercive in Europe. There, as in India, peasants had to be coerced into accepting new relationships to land.

We think of capitalism as being allied with freedom in part because of Adam Smith's idea that it is *laissez-faire*. However, at its beginnings, when capitalism was converting a feudal economy into a primitive capitalist economy, these changes did not occur "naturally," and people did not assent to the change.

Michael Perelman, in his book *The Invention of Capitalism*, uncovers this coercive root of capitalism in the process of "primitive accumulation." This term refers to the process by which feudal peasants were disenfranchised from their land, and thereby forcibly turned into wage laborers. Perelman builds a case for the view that

> Alongside their work on pure economic theory, the classical political economists engaged in a parallel project: to promote the forcible reconstruction of society into a purely market-oriented system. . . . To make sure that people accepted wage labor, the classical political economists actively advocated measures to deprive people of their traditional means of support. The brutal acts associated with the process of stripping the majority of people of the means of producing for themselves. . . . (Perelman 2000, 2)

Perelman takes himself to be uncovering a "secret history of primitive accumulation," a history that was suppressed by leading political economists because it conflicted with the idea of freedom expressed by *"laissez-faire"* capitalism. He grants that this exploitation of labor was "perfectly legal" since peasants did not enjoy legal property rights in the feudal system. They had only traditionally recognized rights to access land for hunting and fishing. The new capitalist producers systematically undercut these rights to access the land.

In a fashion similar to peasants in nineteenth-century India, British peasants' lifestyle depended on regular access to a biological commons for food, medicine, and building materials. In Perelman's words, "Primitive accumulation cut through traditional lifeways like scissors" (2000, 12). Deprived of their ability to support themselves traditional laborers had no choice but to accept the transformation to wage labor.

According to a 1572 statute, for example, beggars (those who had not accepted the new wage labor system) over the age of fourteen were flogged and branded on the left ear. Repeat offenders over the age of eighteen were executed unless someone would take them into their service. Third offences resulted in automatic execution (Perelman 2000, 14).

In England, capitalism required control of what remained of the forests. Perelman provides the example of the Game Laws, laws governing use of the forests that originated in feudal times. The Waltham Black Acts of 1722 provided for strict penalties for poachers who hunted deer on private land. Poaching became such a serious crime that it was equated with treason. Historians report that during this period, "Meat virtually disappeared from the tables of the rural poor" (Perelman 2000, 43). Similar issues played out in France, where the game laws became so unpopular that they were among the first pieces of legislation revoked after the French Revolution.

The privatization of the biological commons, a process illustrated by the game laws, also marked a new public conception of nature. As peasants no longer had intimate relationships to place, nature was regarded as a private resource to be controlled by human mastery. Even the economist Adam Smith weighed in on the new land aesthetic. He criticized manicured landscapes of bushes and trees shaped in the form of pyramids and columns. In their place he recommended a landscape, completely controlled by human beings, that looked "natural."

Perelman depicts Jeremy Bentham, founder of utilitarianism, as the most forthcoming advocate of coercive primitive accumulation. Bentham designed a Panopticon, a prison that would force unwilling laborers to produce for those who exploited them. He proposed a National Charity Company, modeled on the East India Company, "a privately owned, joint stock company partially owned by the government. It was to have absolute authority over the 'whole body of the burdensome poor,' starting with 250 industry houses accommodating a half million people and expanding to 500 houses for one million people" (2000, 21).

The parallels between the East India Company and the proposed National Charity Company make it clear that the process of primitive accumulation was nearly identical in England and in the colonies. The invention of capitalism required the forcible transformation of labor from small-scale, diverse, and direct relationships to place to an alienated form of labor. This transformation occurred by deliberately depriving the peasantry from access to the land so they had no choice but to work against their wills for the very people who exploited them. For those who were already within the system producing for the accumulation of private property, the system was depicted as free and rational. For those outside the system, Bentham's chains awaited.

If the process of primitive accumulation was coercive, we would expect protest in response. And indeed, there were protests, both at the center and at the periphery of colonialism. In India there were forms of resistance, such as poaching and logging from Reserve Forests, and massive protests and strikes. In Potosí, Bolivia, there were strikes against work in the infamous silver mines. In the United States coercive working conditions contributed to the labor union movement.

Anticolonial writers drew on these indigenous voices of resistance to build what might be called an "ethic of resistance." Probably the best known is Mahatma Gandhi, one of the leaders of the nonviolent resistance to British colonialism in India. Other major voices include Aimé Césaire of Martinique, who coined the term "Negritude" as a source of resistance to the colonization of Blacks; Albert Memmi, a Tunisian who explored the psychology of colonization; Frantz Fanon, also of Martinique; and W. E. B. Dubois of the United States.

Although these voices are diverse—some advocating nonviolence, others advocating violence as a response to colonialism—they coincide in their belief that colonialism is fundamentally an attack on one's *identity*. And so, to resist colonization is a matter of reclaiming one's identity and the power to define oneself.

Writing in response to Leo Tolstoy's pacifism, Gandhi explained, "We are our own slaves, not of the British. This should be engraved in our minds. The whites cannot remain if we do not want them" (Gandhi 1996, 38). Gandhi strove to make the British *want* to leave by insisting that Indians' dignity and the dignity of the British were connected. Gandhi used the contradictions in British colonial ideology—holding both that there are basic human rights and that the colonized lack them—to force colonizers to question themselves.

A satyagrahi is trained to disrupt the colonizer's expectation that the colonized will act as a degraded person is *expected* to act. Each encounter with the colonizer is a matter of insisting on one's dignity. As Gandhi said, "the mental attitude is everything" (1996, 33). Each is a matter of insisting on the truth that "man is a self-governing being" (1996, 31).

Gandhi's views were not universally accepted, even within India. One of his major critics was Dr. Ambedkar, the first Dalit to achieve a Ph.D. A reminder of the importance of language comes from Dr. Ambedkar's criticism of Gandhi's language. Gandhi's term for so-called Untouchables was Harijan, or "children of god." Quite understandably, Dr. Ambedkar and other leaders of this community found this term patronizing. They also resented Gandhi's policy of moving slowly on the issue of the treatment of Untouchables during the period of resistance to colonial rule in order to keep up a united front against the British. In response, Dr. Ambedkar and many others adopted the term "Dalit" for this caste. Dalit means "the oppressed"; it is preferred because it is more descriptive of the true condition of these people. Dr. Ambedkar also differed with Gandhi over strategy. He rejected Gandhi's gradualist approach to social matters in India, and he endorsed violence in response to the British.

Aimé Césaire offered the equation: "colonization = 'thingification'" (Césaire 1972, 42). But he also emphasized the damage that colonization does to the colonizer: "colonization works to *decivilize* the colonizer, to *brutalize* him in the true sense of the word, to degrade him, to awaken him to buried instincts, to covetousness, violence, race hatred . . ." (1972, 35). Colonization, he said, is, "neither evangelization, nor a philanthropic enterprise, nor a desire to push back the frontiers of ignorance, disease, and tyranny, nor a project undertaken for the greater glory of God, nor an attempt to extend the rule of law" (1972, 32). It is, in fact, nothing other than "savagery" (1972, 33).

Albert Memmi, author of *The Colonizer and the Colonized*, was extraordinarily insightful in his discussion of the relationship of the individual to the group under colonialism. He emphasized that the colonial situation is *systemic* in the sense that "Colonial relations do not stem from individual goodwill or actions; they exist before his arrival or his birth, and whether he accepts or rejects them matters little" (Memmi 1967, 38). Colonialism is a structure that governs what we can be. This does not deny that there are important differences in the ways a colonizer responds to this structure. There is the colonizer who "refuses," and the colonizer who "accepts" (1967, 19–76). Although the question of individual volition is important, both colonizers and the colonized participate in the systemic colonization of the oppressed.

Memmi is also clear that "thingification" is a matter of treating the oppressed as "animals." He notices when a colonial author found it humorous to observe how "rebelling natives were driven like game toward huge cages." He remarks, "The fact that someone had conceived and then dared to build those cages, and even more, that reporters had been allowed to photograph the fighting, certainly proves that the spectacle had contained nothing human" (1967, 87).

Although all anticolonial writers recognized that resistance is the process of reclaiming one's identity, as I have indicated, they disagreed over methods. Dr. Ambedkar spoke for a rapid rejection of colonialism and caste that might require violence. Frantz Fanon, who was involved in the particularly brutal French colonization of Algeria, claimed that violence is *necessary* as a way of reclaiming one's dignity (Fanon 1986). Even Gandhi argued that active nonviolence needs to be understood as a way of *fighting* colonization.

Looking back on the anticolonial literature, it is notable how human-centered it is. Gandhi insisted that nonviolence must extend beyond human beings. Nevertheless, even in Gandhi the major focus remains on social justice. One searches in vain for a fully developed environmental ethic. Memmi's "thingification" recalls the colonial attempt to colonize people by connecting them with wild beasts, but he did not question the oppression of nature that runs parallel to colonialism.

Perhaps we should say that the writers who resisted colonialism were not *against* an environmental ethic; they just had enough on their hands dealing with the oppression of human beings. This is probably true, but it is dangerous. Waiting for an environmental ethic until colonialism is defeated courts the possibility that postcolonial nations will take the path of resource exploitation as a way of "catching up." This amounts to colonialism from within, as the new ruling class among the indigenous peoples inflicts the lessons of colonial discipline on its own citizens and their relationships to place.

There are also philosophical reasons why colonial writers focused on human beings and excluded nature. One of the major European voices against colonialism was the existentialist philosopher Jean-Paul Sartre. He wrote the introduction to Memmi's *The Colonizer and the Colonized*. The dialog between these two deserves special study, as Sartre, then in a Marxist phase, sought to gently "correct" Memmi's deviances from the Marxist party line, and Memmi deftly avoided being co-opted into a European way of thinking.

Sartre took the naturalization theme farther than Memmi, or any other indigenous anticolonial writer that I know. He asked how the process of claiming one's identity works:

> How can an elite of usurpers, aware of their mediocrity, establish their privileges? By one means only: debasing the colonized to exalt themselves, and defining them as simply absences of qualities—animals, not humans. (Memmi 1967, xxvi)

Here Sartre reveals the lingering influence of the European Enlightenment in his own thinking. To be truly human, according to Sartre, is to transcend nature. Humans are radically free . . . of nature. We, alone, are self-defining. Nature, "animals," are defined negatively, as the *absence* of qualities. Strangely, we find in Sartre, the Marxist/existentialist, the same process of alienation from nature that we found in the ideology of primitive accumulation.

There is a great deal to learn from the colonial resistance literature. However, the themes of this literature are incomplete. A new generation needs to expand resistance to neocolonialism to include a politically informed environmental ethic. I suggest an outline for such a postcolonial environmental ethic in chapters 7 and 9.

In this chapter, I have argued that the economic success of European colonialism was not evidence of European moral superiority. European economic activity was similar to what happened in many other places during the sixteenth century. Europeans succeeded in looting "distant" places largely because of geographical good fortune: the Canary Islands and trade winds provided them with an opportunity that no one else had. Even their "success," having arrived at the "New World," was much more a matter of bacteriology than guns. The European attack on the Tainos and hundreds of other tribes was like a band of armed vigilantes attacking a cancer ward. The patients never had a chance.

Although they were "nothing special," a colonial ideology grew up around these European successes that gave a moral justification to colonialism. European success was taken to be a mark of superior culture and intelligence: Europeans were apes, not gorillas. Free political choice, the exercise of democracy, was confused with *laissez-faire* economic choice, and a coercive process was masked in the flag of unfolding "freedom." People and places were forcibly conscribed.

In the following chapter, I will argue that this process has not ended. The contemporary process of globalization is strikingly similar to colonization. Economically, it is a process of primitive accumulation in geographical areas that were spared earlier in the process. Europe, and the neo-Europes, are still conceived as being at the center, with the "third world" at the periphery. Still, people's identities are at stake. Still, we need an environmental ethic that includes the whole ecological community.

CHAPTER THREE
FRANKENSTEIN OR TARZAN?

I n the fantasy worlds of Burroughs and Kipling the triumph of white men is natural, inevitable. History is the unfolding of genetic neces- sity. Although dominant in Europe and the United States, these atti- tudes were criticized from within "the center." These authors might have listened to a young woman's voice. She had a different story to tell.

Frankenstein is a woman's book. Mary Shelley wrote it when she was nineteen years old. She wrote before Darwin had changed the scientific landscape, but she took the natural philosophy of her day seriously. In fact, she took real science as a way of knowing and engaging nature far more seriously than Burroughs or Kipling did.

Frankenstein is a book, moreover, that emerges from the political Left of the British moral spectrum. If it is not ardently anticolonial, it certainly prescribes caution about colonial intentions, and at an earlier period in British history, when it would have been more difficult to know just how badly the colonies would tarnish Great Britain's claim to the moral high ground.

Despite these contrasts, Shelley asks us to ruminate on the same questions that motivated Burroughs and Kipling: What should we make of reason and its material expression, technology, especially in an age of emerging capitalism? Is nature still a home for humankind, or does the advance of "civilization" and "progress" cause alienation from nature? Does civilization really civilize, or does it corrupt us from within? All these questions are addressed to us through Shelley's version of the "wild-man," who learns to speak so that we cannot avoid the most important questions about our own future, questions we may not want to ask ourselves.

As Viktor Frankenstein goes off to the university for a scientific education, his father cautions him to remember that some kinds of knowledge are not worth having. Victor recalls his father's advice:

> A human being in perfection ought always to preserve a calm and peaceful mind, and never to allow passion or a transitory desire to disturb one's tranquility. I do not think that the pursuit of knowledge is an exception to this rule. If the study to which you apply yourself has a tendency to weaken your affections, and to destroy your taste for those simple pleasures in which no alloy can possibly mix, then that study is certainly unlawful, that is to say, not befitting the human mind. (Shelley 1992, 54)

The two marks of knowledge gone wrong, knowledge unfit for a human being, are *disaffection* from family, friends, and community, and *alienation* from nature. Increasingly, Viktor suffers from both maladies. At the university, he reports, "I shunned my fellow-creatures." The seasons turned, and the leaves withered on the trees, but Viktor remained "insensible to the charms of nature" (Shelley 1992, 55).

The white light of Viktor's scientific imagination was focused on one question only: "the deepest mysteries of creation," the chemistry of life and death. Scientists have penetrated into "the recesses of nature." "They have acquired new and almost unlimited powers: they can command the thunders of heaven, mimic the earthquake, and even mock the invisible world with its own shadows" (1992, 47). But Victor resolves to surpass even these powers. He will not just study life and death, but *create* life by "bestowing animation upon lifeless matter" (1992, 51). Success for Frankenstein is nothing less than godlike powers over what will exist.

Frankenstein no sooner creates life than he begins to shudder in recognition of the horrible responsibility he has incurred for his own creation, for the arrogance of his own will. He fears even to turn his head because "he knows a frightful fiend/Doth close behind him tread" (1992, 58). It will take some time for the Creature to confront Frankenstein, to make him pay for his willing alienation from human companionship and the embrace of nature. But pay he will.

Dr. Frankenstein's Creature learns quickly that he is an outcast. In hiding, he observes the tender family relations of the De Lacey family, a fallen family of gentry whose lives reflect the picture of European social relations. A Lockean tabula rasa, the Creature first gains simple sense impressions, which he does not know how to organize. Under the distant tutelage of the De Laceys, however, he eventually gains social knowledge. He learns to read. He even comes to have complex ideas about human justice and injustice, weapons he later employs against Dr. Frankenstein.

Finally, the Creature, longing for community, reveals himself to the blind patriarch of the family. Other family members discover him, however, and they are horrified by his appearance. They violently cast him out. An outcast again, feeling the painful sting of exclusion, the Creature's longing for equality is replaced by the desire for revenge. The Creature has no place:

> Like Adam, I was apparently united by no link to any other being in existence; but his state was far different from mine in every other respect. He had come forth from the hands of God a perfect creature, happy and prosperous, guarded by the especial care of his Creator; he was allowed to converse with and acquire knowledge from beings of a superior nature: but I was wretched, helpless, and alone. Many times I considered Satan as the fitter emblem of my condition. (Shelley 1992, 126)

Filled with Enlightenment ideas of equality and dignity, yet recognizing that his nature is not fully human, the Creature's demand of Frankenstein is inevitable. Frankenstein must create a mate for the Creature. "My companion must be of the same species . . . ," the Creature insists (1992, 139). If Frankenstein is willing to rectify his mistake, the Creature promises he will retreat with his mate from human society. They will even occupy their own ecological niche. Being vegetarians, not carnivores, the Creature and his mate will have no reason to conflict with carnivorous human beings.

One of the ways *Frankenstein* resonates with a contemporary environmental imagination is in its depiction of nature as a refuge, rather than as something to be conquered. Shelley wrote the book while living on the shores of Lake Geneva with her soon-to-be husband, Percy Bysshe Shelley. In July of 1816 as she was at work on *Frankenstein*, the Shelleys climbed to the Mer de Glace glacier above Chamonix, the very spot at which the Creature finally confronts Frankenstein with his awful responsibility. This sublime experience is put to good use in the text:

The abrupt sides of vast mountains were before me; the icy wall of the glacier overhung me; a few shattered pines were scattered around; and the solemn silence of this glorious presence-chamber of imperial Nature was broken only by the brawling waves or the fall of some vast fragment. . . . These sublime and magnificent scenes afforded me the greatest consolation that I was capable of receiving. (1992, 93)

For Shelley nature was a "presence-chamber," a beautiful expression for the way the senses are heightened in nature. High in the Alps the chains of civilization are pried loose—ego is removed to its normal place—and we cannot help feeling our intimate connection to the "sacred earth." The image of the Shelleys climbing out of the valley of civilization to reawaken their senses among the crystalline spires of the Mer de Glace is hauntingly modern. Somewhere within us we feel the need to connect with place. But this feeling, in turn, betrays the sense that we below, in the realm of humanity, feel disconnected. For Shelley, freedom is not inevitable, as it was (at least for white people) in Burroughs and Kipling. True freedom involves risk. It can lead to recognition of alienation and homelessness.

As Shelley wrote *Frankenstein,* she also contemplated John Locke's *Essay Concerning Human Understanding.* Locke famously believed that the mind is a tabula rasa, a blank slate, which receives and processes sensations from the body. Though its pre-Darwinian science may underplay the role of genetics in determining who we are, Shelley's intentions remain clear. She was trying to connect a theory of knowledge with a political theory of freedom and responsibility. For Shelley, nature is both refuge and the true source of everything we can know. We all start from scratch. We are radically free. The caste categories of Burroughs's Social Darwinism mean nothing. They are the inventions of men's minds.

Frankenstein is full of these images of nature. Recognizing the horror of his own creation, Frankenstein seeks the solace of nature by rowing to the middle of the lake at night, passing "many hours on the water." He would let the boat pursue its own course, giving way to reflections on his own fate: "I was often tempted, when all was at peace around me, and I the only unquiet thing that wandered restless in a scene so beautiful and heavenly." He even contemplates suicide, "that the waters might close over me and my calamities forever" (Shelley 1992, 88). He is drawn back to life, however, by thoughts of his father and brother, and of his betrothed, Elizabeth Lavenza. Nature and human culture are not really at odds. Frankenstein's solitary reflections in nature lead to communion with his family.

The culminating moments of *Frankenstein*, however, are reserved for the mountains. In despair, Frankenstein climbs high into the Alps above Chamonix, seeking to leave behind the "littleness of feeling" that pervades the "obscure world" of human beings (1992, 93–94). As he ascends toward the "light and joy" of the natural world he begins to achieve a distance from himself and his problems that permits him to reflect on the human condition. He wonders why humans boast of superior sensibilities to "brutes." Paradoxically, animals' limited range of impulses—hunger, thirst, desire—renders them "necessary beings" for Shelley. They are "nearly free" because they are not twisted by every breeze or chance word.

Awareness of our own mutability makes us tragically free. Mary Shelley quotes Percy Shelley's poem *Mutability*:

> We rest; a dream has power to poison sleep.
> We rise; one wand'ring thought pollutes the day.
> We feel, conceive, or reason; laugh or weep,
> Embrace fond woe, or cast our cares away;
> It is the same: for, be it joy or sorrow,
> The path of its departure still is free.
> Man's yesterday may ne'er be like his tomorrow;
> Nought may endure but mutability! (1992, 94–95)

So what is Frankenstein's sin, according to this vision of heaven and earth? Isn't it that he has allowed himself to imagine that the scientist is godlike? An "unmoved-mover"? A being who creates, but who is, himself, above creation? Frankenstein has been tempted by the dream that meaning in human life requires immutability, and he must now pay for this mistake. The Creature must remind him that he is not a god, that he is not willing to accept divine responsibility for creation. His denied mutability means he is capable of suffering pain.

Frankenstein is about the existential risk of freedom. From the tragic moment of creation we know that Created must confront Creator. Nature must speak to a humankind that has become more fond of a self-image as God than as Adam, creator rather than created. Nature must demand to know—before it is too late—whether we are truly ready to accept this divine responsibility.

When the Creature tracks down Frankenstein, he appeals not to threats of pain, but to reason, and to the universal light of human justice. The Creature, in fact, takes a higher moral tone than Frankenstein, demanding that he "Do your duty towards me, and I will do mine towards you and the rest of mankind" (1992, 96). Frankenstein is finally won over by the rationality of his Creature's appeal, at least to the extent that he is willing to listen to his story. He commences work on a mate, only to fully confront the horror of his position. He must, again, accept responsibility for the creation of a new species, a species that will perhaps reproduce. If not that, he must accept the certain fate that awaits him. Finally he chooses to destroy the Creature's mate.

The remainder of Shelley's novel anticipates not so much Locke as Hegel or Marx: master becomes slave. The Creature summons all his strength to create in Frankenstein the most agonizing impressions as he is relentlessly deprived—one by one—of the human connections he cherishes most. Viktor Frankenstein's family is murdered, depriving him of all meaningful human connection. We recall that this is just the fate Frankenstein's father warned him against before Viktor left for college.

Shelley believed that if we seek knowledge that connects rather than isolates, if we seek the expansion of the moral community rather than its contraction, colonial greed can be avoided:

> if no man allowed any pursuit whatsoever to interfere with the tranquility of his domestic affections, Greece had not been enslaved; Caesar would have spared his country; America would have been discovered more gradually; and the empires of Mexico and Peru had not been destroyed. (1992, 54)

Colonial violence is a form of arrogance. Colonizers believe they are gods. They pursue the legacy of Burroughs, not Shelley.

Have the questions really changed in the years since an audaciously talented girl of nineteen wrote *Frankenstein*? Or have her visionary questions become urgent demands on our moral attention? In what sense are we still natural? Is nature our home, or do we mark "progress" by the degree of our alienation from nature? Is progress to be measured by the degree of success in finding new ways to colonize nature, and those human beings who can be connected with nature?

The past half century has been a time of "progress" unparalleled in human history. Agricultural production, to take one example, has at least tripled for every major crop, largely due to the green revolution. Transnational corporations have grown to the point that more than half of the world's largest economies are corporations, not countries. General Motors, Ford, and Wal-Mart, along with Japanese industrial giants Mitsui and Mitsubishi, have bigger economies than Greece, Finland, Malaysia, Portugal, Israel, or the Philippines (Anderson, S. and Cavanagh 2000, 68).

One indication of this explosive growth from an ecological point of view is that during this brief period we have consumed more "natural capital" than during the entire remainder of human history *combined*. Furthermore, while species extinction is a natural occurrence, as Darwin taught us, ecologists now report that we live in a period of massive species die-off that is one hundred times the rate of what is considered normal. There has also been a parallel eclipse of human cultural diversity, since most cultural diversity coexists in places with maximum biological diversity. The most biologically diverse countries, such as Papua New Guinea, Indonesia, and Brazil, have been gutted for their natural resources, and their human diversity has eroded drastically as well.

Even considered economically, it is difficult to give a vote of confidence to the Tarzanlike lordship of the last fifty years. In the period from 1960 to 1993 the gap in per capita income between "developed" and "developing" nations tripled. By 1999 the wealth of the world's 475 richest *individuals* was greater than the combined incomes of the world's poorest three billion people (Anderson, S. and Cavanagh 2000, 53).

It is also questionable whether many "developing nations" have developed much during this period. Most such nations are crushed with debt to repay development loans from the World Bank and other development agencies. Combined, these loans now exceed one trillion dollars. By 1997 poor countries paid out more in debt service to repay loans than they received in development aid. During the seven years leading up to 1997 poor countries paid $77 billion more to wealthy countries than they received (Ellwood 2001, 47).

This drain on poor countries' wealth is barely noticed by the wealthy; it is felt by the poor and by the environment. To repay loans, countries are encouraged to develop and export their natural resources in return for convertible currency. This money is often diverted from social goods, such as education or health care, and from environmental goods. In Tanzania, for example, where 40 percent of people die before the age of thirty-five, debt payments are six times greater than spending on health care. In the whole of Africa, where only half of school-age children actually attend school, governments spend four times more in debt service than they spend on schools and health programs.

We need to ask, "How in the name of 'civilization' did this situation occur?" How did a self-described program of "peace" and "prosperity" result in such stark human inequities and ecological disaster? The answer, I am about to suggest, is that this developmentalist project carried forth many of the assumptions about people and place that characterized colonialism. The contemporary project to "develop" the third world is largely an exercise in neocolonialism.

After World War II the United States worked with its allies in the new "first world" to build an engine of economic development that would have astonished even Karl Marx. The United States came to the aid of its postwar partners in Western Europe, the new "first world," with a program of grants through the Marshall Plan. At the same time, the Soviet Union and its allies, the so-called second world, were recovering from the war through massive state-controlled economic programs. The point of contention between these "worlds" was the newly created third world, a strange amalgamation of diverse countries and ethnic groups, many of which were just beginning to emerge from centuries of colonization.

To secure economic stability, the allied powers met at a hotel in New Hampshire to map out the postwar world. On July 1, 1944, conferees at the Bretton Woods Conference agreed to create three mechanisms to ensure continuing economic progress: the International Monetary Fund (IMF), the International Bank for Reconstruction and Development (the World Bank), and the General Agreement on Tariffs and Trade (GATT). A major function of the Bretton Woods organizations was to provide development assistance to these "less developed countries" to ensure they adopted a capitalist economic system.

As its name indicates, the World Bank is indeed a bank; it does not dispense charity. It takes capital from wealthy member countries and makes loans at favorable interest rates to LDCs (Less Developed Countries).

Especially at its inception, the model of development it employed was top-down loans from the Bank to cooperating national governments. These loans were to be used for quick development of infrastructure: dams and hydroelectric projects, roads, agricultural irrigation.

One of the most controversial aspects of the World Bank's legacy is the way it has supported the industrialization of agriculture through support of the green revolution. The green revolution began in 1944 when the Rockefeller Foundation invited Norman Borlaug to leave his wartime job in a Dupont laboratory to direct the wheat-breeding program at the International Maize and Wheat Improvement Center in Mexico. Under Borlaug's direction, the Center produced the so-called High Yielding Variety (HYV) of wheat, which was initially targeted for two areas, northwest Mexico and the Punjab region of India and Pakistan.

In principle, Borlaug's accomplishment was simple. Inorganic nitrogen fertilizer, when applied to traditional varieties of wheat, made the whole plant grow larger. Tall varieties, top-heavy with grain, had the tendency to topple over (called "lodging"), thus reducing the yield. Borlaug genetically engineered a dwarf variety of wheat to concentrate fertilizer in the grain- (and profit-) producing part of the plant. The green revolution was possible because HYVs can accept very high doses of fertilizer.

While the core of the green revolution is simple, the broader impact is complex. As Borlaug himself explained, a whole package of technologies was transferred to the Punjab, including "seeds, fertilizers, insecticides, weed killers, and machinery—and the credit with which to buy them" (Borlaug 1971, 231).

High doses of fertilizer require much greater reserves of water to be effective. Green revolution crops therefore require massive irrigation. In contrast to traditional agriculture, which is based on crop rotation, the green revolution involves plant monoculture. This makes HYVs especially susceptible to pests and diseases, thus the green revolution's dependence on pesticides (Chabousson 1986, 29–36). In contrast to agriculture based on the principle of recycling inputs, the green revolution depends on external sources for seeds, chemicals, and machinery. Green revolution hybrid seeds are not self-pollinating, so they must be purchased each year from a seed company. The biotechnology revolution now occurring in agriculture carries plant monoculture further, to the level of individual brand names. Agrochemical companies are now engineering seeds to respond (or not respond) only to their particular commercial brand of fertilizer, herbicide, or pesticide (see Kloppenburg 1988).

There were elements in Mexico and India that resisted the green revolution as an assault against national autonomy. They were often silenced when food was used as a political weapon. In 1966, for example, President Lyndon Johnson refused to commit food aid to India until it adopted the green revolution as national agricultural policy (Shiva 1991, 31).

Furthermore, there was no strictly scientific reason for directing research exclusively toward improving seeds that undercut the political control of the world's poor. Programs for improving seeds already existed. Richard Lewontin has argued that open-pollinated varieties of seed could have been as productive as HYV hybrids (Lewontin 1982, 16). In fact, under less-than-ideal conditions, traditional seeds are often *more* productive than HYVs. Since most third world farmers work small plots of marginal land with irregular access to water, less-than-ideal conditions are the norm, not the exception. The fact that HYVs were chosen for development, therefore, while programs on open-pollinated varieties were forcibly shut down, reflects the class and gender interests of the green revolution. HYVs are genetically engineered to be a privately owned commodity.

Colonialism has always depended on exploitation of the ecological diversity of traditional agriculture to produce commodities that are sold back to the third world on credit provided by the first world. As early as 1848, for example, the East India Company was collecting plant species in India. In 1853, when Admiral Perry colonized Japan, he collected plant species, including rice (Kloppenburg 1988, 14 and 55). This kind of raid on the biological commons is not news to many residents of the third world. Recently, for example, five hundred farmers in Bangalore, India, stormed and ransacked the office of Cargill, Inc., to protest the intellectual property provisions of the General Agreement on Tariffs and Trades.

The effects of this top-down ideology on indigenous people are both predictable and tragic. Vandana Shiva and Maria Mies have challenged the claim that so-called ethnic violence is responsible for increasing violence in India's Punjab region (Shiva 1991, 189–92). Religious conflict, they argue, is the effect. The cause is the green revolution. The same system of irrigation that caused the Punjab to be chosen in the first place as the test site for green revolution techniques is now causing violence over water rights. Farmers who had the means to mechanize and repay foreign loans have benefited, their acreages increasing rapidly as small farmers are driven out of business. Small farmers—women and men—have been displaced, cut off from their traditional source of security. Men who are displaced by this process seek wage-labor jobs on the large farms, or they migrate to the cities, leaving their families behind. Women who are displaced often are expected to work as unpaid adjuncts to their husbands' wage labor. As is almost always the case in such situations, violence against women has increased in the form of sati, "kitchen accidents," and female infanticide. In many cultures, the same women who grow and prepare the food are the last to eat, even in the best of times.

Although many technical experts may wish to deny it, the green revolution came with a set of ethical assumptions that caused conflict with the recipient culture. Consider, for example, the moral confusion evident in the following passage from the *Journal of the Indian Pesticide Industry* as the author struggles to explain the peasant's relationship to the land:

> [A] more important [difficulty in marketing products in India] is the mental attitude of the agriculturalist about killing. Pesticides spell killing, maybe small and perhaps invisible insects. But it is killing that they are used for. This killing is anathema to the majority of the agriculturalist, be they Hindu, Jain or others. By nature, the agriculturalist is generous, wanting to bestow on others what he reaps out of Mother Earth. He [sic] does not think that he alone should enjoy the fruits of his labor . . . to kill those unseen and unknown lives, though they were thriving on what Mother Earth yields, is foreign to his nature. . . . It takes some time for the simple folk to get acclimatized to the very conception of killing tiny helpless and unarmed creatures. (Lappé and Collins 1978, 61)

The Hindu idea of "ahimsa," or nonharming, puts the violence of the green revolution, and its cultural specificity, into sharp relief. Ahimsa requires a moral universe that includes insects in the moral cycle of life and death. Nature is seen in moral relationship to human beings. We are defined morally by our conduct with nature.

It is telling how often, in practice, development experts fail to perceive this deep relationship between women, indigenous cultures, and place. Third world women, for example, have long depended on grasses that grow along the borders of fields to make baskets and mats. When development experts decide that these grasses have no market value and plan programs that kill them with herbicide, this is arrogant perception. When these same experts decide that public, forested land is "undeveloped," and only has value when it is privatized and "developed" for profit, this too is arrogant perception.

Richard Levins captures the dynamic of center and margin through "seven developmentalist myths in agriculture":

1. Backward is labor-intensive, modern is capital-intensive agriculture.

2. Diversity is backward; uniform monoculture is modern.

3. Small-scale is backward; large-scale is modern.

4. Backward is subjection to nature; modern implies increasingly complete control over everything that happens in the field or orchard or pasture.

5. Folk knowledge is backward; scientific knowledge is modern.

6. Specialists are modern, generalists backward.

7. The smaller the object of study, the more modern. (Levins 1986, 13–20)

Of Richard Levins's seven developmentalist myths, one seems most powerful in explaining the developmentalist's inability to appreciate place: "Backward is subjection to nature; modern implies increasingly complete control over everything that happens in the field or orchard or pasture." In the developmentalist's moral pecking order, one is either dominant over nature or subject to it, either master or slave. The sense of living with nature in a particular place, which is neither subjugation nor dominance, is misread by the developmentalist as backwardness, as a life fit for a slave.

Far from defending the world's poor, the green revolution sought to defeat communism by destroying the world's peasant class. It did this by dividing the peasant economically, politically, and spiritually from the sense of place. Conversely, one could understand much about peasant resistance movements by considering them to be localized defenses of the connection between person and place. It is no accident that Liberation

Theology in Central America and Dalit Theology in India are perspectives that express the particular conditions of peoples. They reject the universalizing tendencies of traditional theology in favor of a theology of place.

The legacy of crippling indebtedness for ventures such as the green revolution began during the 1970s when President Kennedy's Secretary of Defense during the Vietnam War, Robert McNamara, moved to the presidency of the World Bank and declared war on poverty. During the decade of the 1970s the World Bank's stake in the third world increased fivefold. The amount of debt owed by nonoil producing countries also increased fivefold from 1973 to 1982 (Ellwood 2001, 41–43).

The peaceful intent of these loans is called into question when we examine some of its recipients. The Marcos regime in the Philippines siphoned off a third of all the loans made to that country and accumulated a personal fortune in excess of $10 billion. In Argentina during the military dictatorship from 1976 to 1983 fully 80 percent of the loans to Argentina "disappeared" and remain unaccounted for, even as Argentinean taxpayers suffer the consequences of repayment. It is estimated that over $500 billion have been used around the world to prop up dictators (Ellwood 2001, 45).

It is only fair to note that, under its current president, James Wolfensohn, the World Bank has attempted to respond to criticisms that its policies have increased poverty and destabilized the environment. He has said, for example, "People do not want solutions imposed from without, they want the opportunity to build from within" (Wolfensohn n.d.). Quite recently, the Bank has also started to respond, cautiously, to the demand for debt reduction. Yet, despite what may be good intentions, the World Bank itself has generated internal critics in the form of its own former chief economist, Joseph Stiglitz, who is seeking important reforms in the ways the Bank operates (Stiglitz 2003). Other organizations, such as 50 Years Is Enough, are lobbying for the outright closure of the bank (50 Years Is Enough).

The World Bank works in concert with the IMF, and it is the IMF that has been largely responsible for pressuring third world countries to redirect their economies toward debt repayment. The scope of this problem can be grasped by considering that between 1990 and 1997 third world countries paid $77 billion more in debt service than they received in loans. That is, far from developing the third world, the project to develop the third world succeeded in addicting third world countries to borrowed money, and capital flow *reversed*.

The IMF prescription for recovery from this addiction is "structural adjustment programs" (SAPs). To avoid declaring bankruptcy, indebted countries have been forced to agree to strict repayment policies that redirect spending from social programs, public health, and environmental protection to debt repayment. Following structural adjustment in Brazil, for example, the country's budget for environmental enforcement was slashed by 19 percent. Considering that Brazil still possesses 30 percent of the world's rainforests, and that these forests are inhabited by tribal groups that represent much of the world's human cultural and genetic diversity, it is clear that the IMF's policies trade short-term debt reduction for long-term disaster.

The World Bank and the IMF have been subjected to criticisms of this sort for decades. However, the new player, and the one that arguably will have the greatest impact on the future, is the World Trade Organization (WTO). After World War II a series of seven free trade pacts was negotiated under the auspices of the GATT. The goal of these agreements was to spread free trade by negotiating away tariffs and other trade barriers that countries used to protect their workers and products from outside competition.

The seventh round of negotiations, called the Uruguay Round, was especially important. It lasted from 1986 through 1994. At its concluding conference in Marrakech, Morocco, this Round produced a comprehensive 26,000-page document that will govern the trading policies of its 144 member nations. To oversee these regulations, the WTO was created on January 1, 1995.

The WTO has its headquarters in Geneva, Switzerland. Its function is to administer the WTO agreements, and to provide binding dispute resolution in the case of trade disputes. The major difference between the old GATT agreements and the new WTO is that the WTO is a formal international agency that has the power to *enforce* free trade agreements and punish those who are found in violation.

One of the criticisms of the WTO is that it is undemocratic. Ralph Nader and his organization, Public Citizen, have argued that, from the perspective of transnational corporations, "democracy is *itself* the major barrier" to free trade (Nader and Wallach 1996, 94). This is because "GATT . . . rules trump U.S. state and local laws as a matter of U.S. constitutional jurisprudence" (Nader and Wallach 1996, 96). For example, under the old GATT rules, the U.S. Corporate Average Fuel Economy standards were found to be in partial violation of free trade rules. United States laws designed to protect dolphins from being killed as part of the tuna fishing process have twice been challenged on the grounds that these laws violate free trade. In another notorious case, the European Union (EU) had implemented favored nation policies toward several formerly colonized countries in Africa, the Caribbean, and the Pacific that provided for imports of bananas from these countries. The logic behind these agreements was that they supported small farmers in formerly colonized countries who could not compete with giants such as Dole, and who tended not to use pesticide-intensive forms of agriculture. These EU rules were also struck down by the WTO for violation of free trade. Currently, the EU is also fighting to protect itself against the importation of American beef that has been produced with growth hormones such as BST. According to WTO policy, such restrictions would only be allowable if there is confirmed scientific evidence of danger to human health resulting from consumption of bovine growth hormones. Issues that might be raised by animal rights activists, such as the effect of growth hormones on the health of the cows themselves, are ruled out of court according to WTO rules. If all this were not enough, presidents from Richard Nixon on have sought *fast track* authority, which would require Congress to vote yes or no on trade agreements and the changes in law required by them with no amendments permitted.

When there are disputes over WTO rules, they are heard by the Dispute Settlement Body (DSB) in secret behind closed doors by WTO representatives who are appointed by member heads of state. These secret tribunals have themselves been criticized for the fact that they are made up largely of corporate executives with very little diversity of background.

Another concern about the WTO is the effects its rules have on both workers and environments. Consider, for example, the American status symbol, the SUV, and let us set aside the important issue of gas mileage for a moment. The Chevrolet Suburban is made in both the United States and in Mexico. Workers in the United States, because of decades of union activism, were paid $18.96/hour (in 1996 wages). Across the border in

Silao, Mexico, workers making the same vehicle were paid $1.54/hour. And despite the shift in production from the United States to Mexico, the average price for a Suburban rose from around $24,500 in 1994 to $31,000 in 1996 (Anderson, S. and Cavanagh 2000, 51).

Advocates of free trade will point out that economic globalization creates jobs in countries where they are needed. However, notice the fundamental inequity of this situation. Corporations, if they do not like a country's wages or system of taxation, can simply move their factories and corporate headquarters to a new country, where policies are more favorable. Workers, however, cannot freely relocate to follow the jobs. In fact, the border between the United States and Mexico resembles a war zone, all to be sure that "illegal workers" stay put. Corporate "freedom" depends on depriving workers of their freedom to adapt to new patterns of work. Globalization is quickly destroying decades of progress in the United States on child labor laws, environmental protection, blue-collar wages, health benefits, and retirement.

A further innovation of the Uruguay Round was that it provided for international guarantees protecting *intellectual property*. Corporations that had saturated their own markets in the first world saw explosive growth potential in the third world, especially in densely populated areas like China, India, and Southeast Asia. For this potential to be realized, however, companies had to be assured that they would be paid for their inventions, their intellectual property. At the time of the debate over ratification of the Uruguay Round public attention was focused on issues like Chinese illegal copying of music CD's, thus depriving Michael Jackson of his property. The more fundamental issues were rarely discussed in public: agriculture, pharmaceuticals, and the effects on indigenous peoples.

The issue of patenting biological organisms came to a head with a 1980 Supreme Count decision, the case of *Diamond v. Chakrabarty*. In 1971, a microbiologist employed by General Electric, Ananda Mohan Chakrabarty, discovered a type of bacteria that could "eat" oil. General Electric applied for a patent, but the Patent Office rejected the application on the grounds that biological life forms are not patentable. The case was eventually appealed to the Supreme Court. GE argued that "manufactured" life forms should be patentable just like any other form of manufactured innovation. In a five-to-four decision, the Supreme Court sided with GE. Life itself could be patented as long as it could be demonstrated that it was the product of "human-made invention."

As might have been expected, the breakthrough 1980 decision allowing patents on simple bacteria was followed quickly by other patent applications that sought to expand the scope of patentability. In 1985 the U.S. Patent and Trademark Office (PTO) ruled that the *Chakrabarty* decision could also be applied to the patenting of plants and seeds. Many commercial crops are now grown with transgenic seeds, especially corn and soybeans. There are patented tomatoes that include genes from flounder and tobacco. Some potatoes include chicken genes.

Then, in 1987, *Chakrabarty* was extended further to include "multicellular living organisms, including animals" (Kimball 1996, 135). To this point human beings have been excluded from the realm of patentable animals on the grounds that this would violate antislavery provisions in the thirteenth amendment to the Constitution. Genetic material taken from human beings, however, is patentable.

The first patented animal was a mouse, dubbed the "Harvard mouse" because it was partly developed by a Harvard scientist who was working under contract to DuPont. The mouse contains genes from a variety of species, including chickens and humans. It is valuable because it was designed to be predisposed to develop cancer. DuPont sells its patented mouse for use in medical laboratories.

To date, over two hundred animals have either been patented, or there are patent applications pending: chickens, fish, cows, sheep, and pigs are among them. Although humans are not patentable, in 1991 the PTO granted a patent on human stem cells to Systemic, Inc. Stem cells are the fundamental "building block" cells from which all human organs grow. A patent on stem cells provides for the privatization of the human genetic code.

New WTO rules concerning the patenting of life also affect food crops. A Texas company, Rice-tee, asserted its ownership of Indian Basmati rice in patent application 566484, claiming Basmati as its own invention. In fact, Basmati was developed over centuries of rice cultivation in India and its genetic makeup represents the collective work of centuries of cultivators. Not surprisingly, Rice-tee's claims have been strongly disputed by Indian farmers.

Other companies, such as Monsanto, have attempted to dominate whole sectors of the agricultural economy by marketing packages of genetically modified (GM) crops that are resistant to Monsanto's brand of pesticide, Roundup. Roundup is designed to kill all plants that are not genetically resistant to it.

One notable site of conflict has been Brazil, where production of soybeans for animal feed has grown dramatically. Giant single-crop plantations have been planted with Monsanto seeds in areas that were once rainforests. In turn, Monsanto has attempted to drive out indigenous farmers who produce non-GM soya.

Monsanto also built a $550 million factory in northeastern Brazil to produce Roundup. In addition to supplying pesticide for its crops, Monsanto also produces a more powerful form of Roundup that is sprayed from airplanes over coca crops in Columbia, probably by American planes. These tactics, designed to prevent cocaine abuse in the United States, come at the expense of the health of indigenous Columbians.

Another basic human need that has been affected by new regulations on the patenting of life is medicines. Perhaps the most famous case is the neem tree, an evergreen that is common in India. For centuries its many uses have been general knowledge to Indians. Its oil is widely used in toothpaste and soap. Neem oil is also used as a natural contraceptive, important in a country of more than one billion people. It is also used as lamp oil, and its timber is highly valued for building since it is resistant to termites.

Its most important use, however, is for medicines. Various parts of the neem tree are used to treat everything from skin disorders and constipation to leprosy and diabetes. In many third world countries public health depends on dependable access to natural remedies such as the neem tree. To limit access would have a result comparable to suddenly closing all pharmacies in the United States. But it is precisely this public access that has been endangered by WTO rules.

In 1971 an American scientist, Robert Larson, noticed the usefulness of neem in India. He began importing neem seed to his company's headquarters in Wisconsin and eventually patented a pesticidal extract that he called Margosan-O. He then sold the patent for the extract to the multinational company W. R. Grace. In American terms this may seem only fair. After all, Larson's research should be rewarded, and it cannot be rewarded if the discoveries resulting from his research are not patentable.

Larson's research would not have been possible, however, without centuries of more informal "research" conducted by generations of Indians. Their knowledge of the neem tree, however, is not patentable. Indian collective knowledge is termed in WTO language as "the common heritage of mankind." Since it was not the result of formal scientific investigation it cannot be patented. Only scientific innovations are eligible for patent protection.

This imbalance in the legal definition of whose knowledge counts works to the disadvantage of the poor not only because they are deprived of any financial reward for *their* knowledge, but because access to public health is often undependable. Poor people depend on access to the environment, not just for food, but for medicines, shelter, cooking fuels, and clean water. If the neem tree becomes a patented commodity, like Monsanto soybeans, then precious public land will be privatized and devoted to export crops at the expense of local people.

Because food and medicine are so important to public welfare in a country like India, where famine and starvation have been caused not by food shortage, but by hoarding by private companies, India's Constitution prohibited the patenting of seeds and pharmaceuticals. Under pressure from the WTO, India has been debating the question of whether it must change its constitution to comply with WTO rules.

A similar case occurred in Mexico where the constitution recognized the gains of the Mexican Revolution by prohibiting land redistribution in indigenous areas. This provision in Mexico's state of Chiapas, for example, was important as a way of preventing poor peasants from losing their land to large corporations. Under the GATT agreement, however, Mexico changed its constitution, and thus began the wholesale transfer of land from the rural poor to corporations.

My purpose is not to question the integrity or extraordinary talent of the scientists who carry out genetic research. I do not regard my concerns as "antiscientific." We need inspired science if we are to adapt to the future. My concern is that the debate has been one-sided, and that it is entirely informed by the ethical traditions that have landed us in our present condition.

It is significant, for example, that the debate over the patenting of life has taken place entirely within the Enlightenment moral tradition. This tradition, which extols human reason and the progress that results from it, grants integrity to human beings, and thus recognition of the immorality of slavery. However, the moral fiction that this idea requires to get going presupposes that all other beings need not be treated with integrity. The philosopher Immanuel Kant spoke for the Enlightenment perspective when he argued that only human beings, as "ends in themselves," are proper moral subjects. Nonhuman animals are merely property, although Kant did admit that it is probably not good for human character to abuse animals because this may lead to abuse of human beings.

The debate, therefore, is profoundly conservative in the sense that it depends on, rather than examines, traditional Western assumptions about what entities deserve moral respect. In fact, the Western tradition is almost unique in limiting moral standing to human beings. Many indigenous traditions have a far more extensive understanding of the boundaries of the moral community. Human beings are coinhabitants of the community with many other beings. Similarly, across vastly different communities affected by Buddhism, Sikhism, Taoism, and many other religions, humans are far from the only beings that are recognized as having moral standing.

This is important to recognize because, under the global power of the WTO, new regulations on the patentability of crops, pharmaceuticals, and biological materials from animals are constantly coming into conflict with diverse moral viewpoints. We have already seen, for example, the possibility that the extensive use of pesticides conflicts with the moral attitudes of some communities.

Many in the United States like to assume a stance of tolerance and respect for diversity. The present debate over the patentability of life, however, is being conducted under the narrowest possible constraints. If we are to be responsible citizens in the contemporary world, the phenomenon of globalization, which by its very definition causes cultural conflict and novel problems, requires us to "put our moral cards on the table."

Even within the Enlightenment tradition of moral respect for human beings globalization's impact has been inconsistent. Present-day Nigeria has long been the home of several great cultures whose artistic and political achievements are slowly becoming known in the West. It included the "northeastern kingdom of Borno, the Hausa city-state/kingdoms of Katsina, Kano, Zaria, and Gobir in northern-central Nigeria, the Yoruba city-states/kingdoms of Ife, Oyo, and Ijebu in southwestern Nigeria, the southern kingdom of Benin, and the Igbo communities of eastern Nigeria" (Africa Action 1996). It also was one of the great trading regions of sub-Saharan Africa for centuries. Camel trade routes exchanged products across the Sahara with North Africa.

Moreover, because of its location in West Africa, it was the target of slave traders who supplied cheap human labor to the West. As many as twelve of the eighteen million slaves were taken from this region of Africa. One of the effects of this devastation was intraethnic violence, and this was compounded by the British who colonized this region of West Africa.

Nigeria was one of the leaders in the independence movement after World War II: it won its independence on October 1, 1960. Since independence, Nigeria has displayed both extraordinary promise and devastating disappointment as it struggled between democracy and military dictatorship.

No country in Africa has more potential for greatness with its diversity of cultures and its natural wealth. But this mix of diverse cultures with natural wealth has, in fact, been the source of cultural and environmental disaster. Oil was discovered in Nigeria in 1958. Today, oil exports account for well over 90 percent of Nigeria's exports. Oil exploration has been carried out largely by the Dutch-British company Shell Oil, with a lesser role played by Chevron. Shell has had close partnerships with several of Nigeria's military dictators. Instead of resulting in prosperity for Africa's most populous nation, oil wealth has increased the stark division between rich and poor, and it has fueled ethnic violence.

Shell's role in Nigeria is similar to the roles it, and other oil companies, have played around the world in Brazil, Indonesia, and elsewhere. However, in Nigeria it aroused the ire of Ken Saro-Wiwa, a member of the Ogoni tribe whose homeland is the Niger Delta, where most of Nigeria's oil wealth is located. Saro-Wiwa (1941–1995) was a novelist, essayist, and playwright. He came into conflict with Nigeria's military dictators over their support, political and financial, of Shell's pursuit of oil.

Shell's practices in the Ogoni homeland included "flaring," which releases oil vapors into the atmosphere at 1,400 degrees centigrade. Flaring releases thirty-five million tons of CO_2 and twelve million tons of methane each year. Because of the prevalence of flaring, Nigeria's oil fields contribute more to global warming than all the rest of the world's oil fields combined. In Nigeria, 76 percent of oil production is flared compared to 0.6 percent in the United States.

The Ogoni homeland has also been subject to many of the world's worst oil spills, averaging 300 major spills each year with a discharge of 2,300 cubic meters of oil. The environment in the Niger Delta has become a toxic waste dump with lethal concentrations of oil at 12,000 ppm (Human Rights Watch).

For bringing these facts to the attention of the world and for protesting what he called an "ecological war," Ken Saro-Wiwa was arrested, along with many members of his tribe. On November 10, 1995, Saro-Wiwa, along with eight others, was executed by hanging. Shell Oil remained silent through most of the seventeen months of Saro-Wiwa's incarceration. At the last moment the company called for "quiet diplomacy" but it did nothing to jeopardize its relationship to Nigeria's dictators. These dictators, from Nigeria's dominant ethnicity, receive an estimated $10 billion each year from oil profits. Within a week of the executions, Shell Oil signed a new agreement with Nigeria's dictators to build a $4 billion liquefied natural gas project.

Saro-Wiwa wrote until the end of his life. In his "Closing Statement to the Nigerian Military Appointed Tribunal" he said:

> Appalled by the denigrating poverty of my people who live on a richly endowed land, distressed by their political marginalization and economic strangulation, angered by the devastation of their land, their ultimate heritage, anxious to preserve their right to life and to a decent living, and determined to usher to this country as a whole a fair and just democratic system which protects everyone and every ethnic group and give us all a valid claim to human civilization, I have devoted my intellectual and material resources, my very life, to a cause in which I have total belief and from which I cannot be blackmailed or intimidated. I have no doubt at all about the ultimate success of my cause, no matter the trials and tribulations which I and those who believe with me may encounter on our journey. Nor imprisonment nor death can stop our ultimate victory. (Saro-Wiwa n.d.)

In addition to Shell Oil and Nigeria's military dictators, Saro-Wiwa wanted it known that there were two other, less visible, constituencies he held responsible for the Ogoni tragedy:

> If the Americans did not purchase Nigerian oil, the Nigerian nation would not be, nor would the oppressive ethnic majority in the country

have the wherewithal to pursue its genocidal intentions. Indeed, there is a sense in which the "Nigerian" oil which the Americans, Europeans and Japanese buy is stolen property: it has been seized from its owners by force of arms and has not been paid for. Therefore, these buyers are receiving stolen property. (Saro-Wiwa n.d.)

Finally, Saro-Wiwa wanted us to recognize the role of the World Bank and IMF. Nigeria, like most third world countries, was subjected to structural adjustment as a condition for new loans. These adjustments require redirection of economic output to address loan payment. Social projects, such as schools, public health, and environmental protection, suffer. Saro-Wiwa said, "Must we see all those who survive the ravages of disease and famine grow up as zombies because they have no books to read, cannot afford good education, decent housing, transportation and water? . . . methinks the World Bank has to accept that its real instrument of torture is its insistence on growth, its economic theorizing at the expense of human welfare" (Saro-Wiwa n.d.).

What clearer, more concrete evidence could we have of the relationships between (some) transnational corporations, military dictatorships, the World Bank and the IMF, and the buying habits of consumers? These genocidal practices should make us reflect on the precious cost of every drop of oil pumped into the gas tanks of American SUVs. Locally based alternative sources of energy not only make economic sense: they are a moral imperative.

I believe there are important connections between the period of colonialism and the contemporary process of globalization, which I regard as a form of neocolonialism. Both are periods of expansive primitive accumulation in which noncapitalist economies are forcibly converted into fledgling capitalist economies. In each case, the advantage has gone to those who could industrialize quickly and use the benefits of technology and credit.

The economic agenda of each used a moral justification for coercion. Economic changes are justified because they are supposed to harbor civilization and progress. In each case, however, the divide between rich and poor increased. And, while outright military and paramilitary violence was used to support these conversions, in each the basic form of control came through control of personal identity.

Contemporary attitudes toward the third world, then, are a mixture of sincere concern and a set of conceptual tools that tend to harm rather than help. Help is understood as the attempt to make others—the unfortunate—just like us. However, it is now becoming clear that the earth will not allow it, and many of the world's cultures do not want it.

The problems we face are not fundamentally economic, so they cannot really be solved just by changes in the economy, or by adding new cultures to the ranks of those who think of themselves as consumers. The real problems are matters of social and environmental justice.

In the next chapter, I take up a concrete example of one of the celebrated problems we face: population. I suggest, concretely, that our comfortable patterns of thinking actually cause many of the problems we face. What we take to be solutions are, in fact, causes of population problems. When we attempt to help, we often make things worse. The appropriate response to population pressures is fundamentally moral, not economic. Population pressures raise questions of social and environmental justice.

WHAT POPULATION PROBLEM?

A simple, and for many, persuasive, way to look at contemporary population problems reads as follows: there are far too many people living now, and the situation will be immeasurably worse in fifty years. We know that the vast majority of "these people" live in the "third world." And within the third world, women are largely responsible for the dire predicament we face. The conclusion, put succinctly, is: third world women bear responsibility for the looming crisis of population. The "solution" is to prevent women from having babies, ideally through universal availability of birth control and access to abortion services. Failing these approaches, others may be necessary, including involuntary sterilization.

A glance at even the most basic numbers confirms that in the first half of the twenty-first century we will face decisions that human beings have never encountered before. In 1950, world population stood at 2.5 billion. It took twenty-five years to reach four billion, and only twelve years to add an additional billion people. We now stand at more than six billion people, and an additional billion will be added every ten or eleven years for the foreseeable future (World Resources Institute 1994, 29). A widely accepted estimate is that the rate of population growth will stabilize around the year 2050 with a total of roughly 9.3 billion human beings.

This situation has been described in the most dire terms: we face a "population bomb," according to Paul Ehrlich," and a "tragedy of the commons" in the words of Garrett Hardin. Surely, an extreme situation demands an extreme response. And it is just such a response that Hardin recommends: ethical treatment of fellow human beings has become a luxury. We have no choice but to close our borders, cut off aid, and "let them drown" (Ehrlich [1967] 1997; Hardin 1968; [1974] 1994). We have even heard that AIDS might actually be a good thing, if it does the work that we do not have the political or moral will to do.

In this chapter, I make the case that much of our contemporary thinking about population problems stems directly from the colonial discourse examined in the previous chapter. As a result, our thinking about population and the environment often assumes that we must adopt coercive and undemocratic means to stem the tide of the "unreasoning masses." Since gender is a subtext of these approaches, coercive means are often thought of as especially applicable to women: effective control of population in the "real world" requires control of women's bodies, against their wills if that's what it takes.

These attitudes are doubly tragic, I will argue, because (1) they are based on factual and ideological misunderstandings of what the population problem is, and (2) the coercive approach that emerges from these misunderstandings makes the real problems we face *more* difficult, and less susceptible to real change. We need to see that the path to a solution is *more* democratic decisionmaking, particularly for the women who are so often the victims of coercive population policies.

Let us distinguish broadly between *coercive* and *cooperative* approaches to population and environmental issues. The coercive lineage traces back through Hardin to Reverend Thomas Malthus (1766–1834). We have already met with Malthus. Recall that Malthus invented the system of "rent" that was the justification for British colonialism in India. Briefly, his idea was that fertile land produced not just a fair return for the farmer, but an additional income that could be claimed by the "landlord." Thus, in theory, rent taken by the Empire did not interfere with the capitalist production of the farmer. Since the excess was due to the accident of fertile land, not to the farmer, it could be claimed by the landlord with moral justification. Therefore, what the British did in India was not technically colonialism, as it was practiced by France, Portugal, and the other "lesser" forms of economic appropriation.

Malthus was so influential that he was appointed to the faculty of the East India Company's newly founded college, Haileybury, where he held the first chair of political economy in Britain. Aside from the theory of rent, Malthus's other claim to fame was a theory of population published first in 1798 as *An Essay on the Principle of Population*.

The elegantly simple thesis of the *Essay* was that "Population, when unchecked, increases in a geometrical ratio. Subsistence [food] increases only in an arithmetical ratio" (Malthus [1798] 1970, 71). That is, population increases by multiplication: 1, 2, 4, 8, 16, 32. . . . Food production increases, on the contrary, by addition: 1, 2, 3, 4, 5, 6. . . . We can see that, at the beginning of these sequences, population and food production will largely coincide, and this may lull us into a false sense of security that food will always be plentiful regardless of population growth. However, as the mathematical sequences diverge, population growth quickly outstrips available food, and the inevitable result is tragedy.

Malthus describes this tragic sequence, that population will inevitably outstrip food, as a "fixed law of our nature" ([1798] 1970, 70). The "law" follows from two postulates: "That food is necessary to the existence of man," and "That the passion between the sexes is necessary and will remain nearly in its present state" ([1798] 1970, 70). The first postulate certainly seems true. However, concerning the second, we should note that Malthus's claim to the discovery of a "law" requires humans to have no rational control over their reproductive lives. Humans will keep having sex, and producing babies, even if this process amounts to suicide in the long run. Eventually population will outgrow food and there will be a massive dieback of the human species. Humans, like deer, must die in massive numbers when they exceed the earth's "carrying capacity."

And indeed, Malthus is very clear that, "Among mankind," the only real checks on population are "misery and vice" ([1798] 1970, 72). People, by their very nature, will not do what is in their rational best interest and control their sex lives, so population control always, as a matter of law, eludes democratic means of control. People must be coerced into doing what is in their own best interest. For Malthus the three means were war, pestilence, and famine ([1798] 1970, 28).

In the very first pages of the *Essay* we witness two lasting features of the contemporary population debate. First, there is the claim to have discovered an invariable "law of nature." To disagree with Malthusian pessimism, therefore, is to risk being labeled a dreamer, one who attempts to wish away the hard "real world" facts of population control rather than confront them head on. Second, since the Malthusian law depicts the relationship between population and food as inevitably resulting in a crisis, we are encouraged to think of ethics as a luxury we cannot afford. The very nature of "man's" sex drive means that the cold tools of coercion must always win out over cooperation.

As with the debate I imagined earlier between Mary Shelley's *Frankenstein* and Edgar Rice Burroughs's *Tarzan*, Malthus explicitly saw himself as arguing against the "romantics" of his day. The *Essay* is structured as an argument against two optimists on the population issue: William Godwin and the Marquis de Condorcet. Godwin was a political radical, and Mary Shelley's father. Condorcet was a distinguished French mathematician with whom Malthus corresponded.

Condorcet was one of the leading figures in the European Enlightenment, and, as was typical of this movement, he argued that individuals and societies are perfectible through the progress of reason. With respect to population growth, Condorcet recognized along with Malthus that it presented a problem, but unlike Malthus he believed it could be addressed through rational, cooperative means.

Malthus respected Condorcet, so it would not be true to say he rejected his correspondent out of hand. However, the continuing theme of Malthus's critique is that Condorcet was a dreamer whose optimism could not be supported by hard facts: "A few observations will be sufficient to shew how completely the theory is contradicted when it is applied to the real world, and not to an imaginary, state of things." Malthus continues, "Such establishments and calculations [as Condorcet's] may appear very promising upon paper, but when applied to real life they will be found to be absolutely nugatory" ([1798] 1970, 122).

The principal point of difference between Malthus and Condorcet was the mechanism of population control. Condorcet believed that humans possessed the capability to rationally control their lives, including their reproductive lives. In response, Malthus asked Condorcet to examine the French Revolution: "To see the human mind in one of the most enlightened nations of the world, and after the lapse of some thousand years, debased by such a fermentation of disgusting passions, of fear, cruelty, malice, revenge, ambition, madness, and folly as would have disgraced the most savage nation in the most barbarous age must have been such a tremendous shock to his ideas of the necessary and inevitable progress of the human mind that nothing but the firmest conviction of the truth of his principles, in spite of all appearances, could have withstood" ([1798] 1970, 121).

Godwin had argued in his book *Political Justice* that benevolence is the wellspring of human affairs, not selfishness, as Malthus believed. Malthus responded that this was a delightful idea to contemplate, but it was "little better than a dream, a beautiful phantom of the imagination" ([1798] 1970, 133).

At a philosophical level, then, the debate between Malthus and his critics was over the question of motivation in human action. The rhetorical undertones of the debate are clearly recognizable still today: Condorcet and Godwin believed in the possibility of altruism and benevolence; Malthus believed self-interest was the only human motivation. Condorcet and Godwin believed that reason could solve human conflict; Malthus believed that force solved conflicts in the "real world." Condorcet and Godwin believed that, with rational, noncoercive planning, there is enough to meet the needs of everyone; Malthus believed that the fundamental fact of economic life is scarcity. Finally, Condorcet and Godwin believed that humans respect the interests of the larger community; Malthus, echoing the British Utilitarians, thought that the community is a fiction. Only the individual truly exists.

We can witness the ways these conflicts play out in practice in the debate over the "poor laws" that were then being instituted in Britain. The emergence of capitalism had created a new class of urban poor. In response, a Poor Bill was introduced that proposed a payment of one shilling a week to each poor laborer with more than three children ([1798] 1970, 117). But, if such benevolence was understandable and well intended, Malthus thought the real effect of these laws was bound to be the opposite. They will "depress the general condition of the poor in these two ways. The first obvious tendency is to increase population without increasing the food for its support" ([1798] 1970, 97). If people can have children without needing to pay for them this will increase the population, and therefore poverty, since the poor laws did not address food supply. The second problem with the poor laws was that they diverted valuable food resources from the "more worthy," meaning more industrious, members of society, and toward the less worthy, those who do not produce as many goods and services ([1798] 1970, 97). Thinking back to the earlier discussion of coercive primitive accumulation, we can see that Malthus's food policy was literally to starve those who refused to comply with the demand to convert to a new capitalist system of production.

A further problem for the Malthusian pessimists was that, even if the Poor Laws provided money to the poor so they could improve their diets with meat, the actual effect of such charity would be to deprive them of food. Given that there is not enough meat in the market to feed all who needed it, giving money to the poor would only make the meat that is available more expensive. The wealthy would still be able to buy meat, although at a higher price, and the poor would again be left out of the market ([1798] 1970, 94–95). We meet, once again, with Malthus's conviction that scarcity is the basic "law" of economic life. Therefore, we cannot improve the lives of the poor, even if we want to. It's not possible to fool with the "facts of nature."

We can see that Malthus's views of food scarcity and Jeremy Bentham's plan for a prison system presuppose one another. They were designed to make the poor work against their own class interests with the threat of execution if they resisted. Coercion was necessary because, given their analyses of the condition of the poor, there could be no rational motivation for them to work. The poor could never get ahead. Therefore, they had to work under compulsion. Either the law, or the law of nature, would inevitably punish them if they were not compliant.

Two hundred years have passed since Malthus established the basic terms of the population debate. Little has changed. Still today, the Malthusians seem to hold the upper hand, at least in the eyes of the public. Garrett Hardin is the best known of the contemporary Malthusians. He has argued for "Lifeboat Ethics," an idea that scarcely departs from Malthus even in the smallest detail.

Hardin's views are based on what he calls "the logic of the commons." Like Malthus's "laws of nature," the laws that govern the biological commons can be stated simply and elegantly:

The classic paradigm is that of the pasture held as common property by a community and governed by the following rules: first, each herdsman may pasture as many cattle as he wished on the commons; and second, the gain from the growth of cattle accrues to the individual owners of the cattle. In an underpopulated world the system of the commons may do no harm and may even be the most economic way to manage things, since management costs are kept to a minimum. In an overpopulated (or overexploited) world a system of the commons leads to ruin, because each herdsman has more to gain individually by increasing the size of his herd than he has to lose as a single member of the community guilty of lowering the carrying capacity of the environment. . . .

Even if an individual fully perceives the ultimate consequences of his actions he is most unlikely to act in any other way, for he cannot count on the restraint *his* conscience might dictate being matched by a similar restraint on the part of *all* the others. (Anything less than all is not enough.) Since mutual ruin is inevitable, it is quite proper to speak of the *tragedy* of the commons. Tragedy is the price of freedom in the commons. (Hardin [1976] 1998, 194)

The idea of the lifeboat enters when Hardin asks us to imagine the contemporary world in terms of lifeboats bouncing on the rough seas. Those of us in the first world have succeeded in controlling population, so we have enough boats to keep us secure. We even have a few seats left for our future children. In contrast, the third world's lifeboats have already surpassed their "carrying capacity." Their boats are overflowing and people are being tossed around in the sea.

Hardin's question is, "Should we save those who ask for our help?" His answer, emphatically, is that we should not. We should "let them drown." To give them a helping hand by providing them with food aid only makes the problem worse. Like the Poor Laws, humanitarian aid provides only a temporary fix while making the causes of the problem worse. The poor will continue to multiply without improving their ability to produce food.

For Hardin, the facts of the "real world" force us to dispense with ethics, meaning action based on concern for the interests of others. "As a matter of principle," Hardin tells us," we should always assume that selfishness is *part* of the motivation of every action" ([1976] 1998, 197). Selfishness is a virtue for Hardin because scarcity governs human life. That is the inevitable "logic of the commons."

This coercive approach to population issues is clearly very powerful in terms of the elegantly simple analysis it gives to the dynamics of population growth, as well as in the "solution" it provides. Is it too late to hear from the collaborative side of the population debate? Is there more to the contemporary "Godwinian" position than a hopelessly uninformed faith in the ability of humans to act reasonably?

In fact, I think there is a great deal to be said for the collaborative approach. It is morally better, in the sense that it is consistent with the tradition that we, and Malthus, and the utilitarians come from: it treats human beings with dignity. That is, it removes the inconsistency of the Malthusian position, which requires dignified treatment for some human beings, if they are sufficiently like "us," yet allows for coercive treatment of those "others" who are not like us.

Second, however, I believe the collaborative approach is also preferable to the coercive approach on practical grounds. Far from depicting an idealistic "dream world," it makes better sense of the empirical data we now have about the true causes of population growth. It therefore has the greater likelihood of genuinely addressing the coordinated problems of population, the environment, and ethical community development.

Finally, in contrast to the hard individualism of Bentham and Malthus, the collaborative approach allows for the reality of community life. Human beings are not conceived merely as capitalist subjective preference maximizers who will only act in their narrow self-interest. That view of "human nature" is much more a reflection of how Western theories of the self, imbued with the spirit of individualism and the "lawful" nature of capitalism, conceive the world to be. It is the minority view of the self-described "winners" of history about the vast, silent majority of "losers."

More than any of the vexing problems we face today, the population problem needs to be viewed as a problem of the community. Furthermore, the collaborative approach posits that those who are most affected within the community have both relevant expertise and the right to be heard. Solutions to population problems require the active participation of women who, in so many ways, are the unacknowledged experts on reproduction.

The collaborative approach even suggests that our Western notion of the community needs to be expanded. We are, in fact, behind the times in viewing the moral community as exclusively human. One of the things we can learn from third world women as they deal with population issues is that the moral community must be synonymous with the ecological community. Those who are on the front line can only deal with questions of human justice in the context of a community that is committed to environmental justice.

Let us begin by acknowledging that many of Malthus's own predictions have simply not proven true. In 1798 Malthus believed that population had already outstripped food, that humans had exceeded the earth's carrying capacity, and that pestilence could be expected at any time. However, in the decade of the 1980s the earth's population grew by an estimated 923 million people, a figure almost equal to the total number of human beings alive when Malthus wrote (Sen [1994] 1998, 204).

Contrary to Malthus's prediction, food production has kept pace with population. We may have problems with the *way* this increase was achieved—through the green revolution. But that is not the point here. The point is that Malthus believed humans cannot plan rationally for their future. This has not proven to be true. Furthermore, just as the population has continually expanded, so has life expectancy; in fact, people born today can be expected to live almost twice as long as those born in Malthus's time.

To be fair, a careful reading of Malthus indicates that he was aware of some of the ways humans deliberately control population growth. For example, he knew that the average age of marriage has an important impact on the rate of increase in the population. Earlier marriages tend to produce more children; thus it is good to delay marriage as long as possible in the face of population problems. But even here, Malthus's response to this important truth is that it must be met with coercion. Those from the "lesser" parts of society should be kept poor as a constraint on reproducing.

Also, to be fair, Malthus was not aware of the most important invention affecting population: the convenient, safe, and effective birth control pill. Procreation and sex are now separate in ways that Malthus could not have imagined. Birth control has given some humans the power of choice. Condorcet would have been pleased. However, as I will argue later, we need to be careful in concluding that access to birth control always increases women's powers to choose.

Another questionable assumption of the Malthus/Hardin approach is that it depicts population problems as exclusively a phenomenon of the third world. They are not. In fact, what is now occurring in the third world simply replicates what happened earlier in contemporary first world countries.

Nobel Prize–winning economist Amartya Sen has pointed out that the current population increase occurring now in Asia and Africa mirrors the population increase that Europe and North America experienced during the Industrial Revolution. In 1650 the share of world population in Asia and Africa is estimated to have been 78.4 percent. Through the Industrial Revolution, while Europe and North America consistently grew at a rate of 10 percent each decade, Asia and Africa only grew at a rate of 4 percent. Even now, the share of world population in Asia and Africa is 71.2 percent, considerably below their share in 1650 (78.4%). If demographic projections prove accurate and third world population growth peaks in 2050, it is still projected to have 78.5 percent of the population, a percentage almost identical to its share in 1650 (Sen [1994] 1998, 198).

The difference between the first and third worlds is not, as Malthusians would have it, that the "developed" first world has managed to control itself, whereas the "undeveloped" third world has not. Both "worlds" have gone through almost identical periods of population increase. The difference is that China and the Indian subcontinent have had high population densities for many centuries. Warm climates and favorable agricultural conditions produced economic systems that supported many people. The levels of population density at the beginning of a period of population expansion were vastly different.

These points lead to the conclusion that the advent of capitalism is the major cause of rapid population expansion. Recalling the earlier discussion of Michael Perelman's book *The Invention of Capitalism*, the process of primitive accumulation is coercive. It is just this transfer of the means of production from a small-scale barter economy to a protocapitalist economy that coincides with the beginnings of rapid population increases. Far from capitalism being the *solution* to population problems, as Malthus and Hardin would have us believe, it appears to be at least one of the *causes* of rapid population increases.

Let us attempt to apply some common sense to the dynamics of population expansion: primitive accumulation is a process in which people of lower economic classes and social castes are dislodged from their traditional, communal relationships to land. The social and ecological safety net that was once available to the poor for food, medicines, fuel, and water is privatized and closed off by the expansion of capitalism. Land that was once held in common for the public good is seized for the benefit of privatized, more "efficient" capitalist production. Is it unreasonable to conclude that these vast and sudden changes in people's lives produce the sort of insecurity that leads to larger families?

CHAPTER FOUR

We have explored the question of how the utilitarians were active in establishing a colonial policy in India that seized public lands for timber and mining. This process of privatization is regarded by Malthusians as a social and environmental good: the biological commons can be exploited because no one owns it. Privatize land and responsibility becomes clear. Briefly, the idea is that people only take care of something if it is a commodity, that is, if they have a financial interest in it. Hardin's "tragedy of the commons" is based on the assumption that, if no one owns the biological commons, there will be a reckless stampede to feed more and more cattle until the carrying capacity of the land collapses.

However, as is so often the case with Malthusians, Hardin's argument is no "argument" at all. It simply begs the important question by *assuming* that capitalist views of private property are true. Other than abstract stories about cattle and the commons, we get no concrete reasons to conclude that privatization leads to environmental protection. This truism of capitalist ideology assumes that there were no systems for the protection of the biological commons.

The Indian ecologist Madhav Gadgil is notable for research that reveals the importance of traditional systems for preserving the biological commons. One of his most notable discoveries is the human and ecological importance of sacred groves. Groves of sacred trees combine religious practices with preservation of intact ecosystems. Gadgil's research focuses on the human ecology of sacred groves in India, but he recognizes that the same system of commons protection has existed widely in almost every geographical region for centuries.

Gadgil notes that "The protection of patches of forest as sacred groves and of several tree species as sacred trees belong to the religion-based conservation ethos of ancient people all over the world." His research has documented the important connections between human and ecological diversity: "sacred groves and sacred trees belong to a variety of cultural practices which helped Indian society to maintain an ecologically steady state with wild living resources" (Gadgil and Chandran 1998, 1).

This system, in all its diversity, spans the globe. In Australia, for example, "there existed within a clan's hunting territory sacred locations identified by distinct landmarks like rocks, trees, lakes, rivers and ravines where the clans kept their sacred hoards." "In the Caucasus mountains," as well, "each community had its own sacred grove. Especially worshipped

84

were sanctuaries built among enormous age-old trees which were never cut down" (Gagdil and Chandran 1998, 2). Gadgil also notes that the German tribes had sacred groves, and that these sites became centers for intertribal worship as the tribes grew.

Perhaps the best-known examples of sacred forests are those of the Greek and Roman periods. They usually contained large trees and water sources, which were undisturbed by human commercial use. The sacred tree of the Romans was the oak, and the ancient Greeks recognized the goddess Artemis as the protector of plants and animals.

In East Africa sacred groves survived into the 1970s. Research has been conducted on the species of vegetation that were preserved in these groves as it was being lost elsewhere in Africa. Gadgil notes the similarities between Indonesian sacred groves and many in India. In both places springs are often found under mature banyan trees.

Sacred groves apparently vanished from Europe earlier than elsewhere. Scholars trace the demise of the sacred grove to "the rise of dogmatic religions like Christianity and Islam which advocated faith in one god and were explicitly for the eradication of 'pagan' practices" (Gagdil and Chandran 1998, 6). We know that many of the major Christian cathedrals in Europe were constructed over pagan sacred sites. It might even be speculated that the columns of Christian churches are connected to the stately trees that must have stood on-site during the period of pagan sacred groves.

It is in India, however, that we witness the continuing use of sacred groves to connect human and social ecology. Gadgil and his colleagues have documented sacred groves going back to the Buddhist period. The Buddha himself, for example, is said to have been enlightened under a papal *(Ficus religiosa)* tree, and the place of his birth, now in southern Nepal, is said to have been a sacred grove of sal trees. These groves, although frequently connected to deities, rarely contained symbolic representations of gods. Rather, the trees themselves were regarded as sacred.

Such groves were spread to the four directions of India. Today, most seem to exist in the south, particularly in tribal (Adivasi) areas that were relatively undisturbed by the British. In such areas we find access to the biological commons organized according to a complex social system. Agriculture may exist side by side with forest preservation. In turn, forests are often divided into "supply forests," where community access to wood, plant matter, and water is allowed. These are adjacent to sacred groves, which are sometimes called "safety forests."

Gadgil quotes an account of such forests from 1870:

> The forests are the property of the gods of the villages in which they are situated, and the trees ought not to be cut without having leave from the *Gauda* or headman of the village, whose office is hereditary, and who here also is priest (pujari) to the temple of the village god. The idol receives nothing for granting this permission; but the neglect of the ceremony of asking his leave brings his vengeance on the guilty person. (Gadgil and Chandran 1998, 18)

From such accounts, Gadgil concludes that "we may infer that the forests were virtually under the control of village communities within well-defined territories. Thus the common property resources of the village, like forests, were used by a small number of people under a well-regulated social system without the need for policing" (Gadgil and Chandran 1998, 19). The history of British India from an ecological viewpoint is largely a matter of gaining "legal" access to these resources. The Indian Forest Act of 1878, to choose only one concrete example, ceded thousands of hectares of forests to the British. These forests were fenced off to prevent unauthorized access by those who used to live there (Guha 1990). Still today, "tree poaching" is a serious issue: poor forest people sneak into the protected forests, down valuable trees, and receive up to $500 for their efforts. This kind of activity, although risky, is powerfully attractive in areas of the country where the yearly income can average $350.

The general conclusion Gadgil draws from these studies is that "such a system may permit biological resource use at near maximal sustainable level, while keeping the risk of resource extermination low" (Gadgil and Chandran 1998, 17). That is, the Indian system for allocating access to nature in a context of high population density, worked out over many centuries, is a nearly perfect example of sustainable ecodevelopment. Nevertheless, it is precisely this fine-tuned system that was attacked by colonialism, and remains under attack today by the effects of globalization.

The truism that people will only protect what they own seems to be more a projection of the capitalist mind than anything that can be documented in history. As with the poor laws that *created* food scarcity to coerce the poor, ahistorical abstractions, like Hardin's cattle grazing in the commons, only make sense if we make the world operate on a principle of scarcity. Malthusians create what they claim to observe.

A further Malthusian concern is that unregulated population expansion is a threat to the first world because of the pressure to emigrate. Garrett Hardin has even put this in ecological terms: immigration to the United States threatens wilderness areas, therefore the borders should be closed to further immigration. Following the lifeboat image, "we" in the first world have responsibly held a few seats in reserve for our own ancestors. We should do what is necessary to preserve our own options. It may be unfair, according to Hardin, that his ancestors were granted entry while later immigrants were denied, but that's just the hard fact.

Here again, Amartya Sen skillfully argues that the Malthusians have misidentified the causes of migration. Whereas Hardin argues that population flows from Africa and Asia, as well as Central and South America, are due to the fact of overflowing populations, Sen argues that the increase is due to the nature of international capitalism: "The explanation for the increased migratory pressure over the decades owes more to the dynamism of international capitalism than to just the growing size of the population of the third world countries" (Sen [1994] 1998, 205).

We live at a time in which capital no longer knows international boundaries. That, after all, is the *purpose* of the regime being enforced by the World Bank, the IMF, and the World Trade Organization. It is hardly surprising that labor would attempt to follow capital. What needs to be said is that first world countries *filter* this emigration to their benefit, and to the disadvantage of the countries that lose population. Those who are allowed to emigrate are those who already have relatives in the country, and who can demonstrate ability in the workforce: medical doctors, engineers, and computer technicians.

Even the celebrated "undocumented" aliens, who pass over borders illegally, perform critical functions in a capitalist economy: farmworkers and hand laborers. Far from harming the economy, these often-unwelcome laborers are the reason that many food crops, for example, are abundantly available at rock-bottom prices.

If there has been a "tragedy of the commons," as the Malthusians allege, its causes are exactly the opposite of what these pessimists allege. The problem is not, and has never been, that the biological commons are

CHAPTER FOUR

unmanaged. They have been exquisitely managed for centuries in ways that are appropriate to communalistic cultures. The real tragedy has occurred precisely when the Malthusian program has been enforced as part of the coercive process of primitive accumulation. Privatization of land is the *cause* of population problems, not the *solution*.

Perhaps we, in the United States, fail to recognize the coercive effects of privatization because, as Ward Churchill has argued, the campaign to privatize communal access to nature was more "successful" here than anywhere else. The genocide committed against the original inhabitants of North America was so thorough that we can escape thinking about these problems in our own "backyards."

Dealing with the population problem affects all those who must undergo the conversion to capitalist conditions of production, but its impact is felt most powerfully by women. Malthusian policies, pessimistic as they are about the ability of people to control themselves and plan rationally for the future, target the control of women as the main solution to population pressures. Thus, we have had many coercive approaches to population control. We hear that universal access to birth control, sterilization, and other "family planning" devices is the solution. In short, the solutions are often technological and often coercive.

In 1990, an article by Amartya Sen appeared in the *New York Review of Books* titled "More Than 100 Million Women Are Missing." This appalling title reflected some rather simple, but strangely neglected, facts about contemporary population issues. Sen had subtracted the actual number of women alive in Asia from the "normal" number of women one would expect to be alive given ratios of men to women elsewhere in the world. As Sen reported,

> If we could expect equal populations of the two sexes, the low ratio of 0.94 women to men in South Asia, West Asia, and China would indicate a 6 percent deficit of women; but since in countries where men and women receive similar care, the ratio is 1.05, the real shortfall is about 11 percent. In China alone this amounts to 50 million "missing women," taking 1.05 as the benchmark ratio. When that number is added to those in South Asia, West Asia, and North Africa, a great many more than 100 million women are "missing." These numbers tell us, quietly, a terrible story of inequality and neglect leading to an excess mortality of women. (Sen 1990, 61)

88

Sen carefully considers the assumption that many in the first world would make to explain this shocking disparity: that Asia is less developed and more sexist than progressive Western countries. He points out that the South Asian countries with the greatest disparities between men and women, India and Bangladesh, with roughly 0.94 women per man, and Pakistan, with a ratio of 0.90, have also either been governed by women (India and Pakistan), or have had their major opposition party led by a woman (Bangladesh). In addition, the percentage of women in national legislatures is higher than in the United States, as is the number of tenured university faculty (Sen 1990, 65, 66).

One can object that Benazir Bhutto in Pakistan and Indira Gandhi in India both came to power partly through the patronage of their powerful fathers, but a more important fact is that they were able to win popular elections. Gandhi was also capable of putting her son, Rajiv, in power, and upon his death, Gandhi's Italian daughter-in-law has become a powerful presence in the Congress Party. The indisputable fact is that Indians have shown themselves far more willing to accept powerful female political leaders than voters in the United States. It is worth noting, as well, that India's Constitution contains extensive provisions guaranteeing women's rights, perhaps on a scale envisioned by the Equal Rights Amendment, which failed to receive enough support in the United States for inclusion in the amendments to the Constitution.

We should also point out that just because wealthy, politically powerful women are successful does not necessarily mean that they will work to benefit their own gender, or even that they understand the needs of poorer women who have no political power. However, the real reason for the disparity between men and women appears to lie elsewhere. As Sen puts it, "Indeed, economic development is quite often accompanied by a relative worsening in the survival of women . . ." (1990, 62). That is, economic "progress" almost always benefits men and disenfranchises women.

Following the 1979 economic reforms, which doubled China's agricultural production by some reports, the condition of women worsened. The ratio of 94.3 women to men in 1979 declined to 93.4 in 1985. Sen reports that the new emphasis on agricultural output was accompanied by a lessened emphasis on the equality of women. The celebrated "one child family," also initiated in 1979, did succeed in reducing the rate of population growth in China, but it did so at the expense of women. Given the opportunity to have only one child, the Chinese opted for a male child, since male children have long been preferred in China. Furthermore, as agricultural production improved, the resources that were once dedicated to rural health and education programs were diverted to the agricultural sector. So, agricultural progress was often at the cost of women's health and the control they gain through education (1990, 65).

We find similar signs that economic "progress" has been bad for poor women in India. Consider the comparison between two states, the Punjab and Kerala. The Punjab is the wealthiest state in India when measured by per capita income. A major part of this wealth is due to the green revolution, which began in the Punjab, and still has its greatest influence there. The Punjab, in other words, is wealthy because industrialized agriculture has accumulated wealth into the hands of a few wealthy male farmers. So it is significant that the ratio of women to men in the Punjab is the worst of any state in India: 0.86. It also has the lowest percentage in India of women working outside the home (Sen 1990, 64).

In contrast, Kerala is one of the poorest states in India when measured by per capita income. Its ratio of women to men is 1.03, which compares favorably to those of Europe and the United States, and which is extraordinary when compared to the average for India as a whole: 0.94.

There are several important factors for the general well-being of women in Kerala. One reason is the literacy rate, which is approaching 100 percent. Another is that women can have clear title to land, which is largely due to the fact that Kerala is mainly matrilineal. Wealth goes to the females of the family before it goes to the males.

The historical reasons for the almost unique status of women in Kerala are several. Most of Kerala was not part of British India and was therefore spared the transition to a capitalist export economy that ravaged much of the rest of the country. It also had important settlements of Jews and Christians, who valued literacy. In recent decades, residents of Kerala have elected leftist governments that supported extensive public education and family health campaigns (Sen 1990, 66).

This unusual confluence of factors often has unpredictable results. Elsewhere in India the problem of dowry puts extraordinary pressures on families with female children. Females are less valuable economically than males because they, not males, must produce a dowry to marry. In this system, the female moves to live with her husband's family. She may be geographically remote from her own family and at the mercy of her husband's relatives. Often, the mother-in-law abuses the new bride.

The dowry, which began as a simple guarantee of the welfare of a married daughter, has been abused in recent years as new wealth has accumulated. Demands for extraordinary dowries, which preceded marriage, now sometimes continue after marriage, with the health, and even the life, of the new bride at stake. Autos, televisions, and other electronic equipment are sometimes demanded after the marriage. In a few cases, disappointed in-laws murder the new bride in what are euphemistically called "kitchen accidents." Women often cook with kerosene, which is volatile. The mother-in-law douses the bride in kerosene and burns her to death in the kitchen, hoping that the authorities will ignore the murder because it is considered a domestic "accident," and therefore a private matter.

It is typical of the strange ways that gender behaves in situations with rapid economic development that the women of Kerala often experience dowry in a different way from their sisters in the rest of India. Because of their high levels of education, women in Kerala can often find work outside the home. By far, the best-paying source of income for Keralan women is in the Middle East. The result is that Keralan women are often perceived as wealthy from oil money, and they are expected to pay their own large dowries. Keralan women frequently complain, therefore, that the often-cited figures of women's welfare in Kerala are misunderstood. Even those women who benefit from education are often caught in the trap of economic development: they now need to pay for their own husbands to marry them!

Before turning to the question of actual remedies to population problems, we should also mention another class of classic "solutions" to population. They have in common that they are technological "solutions" that are often implemented by experts without sensitivity to the local conditions of women. The most common solution is the universal availability of birth control. Birth control and the availability of abortion are often regarded in first world countries as the remedy of choice for third world women. However, in context, they often lead to disastrous consequences for women. Birth control must actually be used regularly to be effective. However, in many places birth control equates with Western sexual freedom. This is the last thing that many traditional men want to encourage, and most women are uncomfortable with it as well. Men typically want to insist that their wives remain "pure," and this sometimes translates into further privatizing women by keeping them pregnant constantly. Pregnancy is a sign of both fidelity of women to men, and prosperity for men. In such contexts, it is dangerous for women to associate themselves with what appears to be an inappropriate kind of sexual freedom.

The availability of abortion is also not an unambiguous benefit to women. In both India and China, the vast number of aborted fetuses are female because families strongly prefer boys to girls. This pressure becomes stronger when there are government incentives to reduce the number of children. Each birth becomes a more important opportunity for male children.

An additional problem with abortion is that it is often associated with involuntary sterilization. Women who go to the doctor for an abortion, or for another relatively simple medical procedure, are sterilized when under anesthesia. Not surprisingly, when women find they cannot trust a doctor, they are not likely to return in the future, and their health suffers. This leads to cross-generational problems, as mothers with health problems give birth to children who are unhealthy. In turn, the high mortality rate that results causes women to endure more pregnancies in the hope of producing healthy children.

Once again, we have found that the coercive Malthusian approaches to population control confuse the *causes* of population problems with their *solutions*. Rapid economic change is the cause of population problems, not the solution. This is especially true when social, educational, and environmental safeguards that protect less powerful sectors of society do not accompany rapid economic change. Despite what advocates of free market economics suggest, social and environmental justice do not simply take care of themselves. They require careful attention by international, state, and local governments, as well as nongovernmental organizations designed both to protect and to empower the weak.

In response to the Malthusians, I suggest that real solutions to problems of population and the environment are never coercive, and they only incidentally have to do with reproductive technology. Real, long-term solutions derive from the intersection of social and environmental justice as they are interwoven to allow greater freedom for women. Such freedom needs to be understood in terms of greater capability to actually function in the village context.

One of the best-known ways to address population issues is through education. However, we know that one of the ways colonial powers implemented social control was through education, that is, through indoctrination in the dominant ideology. What is needed, therefore, is not just education, but appropriate education, designed to empower women and their families. Appropriate education varies by context. In most contexts, however, women need to be mathematically literate. Women often control the informal economy. Increasingly, they must deal with outsiders in the trade of goods and services. Mathematically illiterate women are victims for those who would shortchange them.

One of the most powerful forms of empowerment for women has been the collective power of women's banks. Although women often do not earn top wages, they have proven to be effective and regular savers of money. Women who join the banking collectives often promise to save only a few cents a month. However, the collective saving power of women adds up quickly.

When women decide collectively on loan applications from other women, the repayment rate is close to 100 percent. Much of the time these funds go to community projects rather than to individual benefit. In the Indian state of Orissa, for example, many women in tribal groups have invested in communal banks. I observed as women in one of these villages discussed the problems they faced with regaining access to land and dealing with a local bauxite mine. The women decided that their major problem was communication: although there were many tribal women, they were separated into dozens of small villages. Apart, they could not exercise power. So, without ever having actually seen one, the women decided that they needed bicycles. They used their collective bank account to provide a loan for any woman who wanted a bike. Within two years the transformation in the villages was striking. Tribal women in long, flowing gowns, with multiple nose rings and earrings, were riding from village to village organizing their lives. They had been successful in gaining recognition of land rights, and a campaign against the bauxite mine was under way.

In addition to mathematical literacy, linguistic literacy is often critical to real community development. In deeply multicultural societies the weak must be able to speak the language of the dominant group if they are to be heard. Outside experts control education, commerce, the government, and the legal system. If women are not able to converse with the powerful it is almost certain that they will be ignored. Often, however, the most important kind of education is the sort older women can provide younger women. This includes agricultural and medical knowledge that is appropriate and inexpensive.

One way to assess where we stand in relation to population is to employ a model devised by the Princeton demographer Frank Notestein in 1945. Notestein's theory held that we can track population growth through three stages:

> In the first of the three stages, the one prevailing in preindustrial societies, birth rates and death rates are both high, essentially offsetting each other and leading to little or no population growth. As countries begin to modernize, however, death rates fall and countries enter stage two, where death rates are low while birth rates remain high. At this point, population growth typically reaches 3 percent a year—a rate that if sustained leads to a 20-fold increase in a century. Countries cannot long remain in this stage.
>
> As modernization continues, birth rates fall and countries enter the third and final stage of the demographic transition, when birth rates and death rates again balance, but at low levels. At this point, population size stabilizes. Countries rarely ever have exactly zero growth, but here we consider any country with annual growth below 0.4 percent to have an essentially stable population. (Brown, Gardner et al. 1998, 61)

The question is how to interpret the causal dynamics of this theory, given what we have learned about primitive accumulation and population. Notestein's theory depicts economic "progress" as the solution to population pressures. The shift from stage one to stage two is caused by modernization as death rates fall, but birth rates remain high. This is what causes rapid population growth . . . and instability, since "countries cannot long remain in this stage." Some countries continue the process of modernization and succeed in breaking through to the third stage, in which birth rates drop to match death rates. The Worldwatch Institute reports that, at this point, "32 industrial countries have made it to stage three, stabilizing their population size" (Brown, Gardner et al. 1998, 62). The solution to population pressures, according to this model, is to push countries through the process of industrialization until they reach the third stage.

However, the Worldwatch Institute also recognizes a troubling, new possibility: many stage two countries may fail to reach stage three, and actually fall back into stage one. They may return to a "preindustrial" condition with high death rates and high birth rates. Such countries would face environmental and social disasters as the basic structures of society disintegrate.

So, what are we really talking about here? The countries that have achieved zero population growth, or at least have a reasonable chance to move from the second stage to the third, are all countries that have gone through the Industrial Revolution with relatively small populations at the initial stages. As Amartya Sen pointed out, industrialization *caused* rapid population increases. But most of the successful countries were able to deal with surges in population through access to wealth and power far beyond their borders.

Of the zero population growth countries, many were former colonial powers: Belgium, France, Germany, Italy, Japan, Spain, and the United Kingdom. Many others were the beneficiaries of the Soviet Union and its collectivist form of industrialization: Russia, Belarus, the Czech Republic, Hungary, Poland, Rumania, and Ukraine (Brown, Gardner et al. 1998, 62). The major countries that are approaching stage three are the United States, another colonial power, and China, which has also identified progress with rapid industrialization and population policies based on gross violations of human rights.

In short, the "successful" countries have been successful because of various forms of economic colonialism. The countries that are lagging behind are largely countries that were colonized and that still suffer from the legacy of colonialism. Many of these countries also started with much higher population densities than the "successful" countries. India, for example, will soon pass China as the world's most populous country. And consider the situation in three precarious countries: Ethiopia, Nigeria, and Pakistan. The fertility rate in these countries is between six and seven children per mother. At these rates, Pakistan's population is projected to grow by 141 percent by the year 2050, Nigeria's by 178 percent, and Ethiopia's by 244 percent, from a population of 62 million in 1998 to 213 million by midcentury.

For Notestein's three stages of population growth to work we must assume that colonized countries can be pushed through to stage three in the same way colonial powers achieved their level of economic development. Is this likely? What distant resources would the colonized exploit? What level of military preparedness would be required? Given the disastrous political climates that still prevail in many postcolonial countries, what likelihood is there that any newly acquired wealth would be distributed in socially just ways? And, given the mad dash to economic development, what chance is there that environmental preservation, or education, or health care, will be a priority?

Consider, further, that many of the postcolonial countries that remain in the most precarious positions are the countries under the most pressure from the World Bank and the World Trade Organization to drop trade barriers and expose their citizens to competition from the winners of the colonial race. This is a process that dislocates the most vulnerable from their land and pushes them into urban slums. And when their governments borrow too much money, it is the poor who are subjected to structural adjustment programs (SAPs) to repay the bank. Money that was spent on education, public health, and the environment is diverted to pay the bank. That is, SAPs destroy the very social structures in vulnerable countries that could address the population problem in an alliance with social and environmental justice. As we have seen, women who are appropriately educated make the greatest difference in controlling their lives, including the birthrate. This is the difference between Kerala and the Punjab.

What Population Problem? The title of this chapter is not meant to indicate that we can happily dance our way into a future of nine billion people. Common sense tells us that increasing our population by a third in fifty years will put an extraordinary strain on the planet. Clean water will be just as hard to come by as good jobs. Conflicts over access to nature are inevitable.

My point is that we need to decide now whether we want to plan to move into the future democratically, or whether we should be content simply to use our power to "keep the lid on" future conflicts. It may seem that the easy way out is to continue to accumulate military and economic power to meet any challenge. But this alternative is expensive economically, and more importantly, expensive to our self-understanding as a democratic people. Our moral identities are at stake.

The tragedy, as I have argued in this chapter, is that the other alternative—more democracy—is more *practical* than force. It addresses the causes of our problems. Force simply responds to the effects of bad policy. This misdirection of public policy will affect, and is affecting, all of us. As the cost of military defense adds up, funding for the social good decreases. The effects of structural adjustment will come home to roost. We will pay with an educational system that doesn't train the young for the future, and a two-tier system of health care in which the wealthy get what they need and everyone else takes what is left.

There is indeed a "third world in the first world," and it is growing. We will all lose if we think of the future as "us against them." Those of us in the first world can learn a great deal from the third (and fourth) world if we will only learn to appreciate the expertise that comes from places where we would not expect to find it.

In the following chapter, I examine one integrated response to colonialism that includes social and environmental justice. Although we think of Mahatma Gandhi's path as relevant only to the third world, I believe we all urgently need to understand his methods and goals as they apply to the contemporary world. If anything, the challenges to people's connections to place are even more urgent than they were in Gandhi's time.

GANDHI'S VISION OF COMMUNITY DEVELOPMENT

We should now be ready to ask several critically important questions: Is all ecodevelopment just neocolonialism in disguise, or are there kinds of human and ecological change that are ethical? Is social justice for humans in conflict with the preservation of nature? When we attempt to help "other" people, does this simply make them dependent on us, or can some kinds of help foster genuine freedom and a healthy self-identity? In particular, what should we say about charity? Does a morally responsible life require us to engage in charity for the welfare of those "less fortunate" than ourselves?

Furthermore, the first world's attempt to develop the third world raises basic questions about the mission itself. If many traditional communities have longstanding versions of an environmental ethic, why do they need "development"? Why do we define "expertise" as the dissemination of Western culture to those "in need" when it is arguable that there are many forms of unrecognized expertise in the cultures defined as needing development? Perhaps they have something to teach us.

If much of the expertise that trickles down to the third world is culturally and ecologically inappropriate, we would expect protest. And indeed, the leading edge of environmental awareness comes from these traditional societies as they resist the "one size fits all" approach of development projects. To understand the cutting edge of environmental ethics today, we need to attend to diverse environmental resistance movements. These are not simply links in the chain of a global environmental movement. These movements arise from specific places, with specific issues that are relevant to certain places.

In spite of the extraordinary diversity of the world's ecological communities, almost every community is now forced to respond to a single source of pressure to change: economic and cultural globalization. We can learn something important if it turns out that these diverse communities are responding in similar, and connected, ways. I would not argue that all of these resistance movements are Gandhian in character. Indeed, many look to mentors in the struggle against colonialism who saw violence as necessary to reclaim one's identity. It may be, as well, that these resistance movements are truly indigenous, in the sense that they depend entirely on local narratives of resistance. The point in getting to know Gandhi's approach well, then, is to provide at least one concrete example of an eco-community resistance movement that succeeded in throwing off colonialism and maintained a "third path" that was not aligned with either Marxism or capitalism.

This chapter can also be viewed as a continuation of the major conclusions of the last chapter. I argued in chapter 4 that a collaborative approach to population issues is both ethically better and more practical than a coercive approach. Women have the right to informed consent on population policies. Women and the poor are often the targets of coercive population control programs, but they are central to cooperative approaches. Women's freedom at the village level is the core of ethical development. The same can be said of the communities that resist globalization. It is both morally right and practical to insist that they have a right to informed consent, and active participation, in the changes that are occurring to them. Real development should be judged by whether it facilitates freedom, dignity, and healthy relationships to place for those who are disenfranchised. Development is not corporate welfare for the economic and political elite.

Fortunately, therefore, we need not start from scratch in thinking about the questions I have just raised. Mahatma Gandhi thought deeply about these issues throughout his life. Moreover, if we are looking for reasons to be optimistic, we might point out that Gandhi's approach succeeded in liberating more than three hundred million people in 1947, at the time of Indian independence, as well as their more than one billion descendents who live in India today.

We have become accustomed to solving problems with violence, but what war has been as successful as Gandhi's nonviolent methods? Gandhi's

99

legacy, I believe, cannot be dismissed as a utopian dream. It is both moral and practical to the highest degree. It is also deeply relevant to the future of this planet.

Mohandas Gandhi was born on October 2, 1869, to a Hindu family in Porbandar on the northwest coast of India. He was devoted to his mother, whom he described as saintly. However, he was in conflict with his temperamental father; these conflicts led him to pursue nonviolent means of dispute resolution later in life. At age thirteen he was married to a girl his own age, Kasturbai, in an arranged marriage.

At age nineteen Gandhi left India to study law in London. He reported that he fervently wished to imitate the British in manner and dress. Later, he came to see this kind of identification with a colonial oppressor as a phase in coming to consciousness of his own identity. He had a lifelong struggle with the question of what it means to establish an identity of one's own in the context of thoroughgoing oppression. Gandhi did not separate the personal from the political.

In 1893, having earned his degree in law, he left for South Africa, also a British colony, to provide legal representation to Indians, many of whom worked in South African diamond mines. For more than a decade, Gandhi remained loyal to the British, even counseling his fellow Indians to emulate the British.

In the summer of 1906, however, Gandhi witnessed the most profoundly transformative event of his life: the Zulu Rebellion. The British violently put down a rebellion by the Zulu tribe, indiscriminately slaughtering men, women, and children. Gandhi was appalled by the sadistic behavior of the British soldiers. It contradicted his favorable view of British civilization. In response, he turned away from the British influence of his law school days, and back to his mother's spiritual nonviolence.

The Zulu Rebellion, therefore, crystallized for Gandhi the connections between the oppressive conditions of colonialism and the treatment of women. In turn, he came to see the connections between the oppression of women and colonialism as distinct, but connected, forms of oppression, which also include racism, classism, casteism, and even the human oppression of nature. Gandhi's response to colonialism was comprehensive and unified.

Following the Zulu Rebellion, Gandhi engaged in his first act of public, nonviolent, collective resistance to colonialism. In a continuing crackdown on resistance to their colonial authority, the British required all Indians to register with the government, and to carry their passes with them at all times. Gandhi, as well as thousands of other Indians, resented the pass law as a public humiliation. They met on September 11, 1906, and committed themselves to public, nonviolent resistance.

The powerful film *Gandhi* vividly depicts this act of resistance as Gandhi and others publicly burned their passes in the presence of British soldiers. They were beaten mercilessly with sticks and dragged away to prison. In the first act of *satyagraha* Gandhi and others—Hindu, Muslim, and Sikh—took the beatings but did not respond in kind.

It is important for us to see that this active nonviolence was designed to reclaim the identity of colonized people in the face of oppression. It highlighted the contradictions in the British claim to respect individual liberty while failing to do so in practice. And it responded to such oppression by living up to the highest standards for treatment of another human being. In short, it forced the British to recognize that they were dealing with human beings.

Gandhi returned to India in 1915 and was joined by Jawaharlal Nehru, later to become the first prime minister of free India, and other members of the Congress Party. On April 13, 1919, an act of British imperialism occurred that was strikingly similar to the Zulu rebellion. Thousands of Hindus and Sikhs had gathered in the northern city of Amritsar to celebrate a religious holiday. General Reginald Dyer took the gathering to be a show of opposition to the martial law that had been imposed on Amritsar. He ordered his troops to fire on the unarmed civilians, killing more than four hundred and wounding fifteen hundred.

The Amritsar Massacre was a turning point in Indian history. In response, Gandhi orchestrated decades of nonviolent resistance to the British. The most celebrated was the salt march, or Salt Satyagraha, in which Gandhi led eighty of his followers on a march to the sea, where they made salt in opposition to the British tax on salt. This symbolic act spurred hundreds of thousands of other Indians to follow suit and make their own salt in defiance of the British.

This event shows Gandhi as an inspiring leader, able to choose telling acts of resistance that exposed British tyranny. At one level the salt march questioned British economic control of India. More importantly, it showed his fellow Indians that the British could continue to rule only if

Indians allowed them to rule: "We are our own slaves, not of the British. This should be engraved on our minds. The whites cannot remain if we do not want them" (Gandhi 1996, 38). The key to effective resistance was for Indians to reclaim their sense of identity as a self-governing people. And, for Gandhi, self-governance begins at the bottom, with those who have experienced exclusion from the top.

Five months after India achieved its independence, in August 1947, a fundamentalist Hindu, Nathuram Godse, assassinated Gandhi. Godse rejected Gandhi's vision of a pluralist India that welcomed all religions. He believed that India should be for Hindus, not Muslims. Indeed, much to Gandhi's horror, at independence India had broken into two countries, India and Pakistan, with millions of Muslims moving to Pakistan, and Hindus moving to India. This breakup was the greatest disappointment of Gandhi's life.

Still today we witness the tensions, now nuclear, between India and Pakistan, especially in the disputed region of Kashmir, which was not granted the right to self-determination after independence, as were the other states of India. Right-wing Hindu nationalists have also reasserted themselves in the form of the Bharatiya Janata Party, which proclaims that India is for Hindus (Bharatiya Janaya Party). The conflict between some (not all) Hindus and Moslems has boiled over into ethnic violence, sadly, in the vicinity of Porbandar, where Gandhi was born.

We have met with Gandhi's form of active nonviolent resistance, which he called *satyagraha*. Part of Gandhi's inspiring leadership was due to the fact that he used key words that are rich with multiple meanings. Satyagraha is most often translated as "the power of nonviolence." A *satyagrahi* is one who practices active, nonviolent resistance. This is a good place to start in attempting to understand Gandhi, since Gandhi certainly wanted to emphasize that satyagraha is not passive. As we will see, satyagraha is fully active in several senses: it requires commitment, training, and a high degree of organization. It also gains power when it is a collective response to violence.

While "the power of nonviolence" is a good place to begin, there is much more to Gandhi's use of the word satyagraha. In order to understand this rather odd term, we need to look carefully at what Gandhi meant by truth. He explained, "The word *satya* [truth] comes from *sat*, which means 'to be,' 'to exist'" (1996, 36). So, a second meaning of "satyagraha" is "truth-being," a person who lives the truth. To actively resist violence is to be a truth-being.

Truth for Gandhi was not just "knowing the facts." Gandhi often described himself as a humble *seeker* after the truth. A truth-being, therefore, engages in a constant *process*. This process never ends for human beings, because we can only glimpse a fragment of the whole truth. To be truly human is to be humble. "Beyond the limited truths [that human beings can know]," Gandhi said, "there is one absolute Truth which is total and all-embracing. But it is indescribable, because it is God. Or say, rather, God is truth . . ." (1996, 35). Only God is a "truth-being" in the fullest sense. Humans are fragmentary, at best; we are humble seekers for the truth.

We see, then, that satyagraha is not just a simple matter of doing the right thing, doing one's duty, and performing the right actions. Given the human condition of fallibility, we need to be suspicious of the idea that there is some simple, abstract *rule* that determines good actions. Gandhi's method was, above all, practical. Gandhi was interested in what sort of *person* we are, what sort of person we *become* through our public engagements. We should cultivate a spirit of humility and nonviolence because, at a minimum, we will not then become fanatics or zealots who hold firm to their version of the truth no matter what. Gandhi called on us to live by principle, in full, daily recognition of life's ambiguities.

Resistance to tyranny, then, was a spiritual enterprise for Gandhi since we must act from firm understanding that we are fragments of the whole. This is one way Gandhi differed from another great revolutionary, Karl Marx. At the beginning of the "age of development" in the years immediately following World War II, there were two responses to global capitalism: Marx and Gandhi. If we want to understand contemporary responses to globalization we should understand something about the origins of these positions.

Marx famously believed that religion is the "opiate of the people." It is a drug used to keep people servile to capitalism: we are "lambs" whose suffering on earth will be repaid in heaven. By using the word "opiate" Marx also intended to convey the idea that religious beliefs, and other cultural beliefs about ourselves, are not real. The "ideological superstructure," as Marx termed these beliefs, is simply the causal effect of what *is* real, the "economic base." Capitalism causes us to have "false consciousness," beliefs about ourselves that we take to be true, but that are really causally determined effects of capitalism. We enslave ourselves, that is, by subscribing to beliefs that hold us in chains.

As a consequence of this one-directional analysis, from base to superstructure, Marx believed that true revolution comes when there is a change in class consciousness. Real change comes when capitalism is destroyed and replaced by a system of economic production that does not split workers into antagonistic classes.

Gandhi often said that he agreed with much of Marx's analysis of capitalism. After all, Gandhi's class consciousness was formed from the perspective of a man oppressed by the capitalist demands of British colonialism. Taken out of context it is hard to know who wrote the following: "Working for economic equality means abolishing the eternal conflict between capital and labor. It means the leveling down of the few rich in whose hands is concentrated the bulk of the nation's wealth on the one hand, and the leveling up of the semi-starved naked millions on the other" (1996, 133). In fact, it was Gandhi. Gandhi also wrote this, part of a blunt response to an American questioner: "Western democracy, as it functions today, is diluted Nazism or Fascism. At best it is merely a cloak to hide the Nazi and Fascist tendencies of imperialism" (1996, 148).

Nevertheless, Gandhi profoundly disagreed with Marx's analysis of the relationship between spirituality and postcolonial freedom, between self-identity and political freedom. A Marxist analysis of oppression fails to include the sort of humility, the sense of unending process that is central to Gandhi's approach to nonviolent resistance. Marx and Gandhi were systematic thinkers in profoundly different ways. Marx thought of his view as a kind of science that could be applied everywhere. Gandhi tried to understand all life as connected, but he believed that perfect understanding is unattainable by human beings. Life is always something of an embarrassment to pure theory.

There were other differences between Gandhi and Marx. Marx believed that it is not possible to really communicate across the boundaries of economic class, since, in capitalism, economic classes are in fundamental conflict with one another. Class conflict is war.

Gandhi was absolutely inclusive in his commitment to communication across borders. He believed that Indians could communicate with their British oppressors about matters of profound importance: the state of their own souls. He believed as well that all the castes and classes of India needed to remain united in opposition to the British, even if they were in conflict with each other. (It must be noted that this conviction was controversial since it made him a gradualist on issues of caste.) In contrast to Marx, Gandhi understood liberation as a process that freed both oppressor and oppressed.

Before moving on to consider other basic ideas, we should pause briefly to consider an understandable suspicion about the practical effectiveness of satyagraha: "How effective would satyagraha have been if confronted by a fascist regime such as Nazi Germany?" This is a fair question, especially since I have been arguing that Gandhi's approach was practical.

To be fair to Gandhi, however, we must remember that he never said active nonviolence works in all cases and under all circumstances. The British were good candidates for satyagraha since they recognized, at least in theory, universal human rights. Gandhi always saw himself as doing the British a favor by demanding that they live up to their own ideals. As a result, he believed the British would eventually leave India as friends. Indeed, that is what happened.

So, what can we say about a racist regime like Nazi Germany, which did not recognize universal human rights? Again, to be fair we must acknowledge that active nonviolence did not succeed overnight. Gandhi worked tirelessly for more than half a century to perfect his methods of organizing people. There were many failures along the way. The most difficult for Gandhi was an incident in the town of Chauri Chaura in which police fired on an unarmed crowd. The police then retreated into their police station as the crowd retaliated, and the crowd set the station on fire. When the officers left the building to escape the smoke, the crowd hacked them to pieces and threw their body parts back into the flames. Gandhi was so horrified that he temporarily called off the campaign of nonviolent resistance.

For Gandhi, nothing in human life is infallible, not even satyagraha. To expect some simple, magical answer to violence indicates a basic misunderstanding of what Gandhi meant when he said that truth will always be a process for human beings, not a final result.

We should also recognize that, in spite of his reputation, Gandhi was not an absolute pacifist. He did not reject violence in every case. In the process of attempting to clarify that satyagraha requires strength and courage, he once said that it is better to be violent than to be weak in one's commitment to nonviolence. This point might be relevant to the case at hand, when there was not time to build a nonviolent collective response to Nazism.

Had the Nazis imprisoned Gandhi, nevertheless, he certainly would have responded nonviolently. Just as certainly he would have been executed. But this is really not a counterexample to what Gandhi meant by satyagraha. A full test of the effectiveness of satyagraha does not come from the execution of one person. Satyagraha requires not just an individual response, even from as great a figure as Gandhi, but a collective response, organized over decades. The force of Nazi violence had to be met with the full force of active nonviolence. This conflict never happened. World War II did not provide a fair test of nonviolent resistance to totalitarianism.

I want to press this point about the practicality of nonviolence further. Gandhi stated his practical opposition to violence thus: "I object to violence because, when it appears to do good, the good is only temporary; the evil it does is permanent" (1996, 43). Responding violently to violence treats only effects, not deep causes. We may temporarily stop violence with violence, but in the long run violence only begets more violence. It is almost always impractical.

We need to distinguish true nonviolence from mere pacification. To violently put an end to violence deals only with effects, so it can never really solve the problem. Nonviolence, on the other hand, deals with causes. It can, therefore, stop the cycle of violence, not just suspend it temporarily.

Consider this image: you are sitting by a pristine mountain lake early in the morning on a perfectly calm day. The water is like glass. For some reason, you throw a stone into the water, but you immediately regret that you have disturbed the perfect beauty of the lake. Responding to such violence with violence is like trying to return the lake to glassy smoothness by reaching out and patting down the waves caused by the rock. Although perhaps understandable, this response will only cause more waves, and more waves again, until there is no calm anywhere on the lake. The real remedy is to act by being still, by not making more waves. Peace in the long run comes from breaking the chain of violence at its source.

Given our fragmented understanding, we can never really know the true effects of violence. Our ignorance only increases the farther we move into the future. Nonviolence is compatible with our human ignorance. It does not require divine knowledge of the future.

Violence responds to short-term threats, that is, to effects. Nonviolence responds to the causes themselves, and it has the potential for real freedom. What could be more practical? One of the oddities of living at a time when we seem to think only in terms of short-term gratification is that it may make violence appear to be the practical solution to conflict.

We are still not quite done with the meanings of satyagraha. Gandhi's term for nonharm was "ahimsa." Of course he meant this to apply to the "big" issues: murder, incest, rape, war. However, it also applies to the smallest details of daily life. Commitment to humility also requires civility: "Civility and humility are expressions of the spirit of non-violence. A non-co-operator, therefore ought never to be uncivil" (Gandhi 1996, 47). Violence in language must be avoided just as much as violence in action.

One of Gandhi's criticisms of non-Gandhian dissenters was that when they confront their oppressors with linguistic violence they betray a sense of egotism, and therefore arrogance. In turn, they betray a lack of respect not only for their opponent but also for themselves: "Speech, especially when it is haughty, betrays want of confidence and it makes one's opponent skeptical about the reality of the act itself" (1996, 49). A satyagrahi, therefore, must avoid psychological violence against one's opponent and also against oneself. Unfortunately, Gandhi would have had differences with many today who protest injustice with violence of speech and action.

Gandhi was quick to warn us that "I trust no one will understand politeness to mean flattery. Nor does it mean hiding our regard for our dharma. To be polite means to show respect towards others while clinging to our own dharma" (1996, 47). By "dharma" Gandhi means something like our true self, which he explained in terms of incompleteness, humility, and civility. To reclaim one's dharma, having been colonized by another, is a humanizing process. It returns one's opponent to true human-being. It also humanizes the satyagrahi.

The last point I want to make about satyagraha is that it is not limited to human beings:

Complete non-violence is complete absence of ill will against all that lives. It therefore embraces even sub-human life not excluding noxious insects or beasts. They have not been created to feed our destructive propensities. If we only knew the mind of the Creator, we should find their proper place in His creation. Non-violence is therefore, in its active form, goodwill towards all life. It is pure love. (1996, 41)

I do not want to push this point about Gandhi's environmental awareness too far. Gandhi was primarily interested in social justice, so it may verge on wishful thinking to ascribe a fully developed environmental ethic to him. But we should also not underestimate Gandhi. I think he was insightful beyond his own time in insisting that all forms of oppression are connected, and must be resisted simultaneously. One must resist all violence, in oneself as well as others, in matters of gender, caste, and economic class, and even in human arrogance toward the rest of nature. Among the great voices of resistance to colonialism, Gandhi stood alone in pairing social and environmental justice.

If we want to understand how Gandhi would respond today to globalization we need to connect satyagraha with his account of positive freedom. Just as we need to be careful not to assume what Gandhi meant by satyagraha, we need to be willing to set aside common assumptions about the meaning of freedom.

We Americans often understand freedom in terms of what has been called "negative freedom." We think that our right not to be harmed by another erects a wall of protection around us. Rights function as a way of marking off "my territory," which you may enter only with my permission.

From Gandhi's point of view, however, this negative conception of freedom ducks a critical question: What is *worth doing* with our freedom? We want freedom, but freedom to do what? The concept of negative freedom encourages us to answer these questions by saying, "It's really none of your business! That's why I want freedom, so I can do anything I like (short of harming others) without having to answer to anyone." Freedom in this sense depicts questions of what it is worth doing with freedom as nothing more than subjective preferences. Choosing to work for the environment, or for women's welfare, might be admirable, but freedom does not require it. If we choose to commit to these things it is almost like saying I prefer Burger King to McDonald's. Someone else might say they prefer McDonald's, but this is not a question we can argue about. Such choices are subjective; we make them without any intrasubjective criteria for evaluating them.

Gandhi disagreed profoundly with the idea that freedom is merely negative. He argued that there is a difference between what he called "independence" and "swaraj," or positive freedom. Gandhi said:

> People generally do not understand the philosophy of all their acts. My ambition is much higher than independence. Through the deliverance of India, I seek to deliver the so-called weaker races of the earth from the crushing heels of Western exploitation in which England is the greatest partner. . . . England can have the privilege of becoming a partner if she wishes. . . . (1996, 99)

Swaraj is a social conception of freedom. It commits us to choices on substantive conceptions of the good. The freedom of one person can never come at the expense of another, or at the expense of the community. The freedom of the human species cannot come at the expense of nature.

Despite the fact that Gandhi wanted the British to leave, he warned that India would not experience swaraj just by throwing out the British. Swaraj requires "a real change of heart on the part of the people" (1996, 99). Without a change of heart, newly free Indians could turn around and colonize each other, since that is what they learned from the British. This would permit ethnic and religious conflict; it would permit "the error of untouchability" (1996, 99). Swaraj, like nonviolence, requires a continuing process for the sake of achieving true self-governance. Positive freedom necessitates active citizenship.

Many of the actual rights that Gandhi thought swaraj could achieve are familiar to a Western audience: freedom of association, of speech, and of the press. It also assumed freedom of conscience and free practice of one's faith based on the separation of church and state.

Some of the rights Gandhi includes under the concept of swaraj, however, are foreign to us. He argues, for example, that swaraj requires "protection of the culture, language, and scripts of the minorities" (1996, 101). This is a policy of *active* support for the cultural heritage of ethnic minorities, not just passive tolerance. It would require culturally appropriate education for minorities in their native languages. In the United States we may offer English as a Second Language programs, but their purpose is to "mainstream" linguistically diverse students quickly. Tolerance for minorities is temporary, not a permanent requirement of freedom, as Gandhi requires.

This is an important point. Negative freedom presupposes a presocial conception of freedom. Our true selves come before our commitments. Gandhi thought the presocial conception fell short of true freedom. Part of our core identity, Gandhi thought, is sometimes our social being. A culture that preserves our "individual" freedom while destroying our ethnic culture—either by active aggression, or by passive neglect—is not truly free.

Gandhi's *swaraj* also went farther in protecting women than we have. He endorsed "Protection of women workers, and specially adequate provisions for leave during maternity period" (1996, 102). Women are to be protected, like all employees, in their places of work. This includes their right not to be discriminated against just because they, and not men, can bear children.

Such rights need to be seen in the larger context that, for Gandhi, human beings have the right to work. Here, Gandhi agreed with Marx that good work is a humanizing force; no person should be deprived of the right to work, therefore, just as no one should be deprived of freedom of speech or religion, there is no "acceptable level of unemployment."

Some of Gandhi's requirements for true swaraj may seem unnecessarily restrictive or prudish to Americans. He insisted that alcohol and drugs must be totally banned, and that usury (lending money for interest) had to be strictly controlled. In context, however, these requirements make good sense. Alcohol and drugs are common instruments through which one class controls another in India. The men in one village often brew grain alcohol and offer it to the men of a lower-class village as a way of "befriending" them. Alcoholism increases, along with violence against women and children, and the end result is total control of those at the bottom.

Similarly, many workers in the third world today simply do not earn enough income to support their families. This is especially true of agricultural workers since their work is usually seasonal. Families then borrow money to get through to the next growing season, but where wages do not rise there is no hope of paying off the loans. In India this condition is termed "bonded labor." Men and women essentially become slaves to a higher economic class, often for what appear to us to be ridiculously small sums of money: twenty or thirty dollars.

The extensive requirements for true freedom laid down by Gandhi lead to the conclusion that true swaraj is freedom at the *village* level. Gandhi was aware that abstract constitutional guarantees of freedom are only valuable if the poorest people can actually exercise them at the village level. India's Constitution provided for extensive freedoms for women, and it abolished the caste system. But what difference do such guarantees make for women who are illiterate and cannot read the constitution, or Dalits who will be beaten if they "pollute" the drinking water of the higher castes? Gandhi remarked,

> External freedom will always be the means of measuring the freedom of the self within. Hence we often find that laws made to grant us freedom often turn out to be shackles binding us. Hence the dharma of those workers who wish to attain true freedom is to try and attempt an improvement in the self. If we understand this simple and straightforward fact, we shall not even utter the word "legislature" but engage ourselves in constructive activity [social reform] day and night. (1996, 107)

Readers who remember the film portrayal of Gandhi by Ben Kingsley will recall his devotion to the spinning wheel. As with much of Gandhi's style of leadership, the spinning wheel symbolized much. England exploited Indian textile workers in order to keep its own textile industry healthy. Thus we have "madras" cloth, which is used in summer weight shirts. It originated in the southeastern Indian city of Madras, but the cloth was finished in England.

Gandhi used the spinning wheel as a daily protest to this sort of dependence on the British. Khadi, as this kind of simple cloth is called, is an example of village swaraj. Gandhi wanted to show Indians that they could support themselves by spinning their own cloth and sewing their own clothing.

Like satyagraha, when we follow out the meanings of swaraj we find that it exists at the local level for Gandhi. There are other connections. Satyagraha is the constant practice of nonviolence and truth toward self and others. It is this kind of "soul force" that is required for the change of heart that constitutes true freedom: swaraj.

A third, more controversial concept must be added to these to round out the Gandhian model of ecodevelopment: sarvodaya. This term is usually translated "the welfare of all." It is controversial because Gandhi meant it in the most literal sense. He believed that no one can truly be free while others are still enslaved: "According to my definition, there cannot be true swaraj as long as there is exploitation" (1996, 134). One of the implications of this idea is that the first world cannot be free while the third world is enslaved.

If Gandhi were to observe contemporary America he would say that we tend to reduce the idea of freedom to mere economic freedom, a kind of negative freedom. But, this cannot be the full meaning of freedom because economic freedom, as we practice it, results in class conflict; it is, therefore, incompatible with swaraj. Positive freedom, freedom of—and within—the community, makes the freedom of one dependent on the freedom of all. A social life means voluntarily limiting one's negative freedoms. True positive freedom for one cannot come at the expense of the freedom of others.

As with satyagraha and swaraj, Gandhi's examination of sarvodaya leads him to conclude that true independence "begins at the bottom" (1996, 149). Although social welfare includes a large measure of control over one's economic life, it goes much deeper than that. It includes the right to work, but it also includes such noneconomic dimensions of life as a sense of integrity and self-worth, and a cultural and ecological place in one's village.

I am aware that to an audience accustomed to the sound of moral individualism, sarvodaya may just tip the scales against Gandhi. If I cannot be genuinely free while others are not, then my individual freedom depends on solving the world's problems. I must address poverty, disease, crime, and war before I can be free. That seems a little much. But let us think in more detail about what sarvodaya really commits us to.

At a minimum, sarvodaya does make us responsible for deep forms of systemic and institutional violence, especially those that benefit us. We have this responsibility to others, and to nature, whether we know it or not. Gandhi would certainly say that we bear responsibility for sweatshops in Central America, especially if we buy cheap clothing because workers are exploited. Simply by being born to a certain economic class, we receive certain benefits whether we know it or consciously want them. Ignorance of the working conditions required to produce our clothing is not an excuse. The oppression is real, whether we know it or not.

There are different ways in which we can be responsible for moral transgressions. All the moral weight of the world does not rest on a single pair of shoulders. When we say that sarvodaya means that we are responsible for the violence that globalization inflicts on disadvantaged workers, we are not necessarily saying that each of us is *individually* responsible, or even that any single person willed this violence. The problem is not individual violence, but, rather, systemic and institutional violence. It is a question of what the structures of contemporary social and economic life permit and encourage.

In the case of globalization the question sarvodaya raises is not whether I, individually, willed sweatshop workers to be exploited. The question is, what should I do with the subtle, sometimes distant, advantages in power—economic and social—that my class gives me? Once I know about these power relationships, the question is, do I exploit such powers to my benefit, or do I refuse such power, as much as possible, and use my knowledge to dismantle relationships that exploit others? We may not be individually responsible for whether there is systemic and institutional violence, but we are responsible for whether we accept or reject the power we gain through such violence.

We might also recall here that Gandhi would never say there is some clean, neutral moral position in the contemporary world from which to issue moral judgments. Opposing globalization is a *direction*, not an end. It is a direction that begins from wherever we happen to find ourselves in the complicated push and pull of the contemporary world.

Given this "positioned response," which is the best that fallible humans can achieve, I believe Gandhi would encourage us to use the particular strengths and skills that we happen to have, and to resist the idea that we can single-handedly achieve a comprehensive solution. Teachers should teach responsibly. Doctors and nurses should provide socially conscious medical care. Scientists should strive to make their research goals consistent with the common good. It is an act of hubris if any of us thinks that we alone can provide the solution to the world's problems. This is why, in discussing satyagraha, I emphasized so strongly that resistance to colonialism must be collective and well organized.

A Gandhian response to the contemporary world is deeply committed to diversity in several ways: we all have different strengths and weaknesses; we all are positioned differently with respect to class, gender, and sexual orientation, and even species, if we take Gandhi's ecological orientation seriously. This leads us to a profoundly important conclusion. Community ecodevelopment is inherently diverse. It must begin at the local level because communities and places are diverse. The only possible response to globalization is an organized, courageous, decades-long resistance in which diverse communities offer their local strengths in response to a global threat.

This extended account of Gandhi's historical legacy as well as Gandhianism in the contemporary world might seem like a long digression. But if we believe that environmental and social justice are intertwined, we need to adjust our understanding of what an environmental problem is. Furthermore, if we do not wish simply to project our attitudes about the relationship of people to place onto profoundly different contexts, we need to pay attention to specific, localized responses around the world that may differ from what is familiar in our own culture.

Gandhi recognized the dangers of globalization long before the term was coined. He still offers us one model through which we might try to think of contemporary resistance movements. Of course, I am not suggesting that all of these actual movements are, or should be, Gandhian. However, I do think Gandhi at least puts us in a position to understand a critically important phenomenon in the contemporary world: *indigenous* resistance to globalization. In contrast to those few appointed executives who sit behind the closed doors of the World Trade Organization and issue decisions on what counts as "fair," resistance to globalization is diverse. The cutting edge of resistance is coming from particular ecocommunities uniting to defend particular places.

We have already met with several important examples of localized environmental resistance. Recall the discussion in chapter 1 of Cree resistance to hydropower projects in Canada. In chapter 2, I discussed the Himalayan hill tribes and their relationship to the deodar forests. In chapter 4, we encountered Ken Saro-Wiwa and the attempt of the Ogoni tribe in Nigeria to protect its homeland against exploitation by the Nigerian government and international oil companies. Also in chapter 4, I recognized the profoundly important example of sacred groves as a place where spirituality and environmental preservation come together. Such sacred groves have existed all over the globe, as Madhav Gadgil argued. In places where they still exist, we can usually expect to find healthy relationships between people and place.

In this chapter, I focus on a variety of contemporary resistance movements from several different locations. My hope is that this survey reveals both the diversity of these resistance movements, since they are defending particular relationships of their people to a unique homeland, and the important connections between them. All are responding to a common challenge: economic and cultural globalization.

India: The Narmada Dam

Since independence in 1947, India's leaders have been enamored with dams. To understand why, it is important to understand that India is not like the Midwest of the United States, the so-called breadbasket. We receive moderate rain throughout the year. India, in contrast, depends on its twice-yearly monsoons. If the monsoon fails to occur it can mean disaster for the agricultural sector.

Indian agriculturists have recognized the need to control water for thousands of years. Many techniques for conserving and damming water were invented as necessary components in systems of agriculture that have supported high population density for centuries. Since 1947, however, the scale and the politics of dams have changed. The largest, and most controversial, project ever undertaken is the Sardar Sarovar project. It will dam the Narmada River and its 41 tributaries with 3,200 dams, including 30 major dams. The completed project will submerge 4,000 square kilometers of deciduous forests. These are dams that cannot be imagined without the support of the World Bank.

In a place like India, dam projects dislodge people as well as forests. A fair estimate is that the project will displace half a million people. More than half of these are Adivasis, the indigenous peoples of India. Where will these people go? India has no functioning relocation policy. The displaced poor have to fend for themselves. As we saw in the discussion of the green revolution, agriculturalists who are removed from their land usually migrate to the cities and into the vast slums that have been caused by industrialization. There are also gender dimensions to these shifts since it is usually the men who migrate in search of jobs. Women and children are often left behind with no access to food or water.

The Narmada project has polarized India along the lines of an earthquake fault. (One of the objections to Narmada is that its largest dam rests squarely on top of the world's most active earthquake zone.) On one side are the World Bank, the Indian government, and large industrialists who praise the dam as necessary for progress. On the other side a resistance movement has formed. The Narmada Bachao Andolan (NBA) was formed in 1986. Supporters from other environmental and social justice groups soon joined; with this broad support in 1988 the NBA called for a cessation of all work on the Narmada Dam project. Active resistance began as many valley residents refused to evacuate their homes, saying that they would choose to drown rather than abandon their homelands.

The Valley was then militarized. On December 25, 1990, six thousand resisters, mainly Adivasis, joined together in an attempt to reach the construction zone where they planned to resist construction with their bodies. They bound their hands together and resisted nonviolently as the police clubbed them and removed them from the site. They were forced back. On January 7, 1991, six resisters announced that they would begin a hunger strike. The international press arrived to witness the event. Unfavorable press caused the World Bank to order a review of its funding for the project.

Stung by international criticism, the World Bank ordered a review of its support for Sardar Sarovar. In June 1991, the Bank appointed Bradford Morse as chairman of the Independent Review. Morse was well qualified to lead the review; he had previously led the United Nations Development Program. The World Bank and the government of India may well have hoped for a whitewash. Exactly a year later, after an exhaustive review, Morse and his colleagues published a devastating report. The summary of conclusions reads:

> We think the Sardar Sarovar Projects as they stand are flawed, that resettlement and rehabilitation of all those displaced by the Projects is not possible under prevailing circumstances, and that environmental impacts of the Projects have not been properly considered or adequately addressed. Moreover we believe that the Bank shares responsibility with the borrower for the situation that has developed. . . . It seems clear that engineering and economic imperatives have driven the Projects to the exclusion of human and environmental concerns. . . . India and the states involved . . . have spent a great deal of money. No one wants to see this money wasted. But we caution that it may be more wasteful to proceed without full knowledge of the human and environmental costs. . . . As a result, we think that the wisest course would be for the Bank to step back from the Projects and consider them afresh. . . . (Morse and Berger 1992, quoted from Roy 1999, 44–45)

To no one's surprise, the World Bank was not willing to accept its own report. Two months later, it sent another team to India. It recommended a set of patchwork "solutions" that allowed the project to continue. Finally, however, the Bank felt sufficient pressure that it was forced to withdraw.

However, leadership of the Project then transferred from the Bank and India's national government to individual Indian states, particularly the state of Gujarat. Work on the dam has continued, despite protests, such as the Monsoon Satyagraha in 1993 when families chained themselves to their homes, saying they preferred to be swept away by the rising water than to be relocated.

The Morse Report cited problems with Sardar Sarovar of several different kinds. It focused on the human injustice of forcing the poorest of the poor out of their homelands without any hope of workable relocation. These are cultures whose literal survival depends on access to rich silt along the river for farming. It cited the religious dimensions of flooding a sacred river literally studded with sacred sites, both Hindu and indigenous. It also questioned the dam conceptually, raising questions about whether, even if judged in its own terms, Sardar Sarovar could provide the solutions its advocates claimed for it.

I have said that water preservation projects are not new to India. Small farmers have long recognized the need to preserve water in a setting that depends on monsoons for rain. However, moving from these small-scale, diverse solutions to the megaprojects of Sardar Sarovar created environmental problems that did not exist before. It has long been noted, even with regard to large dams in the United States, that megadams become less useful over the years as silt, which is disturbed by flooding behind the dam, builds up. What was once rich farmland that supported the poor is tragically submerged behind the dam, eventually filling in the lake created by the dam.

An additional grave consequence of large dams in places like India is the problem of salinization. Dams like Sardar Sarovar are designed to support the irrigation needs of green revolution agriculture. Constant irrigation on land that is not suitable for irrigation raises the water table. It brings water close to the surface that naturally would have found its way down to aquifers that could be accessed by deep wells. As the water moves up through the soil it absorbs salt. The soil becomes waterlogged, and eventually salt is emitted into the air where it affects crops. When the concentration of salt in the air reaches 1 percent it becomes toxic to plant life.

When projects like Sardar Sarovar, then, are sited in places where the soil is susceptible to salinization there is a double effect. They destroy traditional agriculture and further impoverish the poorest of the poor. Paradoxically, in the long run they also destroy the land's capacity to support green revolution agriculture through salinization. In the end, neither kind of agriculture benefits. By that time, funding agencies like the World Bank are long gone and local communities are left to foot the bill for land reclamation. The World Bank's cost estimates for dam projects do not include funding for desalinization.

Before moving on to examples from other parts of the globe, it is worth pausing to recognize certain *positive* consequences of projects like Sardar Sarovar. It is remarkable that Adivasis who were affected by Sardar Sarovar, people who do not normally have the world's attention, organized resistance to the national government and the World Bank to force the Morse Report. Skeptics can say that ultimately the powerful managed to work their way around the Report and continue the Project. However, public statements of the truth function like building blocks that make future misguided projects more difficult. Indeed, criticism of the World Bank from many quarters has demonstrably made the Bank more cautious in the projects it supports. There has been some movement in the direction of insuring that Bank projects recognize human and environmental rights.

In addition, it is arguable that the crisis the Adivasis faced was instrumental in shaping a *normative community* with the strength to articulate and defend its community goods. We need to recognize that, although the word "community" may sound like it expresses something desirable, it is really a word that is morally neutral. Some communities do indeed support their members, allowing them to more fully realize their human capabilities. However, communities can also be oppressive. When communities are divided the powerful can use their power to enforce racism, sexism, or casteism, or to exploit the environment.

In the case of Sardar Sarovar, the crisis the Adivasis faced forced them to clarify their community ideals, and to forge a normative bond around those ideals. There is, of course, no guarantee that the crisis many communities face when confronted with globalization will work to forge a normative community. The sudden pressures of globalization could easily turn community members against one another in an act of mutual suicide. However, despite the "expert" opinion that tribal people are "superstitious" and "backward," these communities do possess extraordinary expertise, developed over centuries, in mediating between the community and their place. They are also far savvier about the intentions of outsiders and "development experts" than outsiders often recognize.

We also need to be honest in looking at the issue of whether these normative, intentional communities that form in response to globalization are nonviolent. These resistance movements are not made up only of saints. Frustration at having control of one's life forcibly removed can easily boil over into violence. We need only look at postcolonial history in places like Uganda and the Congo, and ethnic conflict in multicultural populations like India, El Salvador, and Peru, to see that resistance is often violent. However, while violence always gets more attention from CNN than nonviolence, to be fair we also need to recognize that many resistance movements are nonviolent by choice. The Narmada Bachao Andolan was conscious in its choice of nonviolent methods. The Monsoon Satyagraha adopted methods that had proven successful in India in situations where oppressed people confronted the powerful. Against overwhelming military, police, and economic power, it makes sense, both morally and practically, to adopt organized, nonviolent resistance. The protesters who chained themselves to their homes, like Gandhi taking violence upon themselves without returning it, were successful in dramatizing their plight graphically through their chosen form of resistance.

We should not romanticize traditional and indigenous communities, then, in their struggle to deal with globalization. Communities are fragile. Pressure sometimes brings out the worst in people. The myth of the "indigenous hero" needs to go the way of other stereotypes. However, when we examine real cases, most often we see that crisis brings out the best in people. Crisis forces people to clarify what is important, and they consequently bond together in defense of their homeland. Just as often, as in the case of Sardar Sarovar, intentional communities grow out of common interests. Globalization causes the creation of *intentional* communities in defense of common goals, communities working together at the international level while also defending themselves at the local level.

Malaysia: Native Resistance to Logging

The Asian nation of Malaysia is suffering the most rapid deforestation in the world today. Eighty percent of its tropical wood is exported to Japan, whose national policy supports importation of lumber to spare Japan's own forests. The main point of conflict in Malaysia is in the state of Sarawak, which occupies a corner of an island with Borneo. The forests of Sarawak are the traditional home of 220,000 tribal people, collectively known as the Dayak. Among these, the Penan tribal group has been fiercest in its defense of the forest.

Wealthy families from the mainland are routinely granted concessions to log sections of the Penan homeland. According to one observer, "It is not unusual for the native people to wake up in the morning and see bulldozers and chainsaws leveling their farms, desecrating sacred ancestral burial grounds, and opening roads through their property" (Gedicks 1995, 95).

In February 1987, the Penan appealed to the state government:

> Stop destroying the forest or we will be forced to protect it. The forest is our livelihood. We lived here before any of you outsiders came. . . . Our way of life was not easy, but we lived with contentment. Now the logging companies turn rivers into muddy streams and the jungle into devastation. The fish cannot survive in dirty rivers and wild animals will not live in devastated forests. . . . If you decide not to heed our request, we will protect our livelihood. We are peace-loving people, but when our very lives are in danger, we will fight back. This is our message. (Quoted in Gedicks, 95–96)

Their appeals were ignored. In response, the Penan erected barricades across logging roads to prevent access to logging trucks. The Penan were joined by other Dayak tribes and activists from human rights and environmental organizations. In November 1987, the government responded by arresting protesters, banning three newspapers, and prohibiting public rallies. Malaysian and international groups joined with the Dayak tribes to expose these logging activities to the world. In North America the Rainforest Action Network was particularly active in this campaign. Still, today the tension in Sarawak continues as the Dayak disrupt logging and international organizations attempt to bring pressure on Malaysia and Japan.

Ecuador: Oil and the Amazonian Rainforest

The Oriente region of Northwest Ecuador holds the headwaters of the Amazon River. It is also the most biologically diverse region on earth. Its natural riches support almost five hundred thousand people, many from indigenous tribes such as the Huaorani. In the mid-1960s oil reserves were discovered in the Oriente. Soon a cooperative arrangement was secured between Texaco and the military government of Ecuador to exploit the resources. Neither Texaco nor the government recognized the rights of indigenous people to occupy this land. Paramilitary troops became a common sight as the company pushed its way into the Amazon.

In 1983, after significant international pressure, the Huaorani gained title to a 67,000-hectare reserve named the Yasuni National Park. Although they attempted to protect their holdings by creating borders around their land planted with palm trees, the government continued to cooperate with oil companies to violate Huaorani rights. By the mid-1990s more than twelve million acres of forest had been destroyed in the quest for oil (Gedicks 1995, 101).

Oil companies do not follow the same drilling procedures in Ecuador that they are required to follow in the United States. Unfortunately, 16.8 million gallons of oil has spilled from the Trans-Ecuadorian Pipeline, fouling the waters of the Amazon and affecting people far downriver. Millions of cubic feet of gas have been burned off into the air without any environmental protection. This practice, which separates the oil from the gas, is outlawed in the United States, but it is a common practice in South America and in Africa.

As in Sarawak, the tribes of the Amazon were joined by international social and environmental justice groups to protest the gross violation of tribal rights. The fight continues into the twenty-first century because the government of Ecuador is addicted to oil revenues and the "developed" world shows no signs of recognizing the costs of oil production.

El Salvador: Women's Popular Resistance Movements

The previous examples of popular environmental resistance movements are incomplete because they do not mention the role of gender in resistance movements. Often, environmental destruction has a gender bias.

Men sometimes gain from "development" as they adapt to new wage-labor jobs that are created by logging, mining, and oil exploration. But in many communities women are on the front line when environmental destruction occurs. Women often cultivate crops. They access the forests for natural medicines. When rivers are polluted with toxic waste women see the effects in the damaged health of their children. Since women's interests are often attacked by "development" it is not surprising that women often form the core of environmental resistance movements.

Lois Ann Lorentzen has documented these important truths in El Salvador. This country has experienced the worst environmental degradation in the Americas. Eighty percent of the natural vegetation has been destroyed. Deforestation has had a dramatic impact on farming through erosion and reduction in soil fertility. This situation is worsened when farmers use dangerous agricultural chemicals that are banned as too toxic in the countries where they are made.

The agricultural crisis affects the poor most directly. Eighty percent of children under age five are malnourished. Forty-six percent of the population has no access to safe drinking water, and three out of four have no access to sanitary services (Lorentzen 1995, 57).

El Salvador also suffered from a brutal civil war. The military government pursued rebels with a "scorched earth" policy. Chemicals and bombs were dropped to expose and isolate the guerillas. In the process they killed everything else indiscriminately: civilians, vegetation, animals.

Those in the United States who are now concerned about the cost of prescription drugs can understand the concerns of Salvadoran women. Public health is largely a women's issue, and in poor countries, drugs sold at pharmacies are expensive. Women, therefore, are at the crossroads of human and environmental justice when they promote natural medicines. Women have the expertise to know the medicinal properties of many plants. This localized medical care also keeps an important part of community health within the community.

The National Coordinating Committee for Salvadoran Women (CONAMUS) was founded in 1986 to foster women's solidarity in response to social and environmental degradation. The Coordinating Committee has sponsored programs to support local health and access to natural medicines. It has also promoted reforestation projects, both to supply food and to stem erosion.

In recent years, some economists have drawn attention to the biases in traditional definitions of development. The cases of El Salvador and Ecuador are perfect examples. To an outsider accustomed to measuring development only in terms of increasing gross national product it may appear that these countries are experiencing dramatic economic growth. What happens, in fact, is that there is an unholy alliance between the government, the military, and international corporations to produce exports that help themselves while at the same time further impoverishing the poor.

Gross national product (GNP) or per capita income (PCI) simply measures the productivity of a national economy, or the income produced, on average, by each person. These measures alone can mask gross violations of human rights and environmental integrity. A military dictatorship can govern an economy very efficiently by providing economic benefits to themselves, or to small classes of privileged individuals. When a small group of individuals suddenly becomes wealthy, this can show up as rapidly increasing GNP and PCI. But these increases can also hide the fact that the few have gotten wealthy at the expense of the poor. Increased GNP is sometimes a measure of the effectiveness of political oppression and environmental destruction.

However, all international "development" is not just coded language for exploitation. The United Nations, in fact, espouses a concept of ethical development that conjoins human and economic development with responsible policies toward the environment. The key statistical measure is the Human Development Index (HDI). It was implemented in the early 1990s as a partial remedy to the measuring of development in simple economic terms.

The HDI includes standard economic factors, but it does not equate human development exclusively with economic development. Explaining this approach, the development economist Mahbub ul Haq said:

The basic purpose of development is to enlarge people's choices. In principle, these choices can be infinite and can change over time. People often value achievements that do not show up at all, or not immediately, in income or growth figures: greater access to knowledge, better nutrition and health services, more secure livelihoods, security against crime and physical violence, satisfying leisure hours, political and cultural freedoms and sense of participation in community activities. The objective of development is to create an enabling environment for people to enjoy long, healthy and creative lives. (Haq n.d., 1)

The United Nations Development Programme (UNDP) documents go on to explain human development in these broad—and philosophical—terms:

> Human development is about much more than the rise or fall of national incomes. It is about creating an environment in which people can develop their full potential and lead productive, creative lives in accord with their needs and interests. People are the real wealth of nations. Development is thus about expanding the choices people have to lead lives that they value. And it is thus about much more than economic growth, which is only a means—if a very important one—of enlarging people's choices.
>
> Fundamental to enlarging these choices is building human capabilities—the range of things that people can do or be in life. The most basic capabilities for human development are to lead long and healthy lives, to be knowledgeable, to have access to the resources needed for a decent standard of living and to be able to participate in the life of the community. Without these, many choices are simply not available, and many opportunities in life remain inaccessible.
>
> This way of looking at development, often forgotten in the immediate concern with accumulating commodities and financial wealth, is not new. Philosophers, economists and political leaders have long emphasized human well-being as the purpose, the end, of development. As Aristotle said in ancient Greece, "Wealth is evidently not the good we are seeking, for it is merely useful for the sake of something else."
>
> In seeking that something else, human development shares a common vision with human rights. The goal is human freedom. And in pursuing capabilities and realizing rights, this freedom is vital. People must be free to exercise their choices and to participate in decision-making that affects their lives. Human development and human rights are mutually reinforcing, helping to secure the well-being and dignity of all people, building self-respect and the respect of others. (Haq n.d., 1)

Real human development focuses on "building human capabilities—the range of things that people can do or be in life." As with Gandhi's concept of development, what counts is people's actual capabilities to function in their communities, not just abstract guarantees of human rights.

According to the United Nations, the important capabilities are (1) "to lead long and healthy lives," (2) "to be knowledgeable," and (3) "to have access to resources" that can generate a "decent standard of living and to be able to participate in the life of the community." These goals are reminiscent of Gandhi since they emphasize the importance of direct access to the required resources for a good life. Ethical development is not charity. It is the strengthening of local capabilities so people can exercise their own skills.

This definition of ethical development also recognizes that individual development is connected to the welfare of the community, not just the individual. The ability to participate in the life of the community is at least as important as economic wealth. In fact, the UNDP explicitly endorses the view that economic wealth and human well-being are difficult to connect.

To illustrate these points concretely, the report compares less-developed countries (LDCs) with respect to their human development and their economic development. It found that some countries—Sri Lanka, Jamaica, and Costa Rica—have low rates of GNP, but high levels of human development when this is measured by life expectancy, adult literacy, and infant mortality. In stark contrast, some countries—Brazil, Oman, and Saudi Arabia—have very high GNPs, but poor life expectancy, literacy, and infant mortality rates. Consider the contrast between Costa Rica and Saudi Arabia:

Table 5.1. Measuring Human Development

	GNP per capita ($US)	Life Expectancy (years)	Adult Literacy (%)	Infant Mortality (per 1,000 live births)
Costa Rica	1,610	75	93	18
Saudi Arabia	6,200	64	55	70

(Source: United Nations Human Development Report 1990, chapter 1, "Defining and Measuring Human Development, 1. [United Nations 1990])

Statistics like these make it clear that there is only a weak correlation between income and human welfare. What determines the level of human development is correlated to the amount spent on education and health care, as well as the *way* in which it is spent. Costa Rica has a democratic government; Saudi Arabia a closed plutocracy consisting of members of the royal family.

This kind of discrepancy continues today, after a decade of globalization. The 2002 *Human Development Report* compares income poverty to human poverty. Among the nineteen countries (for which statistics exist) listed as having the "lowest human development," only four do better at addressing human poverty than income poverty. And among those ranked as having "medium human development," twenty-four out of thirty-one score lower on human development than on income development (United Nations 2002, Chart 2: Human and Income Poverty, Developing Countries).

Another telling statistic is the changes in the amount of official development aid (ODA) received by the countries that are lowest on the human development scale. In the decade of globalization, aid to the least developed countries *decreased* in twenty-nine of the thirty-four countries listed considered as a percentage of GNP. As the wealthy countries became wealthier, on average they gave less to the neediest countries.

Even when we switch to considering the countries with the highest rate of income poverty, rather than human poverty, the rate of private investment has been modest at best during the decade of the nineties. Net foreign private investment in these countries rose from .03 to .06 as a percentage of gross domestic product. "Other" private flows of capital actually decreased from 0.7 to −0.2 percent. The negative number indicates that there is more capital leaving these countries than entering (United Nations 2002, Chart 16: Flows of Aid, Private Capital and Debt).

When we combine these two sets of figures we see that official aid transferred from government to government decreased dramatically under globalization, and the transfer of private investments, which is supposed to be the great benefit of globalization, either rose modestly, or actually retreated. For the poorest countries, globalization did not "raise all boats," even when we consider only economic poverty and not human poverty.

Despite very clear evidence that development should focus on the flourishing of human capabilities, and not simply economic goals, the United States recently announced a "New Compact for Development." President George W. Bush described this "new" approach to development to an audience in Mexico on March 22, 2002:

> Many here today have devoted their lives to the fight against global poverty, and you know the stakes. We fight against poverty because hope

is an answer to terror. We fight against poverty because opportunity is a fundamental right to human dignity. We fight against poverty because faith requires it and conscience demands it. And we fight against poverty with a growing conviction that major progress is within our reach.

For decades, the success of development aid was measured only in the resources spent, not the results achieved. Yet, pouring money into a failed status quo does little to help the poor, and can actually delay the progress of reform. We must accept a higher, more difficult, more promising call. Developed nations have a duty not only to share our wealth, but also to encourage sources that produce wealth: economic freedom, political liberty, the rule of law and human rights.

The lesson of our time is clear: When nations close their markets and opportunity is hoarded by a privileged few, no amount—no amount—of development aid is ever enough. When nations respect their people, open markets, invest in better health and education, every dollar of aid, every dollar of trade revenue and domestic capital is used more effectively.

We must tie greater aid to political and legal and economic reforms. And by insisting on reform, we do the work of compassion. The United States will lead by example. I have proposed a 50-percent increase in our core development assistance over the next three budget years. Eventually, this will mean a $5-billion annual increase over current levels. (Bush 2002)

The Bush administration has used development aid, provided through USAID, as an extension of the Chamber of Commerce. Henceforth, development aid will be provided only to countries that accept structural adjustment policies. These are the very policies that have shifted spending from social welfare, education, health, and the environment to debt restructuring and "open" markets. How is this "the work of compassion"?

The Bush administration has also revived the "Mexico City International Family Planning Policy," which was initiated as an executive order by President Reagan in 1984 at a population conference in Mexico. This policy prohibits development aid from going to any foreign nongovernmental agency that supports abortion services, even if the funding for such services comes entirely from other sources, not provided by the United States.

On January 22, 1993, President Clinton issued a memorandum repealing the Mexico City restrictions. The executive order allowed recipients of

USAID grants to use non-U.S. funds for providing abortion services, but they were required to maintain segregated accounts for U.S. money in order to show evidence they were in compliance with the abortion restrictions.

However, on January 22, 2001, President Bush issued a further executive order reinstating the Mexico City policy. As it stands, the United States will not provide funding for any organization that funds abortion services or provides counseling or any kind of public information on the availability of abortion services. This policy also makes it difficult to provide family counseling and birth control information, which is tragic considering its impact on countries with AIDS epidemics.

Planned Parenthood commented, "That's the insidious nature of President Bush's Global Gag Rule: it forces a cruel choice upon doctors and nurses in poor countries, either to remain silent as women die from unsafe abortion, or to cut vitally needed family planning services that can prevent abortion. By forcing providers to withhold information from their clients, it undermines the doctor-patient relationship—an intrusion that would be considered intolerable in the United States." Finally, Representative Barbara Lee of California led a bipartisan coalition to pass the "Global Democracy Promotion Act," which overturned the Mexico City policy and reestablished congressional oversight of development aid (Planned Parenthood 2000).

To this point, I have mainly been considering questions of ethical *human* development. However, we need to raise a further question: does ethical human development necessarily come at the expense of the environment? Is "sustainable development" just a euphemism for economic development?

Sometimes we think that *any* human intervention into nature is violent, and therefore unsustainable. If a morally responsible life requires us to leave nature unchanged then we have no hope of living responsibly. We should notice, however, that there is something odd in this attitude: even if it intends to be an environmental ethic, it depicts human beings as nonnatural. We are depicted as "intervening" into something that is profoundly different from us. It should not be surprising that when we think of our identity as nonnatural that we will have a difficult time arriving at an environmental ethic.

If we think of human life as one more of nature's flourishings, then the picture looks different. The question is not whether we intervene in nature, but how we choose to engage with the rest of nature. We have already made progress in thinking about the "how" question when we distinguish between human development and economic development. Real human development assumes an environmental ethic.

Consider this example: a recent news report carried the news that the Brazilian Amazon was destroyed at a rate of ten thousand acres/year for the year ending in August 2002, twice the amount destroyed the previous year. This acceleration is due mainly to farmers converting rainforest to soybean farms for cattle feed. Twenty percent of the rainforest is already gone, and there is very good reason to think that this has contributed to global warming. Greenpeace estimates that the entire rainforest will be gone in eighty years, given the present rate of destruction, which is fifty to seventy-eight million acres/year (Rainforest Action Network 2003). This is a classic case of increasing GNP at the expense of human and environmental well-being.

Think, on the contrary, about development designed to augment human flourishing. The major elements are longevity, health, and education. As we saw in the previous chapter, these are precisely the sorts of initiatives that tend to reduce the rate of population growth. Combine this with the fact that the recipients of such human development tend to live very lightly on the land, especially in terms of consumption rates, and we can see an argument that real human development is usually environmentally friendly.

Of course, there can never be any guarantee that ethical human development will also be friendly to the environment. People who are attempting only to survive understandably do almost anything to improve their condition, even for a short time. However, if we think about real cases, not just Garrett Hardin's tragedy of the commons, it makes sense to say that when people truly increase their capabilities to function, they take into account the long-term effects of their actions, both for their own heirs and for the environment.

I said at the beginning of this chapter that there are several critically important questions I would like to be able to answer: is all development just neocolonialism in disguise, or are there kinds of human and ecological development that are ethical? When we attempt to help other people, does this simply make them dependent on us, or can some kinds of help address issues of genuine freedom and a healthy self-identity? Is social justice for humans in conflict with the preservation of nature? In particular, what should we say about charity? Does a morally responsible life require us to engage in charity for the welfare of those "less fortunate" than ourselves?

I hope the reflections in this chapter have moved us toward the answers we need. All development is not just neocolonialism in disguise. True development fosters multiple dimensions of human flourishing. This means greater capabilities to function at the local level: better health care, access to the resources required for a meaningful life, appropriate education, a place in one's community. Real development fosters independence, swaraj.

I have argued that social justice is rarely in conflict with the environment. In fact, real human flourishing builds precisely the kinds of localized skills that lead to the exercise of environmental wisdom. Developed people are invested in caring for their "place." Many times, survival depends on it.

Because of the reality of structural violence I believe we are all coresponsible for addressing human and environmental damage. But we should not confuse sarvodaya with charity, if by that we mean giving alms to the poor and the suffering. We may not know what someone else would count as help; sometimes our well-meaning help actually harms. In fact, I believe the main kind of help the United States now offers to developing countries—assuming they cooperate with economic restructuring—hurts at least as much as it helps.

If charity makes its recipients more dependent on their donors, then real development is the opposite of charity. Real development augments freedom, not dependence. I believe we—those of us who "won" because of the location of the Canary Islands—are obligated to help others in the name of social and environmental justice. However, money is rarely the answer by itself. The real question is whether money is well spent. And whether it is well spent can be measured by whether it increases human flourishing and environmental justice. These are substantive goods that money can't buy.

CHAPTER SIX
THE THIRD WORLD IN THE FIRST WORLD

An organization called the International Forum on Globalization Indigenous Peoples' Project recently produced an extraordinary map (International Forum on Globalization 2003). It illustrates the truly global impact of globalization by considering the effects of sixteen factors on indigenous peoples around the world. The range of effects alone gives some indication of the dimensions of the problems: industrial agriculture, biopiracy, cattle, dams, transmigration, fisheries, water, drug interdiction, loss of land, mining, nuclear energy, oil, roads, shipping, logging, tourism, militarization, pollution, and energy.

If the list of countries affected by globalization does not quite span A to Z, it certainly comes very close. We learn that in Angola the government supports tourism, which threatens the Himba people's religious sites, and it works with Chevron and Texaco in ways that threaten traditional fisherfolk. In Botswana, the government has attempted to drive the Bushmen off their lands by cutting off water supplies. It wants the land to promote international tourism, and to explore for diamonds. The government also forced the Basarwa people from their land because they insist on their right to subsistence hunting in the Central Kalahari Game Reserve.

At the other end of the map's list of affected countries is the United States. Here the list does run from A to Z. In Minnesota, the Anishinaabeg oppose attempts by University of Minnesota scientists to determine the genetic code for wild rice and patent it. In Arizona, the Dineh

(Navajo) and Hopi peoples oppose Peabody Coal mines that have caused environmental problems and driven people off their land.

In New York, the Mohawks oppose Alcoa Aluminum, which has allowed deadly PCBs to leak into the St. Lawrence River, leading to persistent health problems and destroying the Mohawks' traditional source of food. Native Hawaiians and Pacific Islanders have seen their land used by the military for bombing practice and as a toxic waste dump. In New Mexico, the Zuni Pueblo protest the Salt River Project, which threatens to strip-mine the Zuni Salt Lake for coal.

This map illustrates that globalization is not simply a "third world" problem. Its effects are felt in every country, including the most "developed." The moral problems of globalization cannot be neatly reduced to the question of whether we are compelled to care about *distant* people and places. Most of the same issues are also alive here, at home. So, I want to turn our attention to the United States and ask how globalization affects us here, within indigenous communities, in urban settings, and in rural agricultural communities. I want to know how globalization interacts with race, and gender, the agricultural and the industrial, the rural and the urban.

Since we are asking about the connections between environmental and social justice, we should expand on the question raised first in chapter 1, a question that not many of us want to address: How did we come to be in possession of this place?

We know that there were important migrations of people, probably across the Bering Strait, to North America. These migrations occurred at least ten to twelve thousand years ago, and probably much earlier. These are the people Europeans met when they colonized the "New World."

Europeans' self-images as moral beings required an ethical justification for occupation of the New World. Scholars often trace this claim of moral legitimacy to two papal declarations from the fifteenth century. In 1452, Pope Nicholas V issued the *Romanus Pontifex* to King Alfonso V of Portugal. As the successor to Saint Peter, on whose "rock" the church was built, Nicholas gave Alfonso the religious authority to capture and colonize distant lands in the names of the Church and God.

This Papal declaration was followed by the *Inter Caetera*, issued by Pope Alexander VI in 1493 to the King and Queen of Spain. It was in reaction to Christopher Columbus' "discovery" of the New World, the Caribbean island he called Española. It provided the same authority to the

Spanish that the earlier declaration had provided to the Portuguese: Christian dominion over the New World. It divided the "New World" into two spheres, one to be dominated by the Portuguese, the other by the Spanish (World Conference against Racism).

There was a second justification for colonial dominion over land and people, the doctrine of *terra nullius*. In his book *Two Treatises of Government* (1690) philosopher John Locke raised the following problem: if God gave the world to human beings through Adam and Eve, then "it seems to some a very great difficulty, how any one should ever come to have a *property* in any thing. . . ." That is, if God gave the world to men collectively, to use as a resource for their advancement, then how can we ever justify private ownership of land? The transition from land held in common to private property is what Locke set out to explain: "But I shall endeavour to shew, how men might come to have a *property* in several parts of that which God gave to mankind in common, and that without any express compact of all the commoners" (Locke 1764, ch. V, sec. 25).

Locke began his argument by putting the "wild Indian" in an original state of nature, before the claim to private ownership arises:

> The earth, and all that is therein, is given to men for the support and comfort of their being. And tho' all the fruits it naturally produces, and beasts it feeds, belong to mankind in common, as they are produced by the spontaneous hand of nature; and no body has originally a private dominion, exclusive of the rest of mankind, in any of them, as they are thus in their natural state: yet being given for the use of men, there must of necessity be *a means to appropriate* them some way or other, before they can be of any use, or at all beneficial to any particular man. The fruit, or venison, which nourishes the *wild Indian*, who knows no enclosure, and is still a tenant in common, must be his, and so his, i.e., a part of him, that another can no longer have any right to it, before it can do him any good for the support of his life. (ch. V, sec. 26)

What distinguishes the "wild" Indian from the "civilized" white man? The white man's labor produces private property; the Indian's labor does not. Locke reasons, the one thing that truly belongs to each man is his own body and, therefore, the labor of his own body: "Though the earth, and all inferior creatures, be common to all men, yet every man has a *property* in his own *person:* this no body has any right to but himself. The *labour* of his body, and the *work* of his hands, we may say, are properly his. Whatsoever then he removes out of the state that nature hath provided, and left it in, he hath mixed his *labour* with, and joined to it something that is his own, and thereby makes it his *property*" (ch. V, sec. 27).

The moral justification for private property is that, through the labor of one's own body, which can never be alienated, nature is transformed into culture, and private property becomes possible. Work effects the transformation from *nature* to *culture*. Therefore, although the native inhabitants of North America predated the colonial expeditions, they had never privatized the land in Locke's view. These earlier inhabitants were all considered to be nomadic, never having established a claim to ownership of particular pieces of property.

The doctrine of *terra nullius*—the land of no one—applied to North America after the European conquest. Land could legally and morally be claimed as private property, as long as the owner actively worked it. It is easy to see how Thomas Jefferson's attitudes toward native North Americans developed from Locke's philosophy: since the Indians were still living in a "state of nature," they could not claim private property rights. That is, as long as they were nomadic they could not own property. Only when the Indians were "civilized" and confined to farms could they effect the transition from nature to culture. It was a convenient consequence of this doctrine that farmers take up much less land than nomadic people, and so farming opened up vast territories, formerly inhabited by tribes, for virtuous exploitation by white men. The doctrine of Manifest Destiny was only possible because of John Locke.

We should also recognize the similarity between Locke's justification of private property and the contemporary arguments that are made for the patenting of genetic material. World Trade Organization rules recognize intellectual property patents for scientists who take the cultural knowledge of indigenous peoples about plant genetics and extract knowledge of the genetic structure of these plants. Indigenous knowledge is held to be "the common heritage of mankind," and therefore it cannot be patented. The process by which the scientist extracts knowledge of the DNA is held to be an innovation. It is something new that didn't exist in the "state of nature." "Innovation" is a stand-in for Locke's concept of labor. It is still the divide between the "natural," the "uncivilized," the "common property" given by God, and the "cultural," "the civilized," and "private property."

The doctrine of *terra nullius* was modified in an 1823 Supreme Court ruling, *Johnson v. McIntosh*. It declared that recognized tribes had a "right of occupancy" to land. That is, if they could not legally own the land, they could at least occupy it. In the earliest treaties, statutes, and cases, indigenous nations were regarded as having a "subordinate" sovereignty related to their "right of occupancy." Denied full sovereignty as independent nations, they were nevertheless regarded as having authority over their own relations among themselves—an "internal" or "tribal" sovereignty (d'Errico 1998).

The right of occupancy doctrine played a role in confirming the legal status of tribes as having "dependent sovereignty." This rather odd expression meant that the tribes had no right to a foreign policy or a military, but they could govern their own affairs internally. Although the meaning of dependent sovereignty continues to be debated, it is now clear that treaties signed between tribes and the United States government have the legal status of treaties between sovereign nations. Many court rulings have held that hunting and fishing rights that were negotiated in treaties are still valid.

In an 1837 treaty, for example, the Ojibwe of central Minnesota and western Wisconsin signed a treaty giving up more than thirteen million acres to the United States. However, they did not give up hunting and fishing rights on this land. Article 5 of the treaty reads: "The privilege of hunting, fishing, and gathering the wild rice, upon the lands, the rivers and the lakes included in the territory ceded, is guaranteed to the Indians, during the pleasure of the President of the United States" (American Indian Policy Center).

In 1850 President Zachary Taylor did issue an executive order depriving the Ojibwe bands of these treaty rights. However, on March 24, 1999, the United States Supreme Court ruled in favor of the tribe. Writing for the majority, Justice Sandra Day O'Connor said, "After an examination of the historical record, we conclude that the Chippewa retain the . . . rights guaranteed to them under the 1837 treaty" *(Minnesota vs. Mille Lacs Band)*. The critical point is that the Supreme Court rejected the claim made by many hunters and fishermen in Minnesota that Native Americans are treated differently—receiving special privileges to hunt and fish—than other Americans. The Ojibwe have these rights because they negotiated a treaty between two governments. These rights have the same status as a treaty negotiated between the United States and Great Britain. Unlike individual property rights, furthermore, the rights that the Supreme Court recognized are community rights held by the tribe in common.

The question of indigenous sovereignty at the international level is still being debated at the United Nations. It issued a "Declaration on the Rights of Indigenous Peoples" in 1994 as a report to the U.N. Commission on Human Rights. Professor Peter d'Errico reports that "The United States took an official position that the word 'peoples' was inappropriate in a statement of 'rights,' because it implied group rights, which would threaten the sovereignty of states. The United States and others argued that 'rights' adhere only to individuals, and that no group may be recognized as having any legal existence independent of a state. Indigenous nations, on the other hand, asserted that the Draft Declaration was meant to embody just such group rights, that these were essential for the survival of indigenous peoples worldwide" (d'Errico 1998).

Setting aside the philosophical question of whether there can be group rights, it is clear at a political level that the United States continues to oppose indigenous peoples in their attempts to speak for themselves. Indigenous peoples can only be represented by recognized national governments, the same governments that often exploit them. And if they are to be heard at all, they must already surrender the more appropriate language of communal rights in favor of the moral language through which they were colonized: the language of individual rights.

Having considered this legacy, it would be easy to conclude that relations between people and place in the United States are so complicated that we have no option but to declare an amnesty and move on. However, I think we ought to resist this temptation. It is true that there is something like a "statute of limitations" on land claims. We would look rather skeptically, for example, on contemporary Italian claims to land based on the history of Rome. Where land claims conflict over many centuries the competing claims can be difficult to sort out, and the results violent. The conflict between Israelis and Palestinians fall into this category.

What about land claims in the United States? Are they too old to sort out? Because many North American natives were nomadic, various tribes can claim title to the same land. Sometimes armed conflict between native groups resulted in migrations and conflicting claims. We know that the Dakota people once lived in northern Minnesota, for example, but were driven south and west by the Anishanabe. Land conflicts were hardly exclusive to the "Indian Wars" between the tribes and colonial settlers.

It may well be that some of these claims are too old, or the legacy of ownership too clouded, to resolve. In some cases, as we have seen, there are clear legal titles to land and land use that courts have upheld. But there are other cases that test our moral consciences. Consider the ambiguous case of whaling by the Makah Indian Nation in the state of Washington. In recent years, the tribe has been asserting their right to hunt gray whales. Whaling was its traditional method of subsistence. Whale oil was also sold to white traders who colonized the Northwest Coast. This source of income allowed the Makah to maintain much of their cultural integrity in the face of invading cultures. The importance of Makah whaling was recognized in an 1855 treaty with the Governor of the Washington Territory. In 1979 the United States Supreme Court reaffirmed the Makah right to fish (Dark n.d.).

Of course, much changed between 1855 and 1979. The gray whale population was decimated by the early twentieth century when its population dropped from approximately 30,000 to only a few thousand. However, because of concerted conservation efforts, the gray whale population has recovered to the level of about 27,000, and sustains a growth rate of 2.5 percent a year. The International Whaling Commission estimates that, at this level, a sustainable catch of 407–670 individuals per year can be justified.

When the United States removed the gray whale from the Endangered Species List in 1994, the Makah filed notice of their intention to resume fishing for gray whales even though the last documented Makah whale hunt occurred in 1926. Because gray whales had been removed from the Endangered Species List, international negotiations occurred to allocate a sustainable catch. Through this process the U.S. government allocated twenty gray whales to the Makah over a period of four years.

Although some consideration was given to returning to commercial whaling, the Makah have decided not to take this route. Whaling is considered to be part of the Makah cultural renaissance, an important expression of their living cultural legacy (Dark n.d.). Although the tribe had a legal right to profit from whaling, they chose to engage in whaling for ceremonial purposes, and for food for the tribe. According to tradition, the

Makah hunt whales in a thirty-two-foot canoe with a nine-man crew. They approach a whale from the left side, shoot it with a harpoon, and then kill it with a World War I tank rifle. A crewmember then dives into the water where he sews the whale's mouth closed so it will not sink. The whale is then towed to shore, where it is ritually butchered.

The Makah reassertion of their treaty rights has been met with opposition from the far left and the far right of the political spectrum. On the left, the Sea Shepherd Conservation Society and its "captain," Paul Watson, have vigorously opposed Makah whaling as part of its broader anti-whaling campaign. Sea Shepherds regularly attempt to prevent Japanese whaling in the arctic, for example, by inserting their ships between the whales and the whaling boats. Their motto is "Sailing into Harm's Way!"

On the right, Makah whaling is opposed by politicians who reject what they consider to be "special rights" granted to Indian tribes that are not available to the larger public. The American Civil Liberties Union gave a Makah opponent, Representative Jack Metcalf of Washington, only a 6 percent positive rating for votes in favor of civil liberties. Despite his claims to be a lover of the outdoors, the League of Conservation Voters gave him only a 23 percent positive rating on votes concerning the environment (American Civil Liberties Union).

During the whale migration in the fall of 1998, Sea Shepherd activists used their boats to prevent a Makah whale harvest. They used loudspeakers to broadcast their opposition to whaling into the Makah villages. There were verbal insults hurled between the activists and the Makah whalers, and there was some physical violence. In 1999, however, Iceland announced its intention to resume commercial whaling, and the Sea Shepherds shifted their attention away from the Makah.

During the conflict the Sea Shepherds have offered a variety of arguments: that the Makah are mere pawns of large international whaling powers (the Japanese), and that Makah whaling is archaic and a roadblock to cultural progress. Others have argued that the Makah are hypocritical in their affirmation of cultural traditions at the same time that they use modern technology, such as electricity and the automobile (Dark n.d.).

Keith Johnson, President of the Makah Whaling Commission, issued a response to the critics of Makah whaling that was published by the *Seattle Times* on August 6, 1998 (Johnson 1998). It repays careful reading of the original text. He began by documenting what the Makah were planning to do, as well as their recognized authority to hunt whales under the provision of the 1855 treaty. He reaffirmed that whaling was to be resumed for religious and cultural reasons. The Makah would not engage in commercial whaling, like Japan, Norway, and Iceland.

Johnson also pointed out that gray whale populations are still increasing by 2.5 percent each year, and that some prominent environmental organizations, such as the Sierra Club and Greenpeace, had refused to join with the Sea Shepherds in their opposition to Makah whaling. Finally, he pointed out that there is opposition to whaling among the Makah themselves. Still, 85 percent of the Makah voted to support noncommercial whaling.

Some of the moral arguments against Makah whaling have come from an animal rights perspective. Whales are highly intelligent creatures, perhaps even self-aware. They are, therefore, aware of their own suffering. This means they have the moral right to be spared from needless suffering, just as we would say that no one has the right to inflict needless suffering on a human being. Concerning these ethical claims against Makah whaling, Johnson admitted that many of those who oppose the killing of mammals are sincere. However, he pointed out that the Makah have lived "with and among" whales for two thousand years. He argued that the Makah and the whales are part of a common ecological community. The Makah know whales, and believe it is important not to romanticize them:

> But we have an understanding of the relationship between people and the mammals of the sea and land. We are a part of each other's life. We are all part of the natural world and predation is also part of life on this planet. So orca whales attack and eat whales and whale calves as well as seals and fish. Those who regard the orcas simply as cute may prefer to ignore this side of their nature. (Johnson 1998)

Finally, Johnson expressed his concern that some of the Makah's critics are guilty of "cultural arrogance" in claiming to know what the Makah should do to avoid being relics of the past, and opponents of modernity and progress. Tellingly, he pointed out that

> Whales have captured the public's fascination. Whales are definitely "in." Does that mean that Indians are "out?" The world has had a similar fascination with us and our cultures, but whenever we had something

you wanted or did something you didn't like, you tried to impose your values on us. (Johnson 1998)

This is a provocative case for those who would like to think, as I do, that environmental and social justice are largely compatible. It involves issues of cross-cultural communication, and differing views of the proper relationship of people to place. It also requires us to sort out legitimate from illegitimate arguments on both sides.

Despite the risks of making cross-cultural judgments, I do believe it is possible to make informed moral judgments even if we are not insiders to a culture. Before we consider the question of our moral response to Makah whaling, however, we should pause, once again, to note that a major dimension of this case is legal, not moral. The Supreme Court has already held that the Makah treaty concerning whaling can still be enforced. If we disagree with Makah whaling, then, we must *negotiate* differences, since they have the legal right to fish.

Some of the moral arguments against Makah whaling do indeed seem to be familiar reiterations of colonial reasoning. The argument that the Makah are uncivilized and backward in insisting on their whaling rights simply assumes the moral high ground of the colonial mind. Concepts like "progress" and "civilization" are not questioned. This fails to consider that cultural development might be understood in a variety of ways.

We also need to be careful not to assume that outsiders are experts on whaling or the Makah. There was a long-established practice of Makah whaling. Keith Johnson discussed the meaning of these traditions in his public letter. It is patronizing to argue, as the Sea Shepherds did, that the Makah are merely pawns of outside forces, or that they are anything less than experts on their own culture. Arguments like these are examples of prejudice, not cross-cultural communication.

The animal rights activists do seem to be offering legitimate arguments. Here again, we should not assume that there is only one "animal rights" argument. There are many. However, it is relevant to point out that whales are highly developed mammals. Not only do they suffer physical pain, but it is likely they suffer something like emotional or psychological pain, as in cases of the reactions of whales to their pod members who are caught in nets.

Since these considerations do seem relevant, I do not think it would be appropriate for the Makah to simply use cultural autonomy as an all-purpose reason to engage in whaling. Every culture needs to be open to the possibility that some of its practices, even old and important practices, cannot be morally justified.

In fact, Keith Johnson did not hide behind the shield of cultural autonomy. He responded to animal rights activists with an argument of his own: he countered, "we have an understanding of the relationship between people and the mammals of the sea and land. We are a part of each other's life. . . ." That is, he claimed, quite rightly, to have some expertise on this matter. He then went on to say that, because of this expertise, he knew that predation is natural, as in the case of the orca or "Killer Whale."

So, the real moral argument appears to be over the moral legitimacy of predation, especially within a culture that has long and important connections to the mammal in question, and whose hunting methods themselves endanger the hunters. What should we think of such claims? Is hunting for flesh-food "natural"? Is there an argument from the fact that orcas kill their own young to the conclusion that whale hunting by Makah is morally justified?

I think we should be suspicious of the claim that meat eating is moral because it is "natural." Despite great similarities between whales and people, there are also some important differences. One is that most humans are not only morally *considerable;* they are also moral *agents.*

To say that a being is morally considerable is to claim merely that it deserves respect. We say that a human baby is morally considerable because it can experience pain, and therefore has an interest in not experiencing pain unjustifiably. But human babies are not yet moral agents. That is, while we need to treat them with respect, we do not believe we can hold them responsible for their decisions. Indeed, in our culture, we treat adults differently from juveniles both in the law and morally because we do not think that most juveniles are capable yet of fully anticipating the consequences of their actions. And if they cannot anticipate the consequences of their actions, they cannot be held responsible for them.

The adult orca may be morally considerable, but it is questionable whether it is a moral agent. I don't think anyone knows for sure. We do know, however, that most human adults are both morally considerable and moral agents. This means that, while it is questionable whether whales can be held morally responsible as agents, human adults can and should be held responsible for their actions.

The possibility of choice implies human responsibility. If we have a choice whether to eat the flesh of other animals, then we are morally responsible for the choice of what to count as food. According to the arguments of some animal rights theorists, hunting other animals is akin to murder, since it unjustifiably deprives the animals of their right not to be harmed unnecessarily. Since it is not clear whether orcas do make this choice, it is not correct to compare the choice of a human diet to the diet of a whale.

A related question, then, is whether it is "natural" for human beings to eat meat. If we really are carnivores, like a wolf, or an orca, then we cannot argue that it is immoral to eat meat. This would be tantamount to requiring suicide. No one can have a moral obligation to kill oneself.

However, the claim that human beings are carnivores is false. We are omnivores, not carnivores. Since we *can* maintain our health with a diet that does not include animal flesh, this means that meat eating is optional. We do not require meat, most of us at least, to be healthy.

For humans, then, who are moral agents, and who do not need to eat meat to survive, the question of meat eating is a moral question. We cannot simply say, "Nature made me do it!" With all due respect then, I disagree with Keith Johnson's argument that predation is "natural" for humans and that it is therefore morally permissible for human beings to kill other animals for food. The orca is a carnivore, and while morally considerable, it is probably not a moral agent. So it cannot be held morally responsible when it eats its young. Human beings, on the other hand, are omnivores; we do not have to eat meat to remain healthy. We should hold adult human beings responsible for their food choices.

However, perhaps we can find another, more subtle argument in the Makah's moral claim to hunt and consume whales. So far, we have considered arguments about the morality of meat eating that apply to all humans, just in virtue of being human. Perhaps we should interpret the Makah claim as saying that there are particular reasons within Makah culture that justify whale hunting.

I have argued for a position I call "Contextual Moral Vegetarianism" (Curtin and Heldke 1992, 130–34). Although the argument is basically in favor of vegetarianism, it does allow for contextual arguments to the contrary. For example, I cannot agree with those who argue that Arctic peoples have a moral obligation to refrain from eating fish and seals. We cannot seriously say that Arctic people should become farmers and grow their own food. Do we want to argue that they should stop acquiring their own food and depend on importing grains from distant places? We have seen that Gandhi, among others, argued that true freedom requires local control of food. Especially in a globalized economy of food production, it seems difficult to make this argument.

The case of Arctic peoples, then, may be a counterexample to the claim that all humans, just in virtue of being human, are morally compelled to be vegetarians. But perhaps this is not the case with the Makah. They are coastal fishing people. However, it would not be impossible to grow food in the state of Washington. So this is a slightly different case from that of the Arctic peoples. If people *can* become farmers, are they always morally *compelled* to be farmers in order to refrain from eating meat?

This Makah case raises a more difficult question: can *culture* provide a sufficient moral justification for meat eating? I would guess that vigorous arguments can be made on both sides. Certainly, being a Native American, coming from a cultural group that has been oppressed by colonialism, does not give one a "get home free card" when it comes to moral issues. However, the present issue concerns whether native peoples are morally obligated to become *farmers*. Colonial land policies made it impossible any longer for them to be *gatherers* and provide sufficient food for themselves. I find it difficult to argue, given the colonial requirement that native peoples become "civilized" by adopting farming, to say that cultural reasons are irrelevant in this case.

I *can*, in contrast, imagine saying to a dominant white culture, which has perfected the global food market and excelled at industrial farming, that we have an obligation to be vegetarian. In fact, the vastness of food choices available to white people in America results in a particularly strong argument for the conclusion that the "winners" in the colonial struggle for power are morally compelled to be vegetarian.

With the Makah, on the other hand, I find it difficult to make this argument. I think there is something to the argument of animal rights activists when they say that moral agents have an obligation not to inflict unnecessary suffering on self-conscious beings if such food is not required for health reasons. But with the Makah, this argument must be balanced against the colonial decimation of their culture, and their legitimate right to reclaim their cultural integrity, having survived colonialism.

Finally, however, it is important that we avoid the temptation to think too strongly in terms of "the Makah," as if there were no diversity of opinion in the tribe itself. There may well be tribal rights that are relevant here, but this should not simply cover up diverse voices from within. The ecofeminist author Greta Gaard has pointed out that "Historically, whale hunting was not a universal practice in Makah tribal society; rather, it was limited to individuals of a specific class, gender, and ethnicity" (Gaard 2001, 15). The Makah traditionally held slaves who were purchased or captured in war. They were excluded from whale hunting. In addition, women of the tribe as well as lower-class male tribal members were excluded.

Whale hunting, then, may have functioned as a sort of male bonding among aristocratic men from the Makah tribe. Outsiders need not endorse all insiders' claims to cultural integrity, especially when traditional practices enforce racist or sexist violence. Female genital mutilation, for example, is hardly justified by the fact that those within the relevant cultures with voices that can be heard are in favor of the practice.

Is Makah whaling sufficiently like female genital mutilation that outsiders should feel compelled to condemn it? Does the *current* practice of whaling among aristocratic males in the Makah tribe still enforce sexist and classist violence, in spite of the passage of several decades during which whaling did not occur and Makah social relations evolved?

Clearly, there are questions of fact here that require clarification. It is clear to me, however, that outsiders to a practice should never feel compelled to support sexist or racist practices just because one part of a culture claims these practices to be important parts of its traditions. In addition, as I have indicated, the taking of another life, especially when that life is self-conscious, is a morally grave course of action. And in this case, the whales are innocent. The fact that they kill their own is morally irrelevant.

Cases like the Makah should make it clear that environmental problems are not simply matters of wilderness preservation or maintaining habitats for endangered species. Although these are critically important, if we think of an environmental problem outside of the historical and social context that created it we are likely to think that politics and environmental ethics are separate.

In fact, an environmental ethic needs to be fully open to matters of race, gender, and economic class. Oppressive patterns of thinking have often connected images of nature as something to be used as a resource with images of Native Americans as "wild," with Blacks as "uncivilized," and with women as "dogs" and "cats." One dimension of these issues is environmental racism.

Environmental racism is the connection, in theory and practice, of race and the environment so that the oppression of one is connected to, and supported by, oppression of the other. In simple terms, in a culture that damages nature there is a tendency to reinforce this by connecting certain people with nature so they can be "naturalized." Conversely, in a culture that oppresses certain groups of people, there is a tendency to connect these groups with justifications for damage to nature.

Is there environmental racism in the United States? The American Lung Association, hardly a "radical" political group, stresses the connections between race and air pollution. It reports that "Over the past decade, there has been increasing recognition that minority and disadvantaged populations are disproportionately subjected to a variety of environmental health hazards, including air pollution. For example, the nation's most severe air pollution problems, including ozone, are typically found in urban metropolitan areas, which are home to many minority populations."

Among the facts it cites are:

— Many minority populations are concentrated in central city areas where air pollution is most likely to be at its worst: 86.1 percent of blacks and 91.2 percent of Hispanics live in urban settings, as compared with 70.3 percent of whites.
— Researchers have found that higher percentages of African Americans and Hispanics than whites live in areas that do not comply with national air quality standards for particulate matter, carbon monoxide, ozone, sulfur dioxide, and lead.
— About 52 percent of all whites live in counties with high ozone concentrations; 62 percent of African Americans and 71 percent of Hispanics live in these areas.
— During the period between 1991–1993, 27.1 million children younger than thirteen and 1.9 million children with asthma lived in areas which did not meet the current national ozone standard of 0.08 parts per million (ppm) over an eight-hour period. African

145

American, Hispanic and Asian American children are disproportionately represented in areas with high ozone pollution levels. Over
61.3 percent of African American children, 69.2 percent Hispanic
children and 67.7 percent of Asian American children live in areas
that exceeded the 0.08 ppm level during 1991–1993, while only
50.8 percent of white children live in such areas.

— Industrial and electricity-generating facilities are major sources of
harmful air pollution. Studies show that these facilities are disproportionately concentrated in counties with high percentages of
minorities. Of all the U.S. counties considered urban, only 12 percent had minority populations greater than 31 percent but these
areas contain 21 percent of the three thousand major air-polluting
facilities in the nation. (American Lung Association)

In the United States, being black, or Hispanic, or Native American means
much greater likelihood of suffering from environmental health problems
than being white.

Critics of the claim that there is environmental racism often argue
that the real problem here is not race, but economics. People of color suffer from these problems not because of racism, we are told, but because
they tend to be poor. The solution, then, is for them to become more fully
integrated into the capitalist economy. Increased earnings will allow people to move to the suburbs where they are less likely to suffer from environmental health problems.

But this argument misses the point. No one claims that race and economic class are identical, as if an analysis of earnings power would mean
that there is no need to examine the ways that conceptions of skin color
work in the United States. The point in focusing on environmental racism
is to show that there are important and systemic *connections* between race
and economic class. Being nonwhite increases the likelihood of environmental health problems. Being poor also increases the likelihood of environmental health problems. Being nonwhite and poor. . . .

Finally, we should note that the effects of globalization have reached
the sector of the American economy that we might have thought would
benefit the most: the American farmer. According to the Principle of
Comparative Advantage, the global economy works most efficiently
when countries specialize in producing what they produce best. It makes
no sense, according to this principle, for the United States to produce

bananas when countries in Central America can produce them much better. The United States would be much better off producing grains in its "breadbasket," especially corn and soybeans. Since the United States can produce these basic food crops at a price advantage compared to other countries, it should be able to export food at low prices and compete effectively on the international grain market. Globalization should, therefore, benefit the American farmer if it benefits anyone. Or so the theory goes.

Despite the common assumption that poverty in the United States is concentrated in urban areas, this is not true. Data collected by the U.S. Department of Commerce's Bureau of Economic Analysis show that forty-nine out of the fifty poorest counties in the country are in rural areas. In 1990, 22 percent of U.S. farm households had incomes that were below the official poverty level, twice the rate of poverty for the country as a whole. Poverty is overwhelmingly concentrated among those who produce food, and in small towns that often depend on agriculture (Mittal 2001).

Land disenfranchisement is not just a "third world problem." It is happening to American family farmers at an alarming rate. The rate of job loss is greater among family farmers than for any other occupation in the United States: 13.2 percent. In fact, the United States now has more prisoners behind bars than farmers (Mittal 2001).

A common response to the plight of family farmers is that they are "inefficient producers": just as the corner drug store cannot compete against Wal-Mart, so the family farmer must expect to give way to corporate farms. The message of the Department of Agriculture and agribusinesses is, "Get Big or Get Out!"

As is often the case, however, such slogans mask a different reality. The facts indicate that American taxpayers are footing the bill to drive family farmers out of business. In 1996, a year after the birth of the World Trade Organization, Congress responded to the new impetus for free trade with the "Freedom to Farm Act." The Act removed subsidies to American farmers. Its goal was to create a one-world food market that was based on the true cost of food production. It put the Principle of Comparative Advantage into practice.

The 1996 legislation produced a crisis in the American farm economy. Many commodities suddenly cost more to produce than they could return at the market. We quickly discovered that the Principle of Comparative Advantage gave no advantage to the American farmer.

In response, on May 13, 2002, Congress passed the Farm Security and Rural Investment Act, which provides $248.6 billion in subsidies to American farmers, more than an 80 percent increase over the provisions of the 1996 legislation. The benefits were directed toward those farmers who least need them: the richest 10 percent of farm corporations collect 80 percent of the subsidies; the bottom 80 percent collect just one-sixth of the subsidies. Almost half of the subsidies go to farmers with average household incomes above $135,000.

United States farm policy supports neither free trade nor fair trade. It is a form of corporate welfare for factory farms, often with absentee owners, and a small group of farm chemical and seed companies, such as Cargill and Monsanto. This has the effect of driving American family farmers out of business, as well as farmers around the world whose governments cannot compete with the American taxpayer. The United States now exports corn at 20 percent below the cost of production. Wheat is sold at 46 percent below the cost of production.

For those who wonder why third world farmers can't seem to compete with American farmers, consider how subsidized American cotton is destroying production of cotton in Africa in countries well suited to cotton production. Artificially low prices deprive west and central African countries of an estimated $250 million/year in agricultural revenues. The World Bank itself estimates that U.S. farm subsidies cost poor countries $50 billion/year. This is roughly the same amount these countries receive in "development aid" (Mittal 2001).

Despite the American message that "free trade will raise all boats," U.S. farm policy is destroying local agricultural markets around the world, and it is providing development loans that sink these same countries deeper into debt. If American family farmers cannot compete against welfare for Cargill and Monsanto, how will farmers in Nigeria?

Farmers here and abroad are also concerned about new kinds of seeds, genetically modified organisms (GMs). At a surface level, it may make sense to say that GMs will help alleviate hunger. Crops whose yields were once reduced by pest damage, for example, can now be engineered to resist pests. Plants themselves now can do the job that once required pesticides.

The debate on GMs is complex, but at least two concerns need to be voiced. One is that GMs are patented by the same companies that benefit from corporate farm welfare, particularly Monsanto. They represent the complete rupture of the genetic circle of open pollinated seeds that farmers around the world have depended on for ten centuries. It is important to ask whether it benefits food security to allow the genome of major food crops to be owned privately, in some cases by a single company. The advantage these crops enjoy is not only genetic. They also enjoy the political advantage of vigorous support from the government of the United States.

A particularly troubling case was reported in 2001 by two University of California at Berkeley researchers, Ignacio Chapela and David Quist, in the scientific journal *Nature* (Chapela and Quist 2001). They found that GM maize (corn) introduced into Mexico from the United States had crossbred with native Mexican maize in two remote states, Oaxaca and Puebla.

Maize is the staple crop of Mexico. Food security for the poor depends directly on access to these food crops. Mexico is also the place where maize was first cultivated, and much of the genetic diversity of the crop still exists there. The reason the *Nature* article was so troubling is that Monsanto had reassured farmers that GM maize could be controlled, and that it would not interbreed with traditional strains of maize. This was not true. The United States ships six million tons of U.S. maize to Mexico annually. GM maize is not labeled, so there is no way for Mexican farmers to tell what they are planting (ETC Group 2002).

The accidental spread of GM maize genes raises the possibility that it will make cultivation of traditional maize impossible. We cannot leave the question whether it is wise to release genetically modified organisms into the environment solely to economists and scientists. We need to know good science and consider the possibility that GMs can help address world hunger. But we cannot ignore the legitimate interest diverse peoples have in controlling their own food security. The United States, Japan, and many other world powers are unwilling to expose their farmers to a free market. Why should politically vulnerable countries be open-air testing grounds for experimental crops that will leave them dependent on multinational corporations?

When we hear the term "third world," then, we have trained ourselves to think of faraway problems and places. This pattern of thinking neglects the fact that North America was also colonized. What happened here was not a "kinder, gentler" kind of colonialism, not when we recall that the indigenous population of North America declined by 98 percent in the period following 1492.

The divide between the rich and poor, between those whose ancestors colonized, and those whose ancestors were colonized, still exists. We cannot go back in time and set everything straight. No one is arguing for such a solution. However, we can recognize treaties negotiated between sovereign nations, as prejudicial to native interests as they were. We can also restructure some of our familiar ideas, such as the idea that white settlers colonized a great "wilderness." It is important to save as much of the natural legacy of North America as possible, but it is not "wilderness."

Another familiar idea that needs to be restructured is the image that poverty only affects the inner cities. It does, of course. A full environmental ethic ought to include recognition of the environmental hazards people face when they live in the core of many American cities. However, the facts show that rural poverty is at least as great a problem as urban poverty. Globalization means that many of the world's people who grow food can't afford to eat. The United States is no exception.

CHAPTER SEVEN
CLEAN CLOTHES/CLEAN CONSCIENCE

Konrad Korzeniowski was a boy of nine in 1866 when he pointed to the white, unexplored spot at the center of a map of Africa. He announced to his school friends, "When I grow up I shall go *there*" (Hochschield 1998, 140). Korzeniowski's appetite for adventure beyond the borders of Europe's grasp was fired by his boyhood hero, David Livingstone. A missionary and explorer, Livingstone crossed Africa for three decades beginning in the early 1840s in search of the headwaters of the Nile. He represented, for Korzeniowski, the highest expression of European curiosity: exploration as the unflagging search for Truth.

In September 1890, after an arduous thousand-mile journey up the Congo River piloting a steamer called the *Roi des Belges*, Korzeniowski arrived at the very spot he had marked as a boy. In the distance he could hear the muted thunder of Stanley Falls, the highest navigable point on the river. There, as he sat under a starry night sky smoking his "pipe of peace" he permitted himself to speak the words, "This is the very spot of my boyhood boast."

But his journey, this place, had by then turned from dream to nightmare. We have his words:

A great melancholy descended on me. Yes, this was the very spot. But there was . . . only the unholy recollection of a prosaic newspaper "stunt" and the distasteful knowledge of the vilest scramble for loot that ever disfigured the history of human conscience and geographical exploration.

151

What an end to the idealized realities of a boy's daydreams. I wondered
what I was doing there. . . . (Conrad 1988, 187)

The "newspaper stunt" has now shrunk in our cultural memory to the
size of a single sentence: "Mr. Livingstone, I presume." But it was perhaps
the most celebrated media event of the nineteenth century. In 1866 Livingstone had set off on another journey to confront Arab slave traders,
convert pagans, and perhaps, at last, discover the source of the Nile. Three
years passed without news from Livingstone, and there was widespread
concern for his fate in Europe and the United States. James Gordon Ben-
nett, publisher of the *New York Herald*, seized on this thirst for news. He
summoned his reporter to a meeting in Paris and issued a directive: find
Livingstone!

Henry Morton Stanley was a virtuoso of self-aggrandizement, the
perfect choice for an assignment to create the kind of news that would sell
newspapers. Based on these accounts, Stanley published the first of his
many accounts of African adventure in a book, *How I Found Livingstone*.

Stanley's account of his travels filled his readers' minds with images of
a barbaric Africa, where Arab slave traders dealt in human flesh. Stanley
and his men slogged for days through alligator-infested swamps under the
burning sun. They suffered illness and near starvation before finding Livingstone on the shores of Lake Tanganyika.

Stanley's racial attitudes made for brutal treatment of his porters, and
of villagers who resisted his demands for food. In Stanley's words, "A barbarous man . . . is like a child which has not yet acquired the faculty of ar-
ticulation. The missionary discovers the barbarian almost stupefied with
brutish ignorance, with the instincts of a man in him, but yet living the
life of a brute. . . ." Brought into contact with the European, however, the
African "becomes docile enough: he is awed by a consciousness of his own
immense inferiority, and imbued with a vague hope that he may also rise
in time to the level of this superior being. . . ." (Stanley 1969, 80).

For Stanley, as for Edgar Rice Burroughs, Africans were subhuman
reminders of Europe's racial past: inarticulate, ignorant, inferior. The pun-
ishments Stanley issued were intended to remind them of their subhuman
status. Porters who broke down on the trail suffered the lashes of a dog-
whip. Prisoners were chained together like oxen. Today, his treatment of
animals would mark him as someone who is pathologically deranged. He

traveled with his pet dog, Omar. For no announced reason he cut off the dog's tail and made him eat it (Hochschield 1998, 196).

Stanley's celebrity brought him to the attention of a powerful bene-factor, King Leopold II of Belgium. Leopold was Stanley's equal in ma-nipulating publicity of high moral purpose for personal gain. Leopold was the king of a small European country, less than fifty years old. He was ob-sessed with the fact that the European powers had long since consolidated their colonial holdings. Without a colony of his own, Leopold had no hope of acquiring the immense fortune he craved. Though he tried over many years to buy, or even rent, colonies from other countries, he failed. The only unclaimed territory remaining by the second half of the nineteenth century was that unexplored white spot at the heart of Africa. Leopold did not have the military might or the financial wherewithal to conquer the Congo on his own. So, he outsmarted his royal compatriots by appealing simultaneously to their morals and to their pocketbooks.

In 1876 he convened a Geographical Conference in Brussels for a group of the most renowned dignitaries and explorers. He welcomed the delegates with a bold proposal: "To open to civilization the only part of our globe which it has not yet penetrated, to pierce the darkness which hangs over entire peoples, is, I dare say, a crusade worthy of this century of progress. . . ."

Having made his appeal to the mandate of civilized societies to wipe out darkness and replace it with the light of progress, he then advanced the puzzling claim that only Belgium was positioned to play the lead role. Just because Belgium is small and neutral, Leopold argued, it could pro-vide free access to competing European powers so they could all trade freely without unnecessary conflict.

By the time Leopold began to levy crushing taxes on the trading en-terprises of other countries it was too late. Leopold had consolidated power in himself. Leopold, not Belgium, owned the Congo. Over a period of twenty-six years he amassed a personal fortune of more than one bil-lion dollars calculated at today's rates. His policies cost the lives of at least ten million Congolese. Leopold's personal agent in the Congo was Henry Morton Stanley.

One of the most remarkable documents in the history of human rights is an open letter written by an American black man, George Wash-ington Williams. It was addressed to none other than "His Serene Majesty

Leopold II, King of the Belgians and Sovereign of the Independent State of Congo." The letter was written at the very same spot, Stanley Falls, at which Joseph Conrad had penned his words of regret only two months earlier, in July 1890.

By the time Williams arrived at Stanley Falls he had already lived a remarkable career: Civil War veteran, soldier in Mexico and in the American Indian wars, minister, attorney, historian, and author of *History of the Negro Race in America from 1619 to 1880*. A devout Christian, he journeyed to Africa largely accepting the Euro-American moral rationale that colonization is necessary to convert Africans and lift them to civilization. Williams was horrified by the activities of Afro-Arab slave traders: he had been offered slaves at Stanley Falls, and had witnessed canoeloads of slaves chained together by the neck. He also had harsh words for some of the tribes he met while traveling up the Congo River, tribes that sacrificed human beings.

But the clear target of his letter was Leopold himself, as well as his agent, Henry Morton Stanley. The letter opens with Williams's vow that he will speak "the whole truth" about things that he had witnessed. It must have taken extraordinary courage to remind the king that Williams was duty-bound not only to "History," "Humanity," and "Civilization," but to "the *Supreme Being*, who is himself the 'King of Kings.'"

Williams wasted no time in telling Leopold that his title to the State of Congo was "badly clouded." The contracts supposedly extracted to native chiefs by Stanley were "tainted by frauds of the grossest character." The lore of Stanley's methods was still alive among the people Williams met, and his account has the ring of a report from a direct witness:

A number of electric batteries had been purchased in London, and when attached to the arm under the coat, communicated with a band of ribbon which passed over the palm of the white brother's hand, and when he gave the black brother a cordial grasp of the hand the black brother was greatly surprised to find his white brother so strong, that he nearly knocked him off his feet in giving him the hand of fellowship. When the native inquired about the disparity of strength between himself and his white brother, he was told that the white man could pull up trees and perform the most prodigious feats of strength. (Williams 1988, 104)

Another favorite of Stanley's was the lens trick. He used a lens to light his cigar, explaining that this demonstrated his intimate relationship to the sun. If petitioned, the sun would also "burn up his black brother's village." The third trick Williams reports is the gun trick. Native chiefs were handed a gun loaded only with a cap. They were encouraged to "shoot" Stanley at a distance of ten feet. After the explosion Stanley would retrieve a bullet from his shoe, proving that even the strongest weapons could not harm him.

When such tricks failed, Stanley dropped the pretense and "sequestered their land, burned their towns, [stole] their property, enslaved their women and children, and committed other crimes too numerous to mention in detail" (Williams 1988, 106). It comes as no surprise that "Henry M. Stanley's name produces a shudder among this simple folk when mentioned; they remember his broken promises, his copious profanity, his hot temper, his heavy blows, his severe and rigorous measures, by which they were mulcted of their lands" (1988, 111).

What should we make of George Washington Williams' legacy? Did he have the moral standing to address the King of Belgium as he did? He was not Belgian or Congolese. Was it his standing as a black man, a man who knew the meaning of slavery, that gave his voice such moral resonance? Yet, even in his own country Williams suffered the blows of racism. His accomplishments meant nothing to the majority of white people. Williams's moral criticism was very much in the minority during his own time. There was little likelihood that his protests would even be heard.

Is it enough to respond to the story of George Washington Williams, as many do today, "You need to live in the real world!" "Who's to say that colonialism was bad? We can only judge our own times." "We can only judge our own culture."

These responses sound like excuses rather than reasons. Williams's moral condemnation of slavery and colonialism seems remarkable today because he was ahead of his time. The great majority of us today have come to *agree* with Williams. In a morally confusing world, slavery and colonialism are among the few injustices we all agree to condemn.

Who was the right man to condemn the King of Belgium? Clearly, the answer is that George Washington Williams *made* himself that man. Despite all odds, he spoke the truth to military and economic power. And despite the dim prospect that his voice would be heard, we all—you and I—now know his legacy. Against all odds, George Washington Williams's voice prevailed. The colonial empire of Belgium no longer exists.

How is Williams's legacy relevant to us today? We need not look far. When the Belgians left Congo, they took vengeance on their former colony by destroying its infrastructure and turning tribal groups against each other. Today, the Democratic Republic of Congo is one of the world's most violent places. More than three million people have died in a protracted civil war; its neighboring countries, Rwanda, Burundi, and Uganda, intervene regularly to make the situation worse.

The eastern Congo is rich in a metallic ore, called columbite-tantalite. It is refined into tantalum, a powder that is heat resistant and that can hold an electrical charge. It is used in almost all computers and cell phones. Tantalum is literally worth its weight in gold.

Miners have invaded eastern Congo's national parks in search of columbite-tantalite. It is easy to extract with strip mining, often in rivers and streams. The ore is separated from unwanted rock and soil with sieves. The waste pollutes the rivers.

The major problem, however, is that the land cleared for mining is a habitat for Congo's gorillas and elephants. Miners kill both indiscriminately for food. In Kahuzi Biega National Park, for example, the gorilla population has been cut almost in half in the last decade, from 258 to 130.

Mining also fosters human violence. Warlords use profits from illegal mining to finance their military campaigns. The Rwandan army made over $250 million from columbite-tantalite in eighteen months; none of it was mined in Rwanda (Chadwick 2001). Under vigorous pressure from the United Nations, some suppliers have agreed not to purchase columbite-tantalite from sources in the Congo region. It is available from other locations, such as Australia.

It is true, as some people say, that we cannot continue to blame the effects of colonialism for contemporary violence. We cannot change the past. In spite of the problems the Congolese inherited, the future depends on learning from, and refusing to perpetuate, the violence of the past. However, if we want to improve on the past, we must at least appreciate how we arrived at the present situation. In fairness, we must also recognize that the problems illustrated by columbite-tantalite mining are *contemporary* problems. If you own a cell phone or a computer you are morally compelled to be concerned about the future of columbite-tantalite mining.

Let's admit it: knowing how the world really works these days can be pretty discouraging. Many of the readers of this book will live in a world of nine billion people. Much of what counts as "development" is a euphemism for new forms of capitalism: capitalism down to the level of the gene pool, and up to the level of the biosphere. Governments everywhere seem undeterred in their zeal to promote agreements and agencies that deprive the ever-expanding majority of people of the ability to control their own lives. Even those of us at the "center" are seeing the effects of globalization as the wealthy become wealthier, and marginal rural and urban economies decline. Often, Gandhi's dream of community development that empowers people and cares for the environment seems to be just that, a dream.

Is there no alternative, then, to "keeping your head down and taking the money"? Can we still claim the power of self-definition when the world seems to be powered by large, anonymous, nondemocratic forces? Is it possible to claim an identity that involves more than being a consumer? Is real citizenship—including a commitment to social and environmental justice—still possible?

Will there be room for ethics in a world of bare necessity?

I believe there is room for optimism, a sobered, informed, realistic optimism that leads to concrete, meaningful choices about one's life. The values of those who are troubled by globalization are *life affirming* in the broadest and deepest sense. A commitment to treat other people with integrity is also a commitment to treat one's self with integrity. Relations with others cannot be sustained without proper respect for oneself. A humble recognition of oneself as a "plain citizen of the biotic community" is only possible when we live the truth that citizenship is never solitary. The moral community is not confined within the boundaries of human civilization. Healthy resistance to globalization begins with the recognition that the vast majority of the world's peoples and places are "in this together."

Although we may sometimes give way to the feeling that we are alone in responding in the ways we do, in fact, we are never alone. The task is to recognize and build on this consensus about what constitutes a meaningful human life. A meaningful future depends on building intentional moral communities that affirm life.

We normally think of ethics as distinct from medicine. But there is an important connection. Ethics is not just a matter of following abstract rules, doing what an authority figure tells you to do. Living ethically is a matter of building a healthy, whole, integrated life. A healthy life is not an accident; it results from deliberate choice. It is a matter of being able to look back after decades of engagement with others and say truthfully, "That was well done."

When we get down to it, the general patterns of an ethical life are quite simple. A healthy life, psychologically and ethically, is a matter of how we relate to others, as well as what we become through these relationships. If I treat others deceitfully, eventually I become deceitful. Deceitful people are just as ready to deceive themselves as others, perhaps even more so. If I live a life in denial with my head in the sand, just taking life as it comes, I may end up a slave rather than my own master. Is a worse life imaginable?

The values affirmed in opposition to homogenization are no mystery. They are the values that are conducive to respect and love for others, as well as respect and love for oneself. Real human development is a matter of growth from within that allows one to take one's place in a community of others. The healthy interdependence of a vibrant community is the opposite of mere dependence.

Thinking ecologically, it is important that we can view ethics as a matter of scale. We all operate on many levels: as children and parents, as neighbors, as contributors to the local community. We participate in state and national government through the right to vote, the right to lobby, and the obligation to pay taxes. Today, there is the emerging sense that citizenship can no longer be understood simply in terms of one's obligations to state and country. We need to learn to think of ourselves as transnational citizens with obligations to real, but sometimes difficult to identify, sources of power and identity. Transnational citizenship usually operates at an intermediate level today, through social and environmental organizations and allied nongovernmental organizations that grow out of local experience and provide the authority needed to stand between corrupt governments and corporations and their visions of progress.

Ethics, then, is a matter of clarity of purpose, integrity and compassion at each level of scale, and integrating these values throughout the smaller and larger scales of modern life. We function best, I believe, when our commitments to family, friends, and local community integrate with our commitments on a broader scale. Put negatively, it is a less than fully human life that treats family with love and compassion, but treats people we define as distant with disdain.

Despite the odds, the best contemporary life is also cautiously optimistic. We have only one life. It is far better to act on the assumption that we can define our identities in the contemporary world than to surrender and let those large, anonymous forces do the job. Because they will if we let them. Perhaps if we reflect carefully we will find more room for creative self-definition than we might think possible, given the weight of the problems. The solutions are there, if we will work together to achieve them.

Anyone who has vacationed in Mexico or Jamaica knows the relative economic power that middle-class Americans have. What would happen if we pooled this power together and consciously directed its use, instead of letting it direct us? Where might it lead us if we tried to think through this comparison: just as men in a sexist society must use their power as men to oppose sexism, so those who are relatively well off in a globalized world must use their power to . . . what? What would George Washington Williams advise us to do?

I have argued that much of the economic well-being we enjoy today in the "developed" world is due to the legacies of colonialism and neo-colonialism. Colonial rulers became phenomenally wealthy over a period of five hundred years by stealing what was not theirs. They robbed countries of their natural wealth, the same wealth that might have been devoted to the well-being of colonized people. Today, the attempt to develop third world countries has left them mired in debt. Funds that might be devoted to schools and medical care are diverted to repay loans. Despite the attitude of many Americans today that "they" should "pull themselves up by the bootstraps just like we did," there is no level playing field today, economically or ethically. Whether we will acknowledge it or not, our benefits are systemically connected to the deprivation of others. The question is, "What should we do about it?"

Since a large part of the problem is economic we can begin by focusing concretely on our roles as consumers. Some positive steps are possible without the slightest sacrifice. If you have a telephone in your home, for example, you might buy your long-distance service from Working Assets, a company that uses its profits to support the causes of social and environmental justice (Working Assets). Since 1985 it has donated more than

$35 million to nonprofit organizations working for "peace, equality, education and a cleaner environment." These groups include Planned Parenthood, the Rainforest Action Network, and the American Civil Liberties Union. The company even provides free long-distance calling to your representative in Congress.

Working Assets also offers credit card and cellular phone services that donate a percentage of the monthly bill to progressive causes. And for once, you may actually enjoy opening your bill: Working Assets' monthly bills come with information on issues relating to social justice movements and the environment. A related website is Shopping for Change. Here it is possible to buy books, clothing, flowers, gardening supplies, and environmentally friendly products online, with up to 5 percent of the purchase going to progressive causes.

Another website that helps consumers dedicate their purchases to social and environmental causes is Responsible Shopper. This site contains information on over two hundred well-known companies on a variety of social and environmental issues. It is easy to investigate entire industries, and then to compare alternatives within those industries.

One of the important issues that can be traced through this site is sweatshop labor, perhaps the clearest example of how our lifestyle depends on the oppression of others. Sweatshops have been common in the garment industry from the beginning. In the 1890s activists such as Jane Addams and Florence Kelly helped garment workers organize campaigns to reform the conditions of work. Out of these efforts grew the International Ladies' Garment Workers' Union in 1900, followed by the Amalgamated Clothing Workers of America, founded in 1914. Together, they won contract concessions for the workers that included better wages, safer working conditions, and health care and pensions (Botz 2002).

By the 1960s, however, clothing companies began to leave the Northeast, which was heavily unionized, for locations in the American South and to countries around the world where labor was still unregulated. In the 1990s this movement gained power through the process of globalization. Trade barriers came down. Capital could pass across national borders freely, while labor was still contained within national borders. Gains that had been made through a century of union organizing were quickly eroded as the garment, electronics, and automobile industries relocated to foreign soils where there was not a strong labor union presence. Globalization brought the owners of the means of production together in organizations like the World Trade Organization, while it split workers apart. Autoworkers in Detroit were put in direct competition with workers in Mexico. Gains in health care, pensions, and working conditions were quickly sacrificed for cheaper prices at the market place. In the 1990s we witnessed yet another phase in the history of coercive primitive accumulation.

In garment sweatshops, the workers, often women and children, typically work for less than one-third of the country's official poverty level. Workweeks are commonly double the number of hours that unionized American workers spend on the job. Health care is minimal and work conditions can be dangerous. Workers are fired at the hint of unionization, and there are frequent charges of sexual harassment from female workers.

Seventy-five percent of the clothing Americans buy is made with sweatshop labor. Some of this labor is domestic: as the costs of doing aboveboard business have risen, illegal sweatshops in Los Angeles and New York have been discovered using undocumented workers from Mexico and Central America. Most sweatshop clothing, however, comes from factories in China, India, Thailand, and elsewhere.

In a poll conducted by the Marymount University Center for Ethical Concerns, three-quarters of polled consumers reported that they would avoid shopping at a retailer if they knew it sold sweatshop clothing. Eighty-six percent said they would be willing to pay an extra dollar on a twenty-dollar garment if they could be sure that it was not made in a sweatshop. The great majority of Americans actually oppose sweatshops (Marymount University Center 1999).

The poll also showed, however, that respondents in the 18–34 age range were the least concerned about sweatshop labor. Even in this age group there are important exceptions. College students are raising awareness of the sources of clothing sold in their college bookstores. Caps bearing the Harvard logo sell on campus for $17. The women who sew the caps in Bangladesh, however, are only paid 1.6 cents for each cap, or less than 0.1 percent of the retail cost (Hayden and Kernaghan 2002). In response, students have built coalitions between themselves and labor unions. There are active student organizations for both colleges and high schools (UNITE!).

One of the major campaigns is against Gap for its use of sweatshops. Gap is the largest name-brand retailer in the United States, and the fifth-largest retailer of clothing in the world. It markets clothing under a variety of names: Gap, Banana Republic, Old Navy, GapKids, and babyGap. Gap contracts with more than 3,600 factories worldwide in over fifty countries.

The National Labor Committee started the campaign because of Gap's attempt to prevent union organizing in El Salvador. Eventually Gap agreed to a system that monitors labor conditions in El Salvador. However, it has resisted pressure to implement the same agreement in other factories around the world.

Gap claims that it cannot be responsible for the working conditions in independent businesses that are not owned by Gap. There are simply too many factories, and they are too widely distributed around the world. Under pressure from watchdogs such as Global Exchange and the Clean Clothes Campaign, Gap has agreed to withhold business from known sweatshops, but it will not actively seek out information on which of its subcontractors uses sweatshop labor. It only responds when pressured by outside organizations, and even then, it is usually among the last companies to change its policies.

Gap is among the companies that have been sued over their use of sweatshops in Saipan, in the Northern Mariana Islands in the western Pacific. Saipan is an American protectorate, so garments made there can carry the "Made in America" label, and they are exempt from import taxes when shipped to the United States. However, workers, who are mainly young women from Asia, are treated as indentured servants. Often they must pay large recruitment fees to be hired. They work twelve hours a day, seven days a week without overtime pay, and in unsanitary conditions.

On January 13, 1999, a suit was filed against eighteen American clothing companies in an attempt to reform labor practices in American protectorates. Companies named in the suit include Gap, Tommy Hilfiger, the Limited, J. C. Penney, Wal-Mart, and Sears. In August of the same year Nordstrom, Cutter & Buck, J. Crew, and Gymboree agreed to a settlement that provides back pay, reimbursement for immigration expenses, and the implementation of a monitoring system. To date, twenty-six retailers have signed the agreement. Only Levi Strauss has refused to sign (Global Exchange, Saipan Campaign).

A similar campaign seeks to raise awareness of working conditions in China, where young women work sixteen-hour days, seven days a week during peak manufacturing periods. To gain employment they are forced to make deposits with the company that are returned only after completing two years of work. Disney makes much of the clothing sold in its theme parks in Chinese factories. Wal-Mart and Gap also contract with these companies. However, three companies, Reebok, Levi Strauss, and Mattel, have agreed to a basic set of human rights that apply to working conditions there (Global Exchange, China Campaign).

Consumer awareness is also important in actively supporting companies that commit to fair labor and environmental standards. Ben Cohen, cofounder of Ben and Jerry's Homemade, Inc., recently invested $1.5 million in a Los Angeles clothing factory to produce casual clothing under the SweatX label. The employees are unionized, and they start at $8.50 an hour with full health benefits, a pension plan, and profit sharing. It is no longer difficult to find clothing that is sweatshop free (SweatX).

Some clothing companies also take environmental responsibility seriously. Patagonia, a manufacturer of outdoor clothing, makes many of its fleece garments out of postconsumer waste. It also sponsors the Sustainable Cotton Project, and uses only organic cotton in its T-shirts.

Patagonia has pledged not to use any forest products made from clear-cut old-growth temperate rainforests. Compare this record to that of the Fisher family, owners of Gap. They used profits from Gap to purchase 230,000 acres of forestland in Mendocino County in California, where they have been logging old-growth redwoods. Where we choose to spend our money does make a difference (Responsible Shopper).

These stories provide reasons for optimism. In a globalized world where companies can profit from unethical treatment of workers and the environment, it is difficult for ethical companies to compete. Health care, a living wage, safe working conditions, and retirement benefits cost money. There is no incentive built into the economic system itself to balance the need to cut costs. However, consumer pressure against these companies has been successful. When it becomes an issue, most Americans make the choice to consume responsibly. Companies thrive by providing products consumers want to buy. The key is for consumers to loudly articulate their preferences.

Another important area of concern is food production. One celebrated boycott is against the Swiss company Nestlé. In the late 1980s

Nestlé executives became concerned that the market for its products in the first world was becoming saturated. It launched a campaign to advertise its artificial infant formula to third world women. The campaign encouraged the switch from breast-feeding to bottle-feeding with ad campaigns depicting white women bottle-feeding their babies. Poor women were encouraged to think of bottle-feeding as more civilized. Often, free samples were provided to women with newly born infants.

The problems begin when poor women have difficulty buying enough formula to provide their infants with a healthy diet. Because of the lapse in breast-feeding, many women find they can no longer nurse their children. To save money they dilute the formula, leading to undernourishment. Much of the water that is available to poor people is dangerously polluted. When the formula is mixed with polluted water it causes severe health problems in infants, such as dehydration from diarrhea. Bottle-fed babies are twenty-five times more likely to get diarrhea than breast-fed babies. Four thousand babies die each day from the effects of bottle-feeding.

An international campaign against Nestlé began in support of third world women and their infants. Nestlé eventually gave in to consumer pressure and pulled its formula from the shelves in poor countries. Once out of the spotlight, however, Nestlé once again began marketing infant formula, and the campaign continues (Baby Milk Action).

The coffee industry is a sector of the food economy where the choices are especially clear. Some of the most powerful companies in the market are Nestlé, the Altria Group (formerly Philip Morris), and Starbucks. All of these companies have been criticized for their refusal to support coffee workers' rights and ecologically responsible growing practices; or, in the case of Starbucks, they have dragged their feet. All three companies buy cocoa from the Ivory Coast in West Africa, which uses children as slave labor. Children as young as eleven years old have been forced to work as indentured servants to produce cocoa for the international market.

They also give little or no support to the Fair Trade movement, which guarantees a fair wage for workers on coffee plantations and attempts to eliminate the middlemen by dealing directly with confederations of responsible coffee growers. The same goes for organic and shade-grown coffee. These are ecologically sustainable methods for growing coffee, where beans are grown without pesticides and herbicides under shade trees.

With such practices, the land can be used up to three times longer than what is possible on large plantations, where the plants are exposed to the direct sunlight. Shade-grown coffee also preserves habitats for birds, does not require rainforest destruction, and limits erosion.

Clear alternatives to exploitation in the coffee industry are available with a little investigation. Equal Exchange is a worker-owned cooperative in Boston that imports and sells Fair Trade Certified coffee. The Fair Trade designation means that the coffee was grown in plantations with ecologically responsible growing methods where the workers are guaranteed a fair wage. All of its coffees are purchased directly from democratically organized small-farmer organizations. Similar practices are found at Green Mountain Coffee Roasters in Vermont, Counter Culture Coffee in Durham, North Carolina, and Sacred Grounds Coffee in Arcata, California (Responsible Shopper).

The use of child labor in Ivory Coast cocoa plantations illustrates the critical problems many of the world's children face. Several other industries depend on child labor. In Nepal, Pakistan, and India children as young as five work fifteen-hour days producing rugs for the export market. It takes ten days of solid work for a child to produce an eight-by-ten-foot carpet. Children are valued for this sort of labor because of their small fingers. Poor families sometimes give their children to the carpet industry because they cannot afford to feed them.

Fortunately, there is a nonprofit organization, Rugmark, which monitors carpet factories and other industries in these three countries. It provides a Rugmark certification tag on carpets that were produced without child labor. To receive this certification, rug manufacturers must agree to random, unannounced inspections of their factories (Rugmark).

In turn, the Rugmark Foundation provides support for rehabilitation of child workers through funding for tuition and school expenses. In some cases, it has built its own schools to educate children who were bonded laborers and give them vocational training.

Most first world consumers are rightly disgusted by child labor. It was one of the first abuses eliminated by the trade union movement. How is the situation different when other people's children are exploited? With the Internet it is now easy to shop responsibly. The Rugmark site lists retailers in almost every state that offer rugs from makers who do not use child labor. We can shop responsibly without sacrificing price or quality.

CHAPTER SEVEN

A common response heard from American consumers is that "We are providing people in poor countries with jobs, which they wouldn't have otherwise. Some work is better than none." This is another example of denial. Let's look at the facts.

In El Salvador at Doall Enterprises, a sweatshop, workers earn $0.60/hour. To live in "relative poverty" the average Salvadoran family needs to earn a minimum of $287.21/month. Doall's hourly wage equals only 51 percent of the relative poverty standard. Sweatshop work is not relief from poverty. It plunges workers deeper into poverty.

The Evergreen factory in Honduras, which manufactures clothing for Wal-Mart, pays only 54 percent of the cost of survival. A living wage in China is estimated to be about $0.87/hour. However, Shanghai's minimum wage is $0.21/hour, and Guangzhou's is $0.26/hour (Sweatshop Watch). When we buy clothing made in sweatshops we make life worse for these people, not better.

Furthermore, when we hear that sweatshop workers at least have jobs that they wouldn't have otherwise, we need to remember that many have been forced into sweatshops by the collapse of the rural agricultural economy. As industrialized farming has taken over small farms, and mechanization has replaced human work, the disenfranchised have been forced to migrate to cities to find factory work. What skeptics depict as an *opportunity* really is an act of *desperation*. When people earn less than the minimum needed to survive, they have no choice but to go into debt. This is the situation of bonded labor. Small loans received periodically can mean a lifetime of exploited labor.

The response that sweatshops and bonded agricultural labor are *good*, or even not as bad as we might think, conveniently ignores the other side of the equation: it would be much *better* if these workers had the right to unionize the same way American workers do. It would also be better if American workers were not being deprived of decades of advances in health care and pension coverage for the sake of the cheapest goods at any cost. A more informed and responsible position would be that cheap prices also come with the obligation to pressure companies into adopting labor and environmental policies that allow us to purchase clothing, food, and home furnishings with a clean conscience.

Two immediate responses to this transnational exploitation of workers are especially important: the need for cross-border union organizing so workers cannot be pitted against each other, and the need for consumers to be able to make informed choices. Despite the feelings of many that consumer pressure on companies does not work, the evidence shows that many companies do respond to criticism. If workers and consumers act together, real change is possible. To see what is actually being done, look at UNITE!, the campaign of the Union of Needletrades, Industrial and Textile Employees, a part of the AFL-CIO (UNITE!).

A third, deeper change in thinking may take longer. Most Americans are upwardly mobile. We see ourselves as succeeding if we can become white-collar workers. Most college students, perhaps with the exception of teachers and nurses, can't imagine themselves needing the protection of a labor union. But this shows a lack of class consciousness that will hurt Americans in the long run. Perhaps because of the myth of the American Dream, the belief that "I'll make it to the top by myself," American voters consistently vote against their own class interests. They vote for candidates and policies that will benefit people other than themselves. Cheaper prices at Wal-Mart also mean lower wages and no health insurance.

Looking toward the future, we can imagine a society in which it is not only *possible* to determine the social and ecological costs of consumer purchases, but *easy*. In the United States we have already established that it is a consumer's right to know the nutritional value of the food products we consume. We require this information to be printed on each food item we buy. We have also established that consumers have the right to know about the health risks of certain products. Everyone now knows that smoking can be dangerous to your health.

Why shouldn't we establish the right to know the social and environmental costs of the products we choose to purchase? Each product might be labeled with a list of the raw materials that went into the product, where they originated, the environmental costs of production in terms of pollution and toxic by-products, and the conditions of labor employed to produce the product. Some of this is happening already. The can of shaving cream I use displays an "Eco-Info" label. It says that the can was made of recyclable steel, and that the product was made without the use of CFCs or any other substances that deplete the ozone layer.

If all this is too much to expect on each label, we can imagine a series of compact symbols on each product that clearly display information on the conditions of production. It would be easy to direct consumers to a website where full information is available. If such a plan seems far-fetched, we might ask why. Why do we think consumers have a right to know how many grams of fat are contained in their candy bar, but they have no right to information on the social and environmental impact of their purchases? Why are we more concerned about physical health than moral health? Don't we consider the consumer's right to know basic in a free society? Insisting on the consumer's right to know does not require a major change in attitude. It is simply a matter of carrying through on principles we already accept. In good capitalist fashion, manufacturers might learn to highlight such information in an effort to gain access to a young, environmentally conscious audience. It's a simple matter of meeting market demand.

Environmental writer and businessman Paul Hawken has proposed other creative solutions for including environmental costs in the original cost of a product. Right now, much of the true cost of an item is not charged at the time of purchase. These costs literally go up in smoke. The environment is used as a communal waste dump, and that shows up in problems like ozone depletion, global warming, and toxic waste in streams, rivers, agricultural land, and our cities. Then cleanup becomes a burden to everyone, even if they had no interest in purchasing the product. There are also problems of pinpointing responsibility when pollutants cross over state or national borders. When acid rain from factories in the United States damages the environment in Canada, who should pay?

Hawken proposes that it would make much more sense to include these real costs at the point of sale, rather than as public health problems later on. Automobiles, for example, might include the cost of recycling the auto when it becomes junk five or ten years down the road. This would raise the cost of an automobile, but it would reduce many other costs. Automobile manufacturers would also begin to design their automobiles so that they can be disassembled and used again, rather than scrapped in the junkyard. Materials would be used that are environmentally friendly and easily recyclable.

Hawken's proposal makes sense especially when applied to "durable goods," large consumer items like refrigerators, stoves, washing machines, and dryers, as well as automobiles. We have already seen some positive changes in this direction, for example, the replacement of Freon as a refrigerant with more environmentally friendly products that do not contribute to ozone depletion (Hawken 1994).

The basic argument here is that fairness and economic efficiency can coincide. In the case of agricultural products, for example, all of us pay for subsidies to the meat industry, whether or not we eat meat. So the fast-food hamburger appears to be cheap when, in fact, it only appears cheap because of taxpayer subsidies. It would be understandable if vegetarians didn't wish to support the meat industry with their tax dollars. Hamburger is really a luxury. Why shouldn't its price reflect that reality? If we view things in a larger perspective, high-priced hamburgers might be good for everyone: an expensive hamburger should lead to lower income taxes.

None of these ideas is really radical. None even challenges capitalism as an efficient economic system that produces high-quality goods at a low price. Nothing fundamental needs to change to more fully recognize the consumer's right to know, and the principle that those who buy a product should pay what it really costs. Although the odds may seem great, such changes are certainly no less likely than the thought a few short years ago that the tobacco industry would accede to congressional pressure and allow health warnings to be printed on every pack of cigarettes. We need to find ways to balance the rights of consumers with the power of corporations.

Moving from our identities as consumers to our identities as workers, we can see that work itself can be a socializing process. It can draw out what is distinctively human in us. "Right work" is work that expresses one's personal and social identities. One of the basic critiques that Karl Marx lodged against capitalism is that work, under conditions of private ownership, is alienating. If we imagine working on a production line, for example, the goal is to make the costs of production as minimal as possible, while charging the highest possible price for the product. The owner needs to maximize the difference between the costs of production and price in the marketplace. Among the costs are the cost of raw materials, the equipment, the efficiency of the machinery, and the efficiency of the workers on the production line. In human terms, the process is a matter of making the owner richer, and the production line worker poorer. So, according to Marx, such work alienates us from our own work, like being forced to dig our own graves.

Consider, on the other hand, a potter who produces functional pottery. We can easily imagine that one of the reasons such activities are attractive is that they express who we are. The finished pot expresses "myself in the world." Put in Marx's terms, the pot allows the potter to connect with herself, with the social world that appreciates the creation, and even with the broader natural world through giving shape to the clay. Real work is a humanizing process, not the process of alienation.

We don't need to accept all of Marx to appreciate some of his ideas about work. Clearly, in our society many people *do* feel alienated from their work. We have a clear distinction between work, which many regard simply as a means to make money, and *free time*, weekends and evenings when we can express who we really are. Think about beer commercials during sports events. They celebrate "kicking back" and maximizing time away from work. It's a world where beautiful women regularly fall into your lap. Weekends are when our "real" personalities are supposed to come out.

Still, some people in our society choose their professions because they express their personal and social commitments. Nursing students often express a sincere desire to "help others." The motivation is hardly ample pay. Many medical students express the same desire as fundamental to their choice, even if they can expect to be well paid. Teachers and many others in social service professions express similar sentiments. Many young people choose to do environmentally and socially responsible work for nongovernmental agencies, despite low pay.

Of course, it would be better to do good work and also make a good salary. It says something about our society that we like to talk about the importance of the caring professions, but consistently underpay those who perform such work. In the end, however, people choose this kind of work because they find it intrinsically rewarding, an expression of self. Good pay helps, but it is not an end in itself.

We can also argue that many other kinds of work can be good work. An entrepreneur shows courage, timing, self-control under pressure, and many other qualities we regard as good and humanizing. When successful, the entrepreneur also creates work for others. But, thinking back to the comparison between Patagonia and Gap, we can see that either company might be described in terms of the abovementioned qualities. So, it is clear that the critical thing is not courage or timing in itself, but what we *do* with these skills. Skill used to destroy old-growth forests is not admirable. The courage it takes to build a successful business built on social and environmental goods is admirable.

It is understandable when young people in our culture feel that their choices don't make a difference. No matter what, you are still part of "the system." But it is important to resist this form of self-delusion. Well-educated people in the world's wealthiest country have more choices than others, not less. The type of work one chooses makes the difference between being the person who supports the system, and the one who resists it. These choices are among the most significant we can make.

I argued in chapter 5 that Mahatma Gandhi should be understood as a pragmatic campaigner for human and environmental rights, not as a hopelessly naïve idealist. He admitted that satyagraha can fail, and when it fails, it fails disastrously. He spent decades working patiently to get Indians to believe that colonization was not "natural." Clarity about the economic and spiritual dimensions of their condition allowed Indians to work together across the lines of class and caste. Solidarity of the Indian people ultimately expelled the British, not Mahatma Gandhi.

We in the first world can still learn from Gandhi. We are like the Indians before they gained a clear understanding of their condition. We still think it is "each man for himself." We still buy enough of Malthus, Burroughs, and Social Darwinism to think that we are destined to be the carnivores in a world of vegetarians. We still identify freedom with mere individual autonomy. When asked who I am in a moral sense, I am encouraged to answer in a defiantly individualistic way: "Well, I'm just me, Deane Curtin, not you." Questions of race or gender or species may be interesting facts *about* me, but they are ultimately incidental. I may happen to have white skin, but I *am* just me, a solitary free agent.

These ideas about who we are may be particularly seductive to those who are part of a dominant culture. We want to believe that our success is due to nothing but individual hard work. Whiteness, therefore, is considered to be an accidental fact about me. But in a racially charged culture, blackness is treated as an essential characteristic of "black" people. I am a cultural free agent; people of color are defined by their race. The same can be said about being male. When men succeed it is because they have the individual talent, motivation, and will to succeed. When women succeed it's because of the fact that women receive "special" privileges.

Suppose we attempt to think of ourselves not as solitary cultural free agents, but as being defined partially by our race, gender, or species. Such definitions may not be correct, as I have suggested. Colonialism seeks to define us in ways that facilitate exploitation. We can exploit ourselves by accepting an oppressive self-image. However, this form of control might also be turned on its head. It might come to function as a path to freedom. By becoming conscious of our position in society, we can begin to work in solidarity with others for substantive changes. In the United States the majority can vote their consciences and insist on humanizing changes in government and commerce. The question is whether we will use this power. If we continue to vote pragmatically within the narrow range of choices offered by our two major political parties nothing will change. It is important to vote with our consciences, as an expression of the persons we hope to become.

This active approach to self-definition also helps us think about our relationships to "distant" people. One might work to define oneself intentionally, for example, as a woman. Part of one's healthy self-identity might involve coming to function as part of an evolving intentional culture of women, or women and their supporters. An emerging culture is intentional because women are extraordinarily diverse, and it would be important to discover ways of engaging in practices that are not colonizing. The feminist movement went through this phase in which first world feminists spoke for the interests of third world women. This is why most forms of contemporary feminism assume that they will always speak with a plural voice. The goal is no longer the single voice of authority.

When we look at the world through a different lens, the difficulty of making judgments about "foreign" cultures diminishes. If my intentional moral community is the world of women, however diverse that might be, the pressing moral question need not be how I make the leap across continents of difference. The relevant categories need not only be "American" and "foreign."

Why do we so often define ourselves as "Americans," making the question, "How can people who live in America (the U.S.) judge—or help—people who live in Somalia or the Sudan?" Why can't the question we want to answer be, "How might *women* evolve a practice that allows women to judge and respond to the common problems of globalization?" Why can't human beings evolve a practice of living in greater harmony with nonhuman coinhabitants of the earth? Ethics is not a matter of describing what people believe; it is partly a matter of prescribing how the world should be. Philosophy is the art of asking the right questions.

Without the right questions it's highly unlikely that we will ever arrive at the right answers.

Finally, I also want to say a word in favor of patriotism. Patriotism is not unthinking loyalty. People who don't think are slaves. Real patriotism is an informed and judicious appreciation for one's country. In the United States there is much to appreciate. We have abolished slavery and made progress toward a just society. We have done much to eradicate discrimination against women. The United States has also enacted legislation to protect endangered species, as well as other important environmental legislation.

Globalization, on the other hand, requires corporate executives to demonstrate loyalty to company before loyalty to country. Jobs are exported to countries that have not rejected child labor or environmental protection for the sake of market advantage. Although those who protest globalization are often portrayed in the media as unpatriotic, the exact opposite is true. Concern for the welfare of American workers is patriotic.

Let me say this plainly: if George Washington Williams were alive today he would tell us that when we support sweatshops we are supporting slave labor. Our globalized economy is the contemporary version of the 1800s economy that provided cheap cotton for clothing. Cheap prices at the marketplace come at the cost of universally recognized standards of human and environmental justice. To rationalize sweatshops, or plead ignorance, will look a century from now like defending slavery. People will ask how "those people" back in the twenty-first century ever could have thought that they were doing a good thing when they purchased goods from sweatshops, Wal-Mart, and Levi Strauss.

CHAPTER EIGHT
DON'T TOUCH THE ROCKS!

Τhis journey we have embarked on through the landscape of contemporary life takes courage. Facing the world as it really is is difficult. Without forgetting the desperate condition many people
who live at the edge of bare necessity face, I would like to change pace in
this chapter. Colonialism is not just a form of economic control. It also
controls the ways we think of ourselves and experience the world. It thoroughly pervades our popular culture. To appreciate this I invite you to take
a trip to the Mecca of American culture: the shopping mall.

America is a culture of images. Roland Barthes said: "Consider the
United States, where everything is transformed into images: only images
exist and are produced and consumed" (Barthes 1980, 118). The American social critic Susan Sontag put a similar point bluntly: "Needing to
have reality confirmed and experience enhanced by photographs is an aesthetic consumerism to which everyone is now addicted. Industrial societies turn their citizens into image-junkies; it is the most irresistible form
of mental pollution" (Sontag 1973, 21).

Think about it: images of nature are everywhere in American culture.
Stroll through any mall at Christmas and you will come upon a store devoted exclusively to calendars. Take note of the nature calendars. There are
calendars from nature organizations: the Sierra Club, the Nature Conservancy. There are calendars for every breed of dog and cat. There are calendars celebrating the natural beauty of every state and region. There are
penguin calendars, bear calendars (Polar, Grizzly, Panda, and more), and
fish calendars. There are songbird calendars and birds of prey calendars.

There are whale calendars and weather calendars. Ansel Adams calendars are a subindustry of their own.

An outsider might easily conclude that our love of images of nature reveals the deep connections Americans feel with nature. There is certainly some truth in that observation. However, some have looked at the same evidence and arrived at very different conclusions. The novelist John Berger has said: "The 19th century, in Western Europe and North America, saw the beginning of a process, today being completed by 20th century corporate capitalism, by which every tradition which previously mediated between man and nature was broken. Before this rupture, animals constituted the first circle of what surrounded man" (Berger [1980] 1991, 3).

On Berger's reading the pervasiveness of nature photographs could mean that they are *memento mori*, reminders of the dead and distant past. Perhaps nature images function for us the way zoos functioned for colonial powers. Zoos began as instruments of colonial power used by European royalty and American industrialists to demonstrate their global reach. The elusive, the rare, the exotic became visible, indeed unavoidable, in their small cages. The justification for zoos has evolved. They now justify the captivity of ever-rarer species on the grounds that they preserve genetic material, which has become extinct in the wild.

Nature photographs also reassure us that the wild, the unpeopled, still exists, at least in the realm of images. In a culture that has very little real connection with nature, images of nature can medicate the pained conscience: if we no longer experience nature, we at least surround ourselves with "virtual nature."

In a consumer culture do these images of nature still speak the Truth? Or do they hide what we know, but do not wish to acknowledge?

Image: Deep in the Boundary Waters Canoe Area Wilderness in northern Minnesota. Waves slap against a smooth slab of overhanging rock. On the rock, there is an image of a moose painted in ochre, centuries ago. It is still alive.

Why do I feel that this image, this human presence, *belongs* here?

Why, supposing that I could paint such a figure, would it be nothing more than graffiti? A bad joke? A stain on this sacred place?

> **Image:** The state of Orissa, east central India. I have spent several days in tribal villages high up in the hills many kilometers from the coast. This afternoon I am to return to the coastal city of Vishakhapatnam.

My driver is a young Moslem. He is from the city, as out of place here as I am. He fingers for his watch, which appears from under the sleeve of his expensive pin-striped button-down shirt. It is a showy chunk of silver metal. How different from the silver jewelry women wear in the villages I have left behind: multiple rings adorning their ears and noses.

We must leave now, he says, or we will get caught in the Hindu villages as night falls.

We drive for an hour through brilliant green fields. Then, we reach the edge of the high plateau and begin to descend switchbacks through scattered villages, no longer tribal, but Hindu. My driver leans forward and races through the first villages, recklessly I think, though I try not to let him see me flinch as we cut a path through the gathering humanity.

As the darkness overtakes us, people return from work in the fields, and nearly deserted villages quickly fill with all manner of life. Shops come to life with small transactions, gossip, jokes. Hindu movie music crackles from tinny loudspeakers.

My driver becomes more agitated. A dodge-em game has turned serious, and his face now has a malevolent look as he leans ever more frequently on the horn. I am seated next to him in the front seat, witness to this unfolding battle between cultures.

There, ahead, a passage opens momentarily; my driver accelerates and we surge forward. The left rear flank of a cow appears out of the mass of humanity, near the right front tire. I hear the dull crunch of splintering bones. I turn my head right; the warm body stumbles as it passes near me. As I look left toward the rear-view mirror, there are faces. First, there is recognition. Then rage. Men who have been absorbed in conversation square up and begin to chase the car. Another clearing opens ahead of us. My driver pushes through and out the other side of the village. He is shaking.

Later, when we reach the hotel, he tells me that we were lucky to make it out alive.

> **Image:** It is Saturday morning. I decide to take my children to the zoo I have not visited since childhood. I have sweet memories of the place, of my grandparents who are visiting from New York. The fragrant smells of exotic flowers in the Conservatory recall the touch and smell of my grandmother's silk dresses.

Much has changed, but I recognize the old zoo building. Rows of cages on the inside connect through heavy wooden doors to cages that line the outside of the building. Animals were easy to find. An empty cage on the inside meant the animal could be found sunning itself on the outside. Today, the rows of cages are empty.

In unison, my children, far too young to indulge in political thinking, recall the experience of visiting an abandoned prison while on vacation in Montana some months earlier. There were the same rows of cells. The heavy echoes of steel door against cage are the same. One of the prison cells held a man who went insane and convinced himself that he was the prison warden. He issued "checks" to other prisoners and kept careful books.

The zoo animals have been moved to new exhibit spaces, each designed to recall a natural habitat. Casey, the mountain gorilla, sits on the other side of a moat twenty feet above a cement landscape on a jungle of lumberyard timbers. He picks out my son's voice and gives us a darting half-look. Again his eyes flick at us. My sons ask, "Why is he looking at us?"

Why do gorillas look? What do they remember?

> **Image:** The Mall of America in Bloomington, Minnesota. A store, "Colorado," sells clothes that are "functional yet fashionable."

Logo: "Colorado isn't only a store: it's a state of mind."

At the back of the store is a photomural of the Maroon Bells, in the Colorado Rockies.

I am drawn back to teenage years, when I first saw a photograph of the Maroon Bells and I resolved to go there.

The peaks are gloriously symmetrical, but the rock is bad and the climbing is a long, wet slog. My hands are bloody, my feet cold. This is a *real* place, not just a state of mind.

Image: I lived for some months in a house in Madras (now Chennai), in southeastern India. The house had a kitchen on the first floor. Being an early riser, I often found myself alone in the morning making coffee. I say "alone." Actually, I learned quickly to make way for company. As I turned on the lights, most mornings the rats would bound out from behind the silver mixing bowls, knocking everything in their way onto the floor as they scrambled for a place to hide. These were big rats. Maybe ten inches long, not counting the tail. They were greasy.

One morning I was sitting at the kitchen table drinking my coffee when one of the rats appeared at the screen door, up on its hind legs, pawing to come in. I had had enough, so when my housekeeper arrived that morning I asked her to "do something" about the rats.

When I came down the next morning no rats flew off the shelves. There, next to the refrigerator, was a large green metal trap with a spring-loaded door, looking like it had just come from military surplus. Sticking out from under the door was a long tail. No, two tails. Actually, three. They must have been hungry. All three had somehow gotten inside before the spring snapped shut. I kicked the trap out the back door.

When my housekeeper arrived, thinking nothing of it, she picked up the trap by the handle and walked over to the high stone fence surrounding our compound. There, she whipped the trap forward with such force that the door opened and the rats flew over the fence, onto the neighborhood's communal pile of garbage.

When she returned to the kitchen I asked her casually if she had taken care of the rats. "Yes," she said, "I put them back where they belong." The rats had their place, as everything else does. The only problem was that their place was the garbage pile, not the kitchen. My housekeeper had taken care of the problem by returning the rats to where they belonged.

Later in the day we visited some German friends who had a house across the compound. We now recognized the military hardware in their kitchen and told them the story of that morning's events. They said, "Yes, we catch them too. But they don't come back. We boil up a big pot of water and immerse the whole trap. It's the only way to deal with rats."

There are two sides to this story. One, the familiar reading, has to do with European cleanliness and efficiency. According to the other side, everything—even the rat—has its place in nature. This story is not intended to be about racial stereotypes. Our German friends were kind and gentle people. The same can be said of our housekeeper. My point is simply that often we do not even recognize our assumptions about life until we leave the confines of our own culture. We certainly value cleanliness and efficiency above all else. We find it remarkable when we discover that others have profoundly different assumptions.

Let us reverse this situation. Imagine, now, that you are from a distant culture, visiting the United States for the first time. In my part of the country, most people want to visit the Mall of America in Bloomington, Minnesota. What would your visit tell you about the ways "these people" live? What would it tell you about the ways they connect with nature? Please indulge these notes, jotted down soon after returning from India, just before Christmas:

"And now the adventure begins." The restaurant hostess delivers her line in a flat, mechanical tone that deflates its intended meaning. As she reaches for a stack of colorful plastic menus, she beckons another party of hungry adventurers to fall into line behind her for their trek into "The Rainforest Cafe, A Wild Place to Shop and Eat."

Outside, more than a dozen parties of fellow adventurers mill around at lunchtime. They eye their "Passport to Adventure," which contains information about denizens of the Rainforest and marks the time of each Safari's departure.

The passport promises diners will be "immersed in a tropical wonderland with dazzling special effects: cool mists that permeate through cascading waterfalls; gentle tropical rainstorms, thunder and lightning; huge mushroom canopies, fabulous animation featuring Tracy the Talking Tree, whimsical butterflies, crocodiles, snakes and frogs, trumpeting elephants and other spectacular wildlife; all moving within the surroundings of larger than life banyan trees, with the sounds and aromas of a tropical rainforest."

Out front, two earnest souls dressed in zookeeper khakis entertain prospective customers with live parrots. The passport is reassuring: these are the "Rainforest Cafe Resident Parrots" who live "on-site in special habitats, designed just for them." They are second and third generation, domestically bred and hand-raised, cared for by a full-time curator. The mix of the real, if safely domesticated, with inventions of the human imagination is sometimes startling. Other parrots, taking a break from work, sit on perches above a pool that is sprayed with artificial misters. Mysterious! Next to them, mechanical butterflies flap slowly in a virtual wind. At regular intervals, recorded thunder and lightning shake the tile floor. Real birds, and brightly colored tropical fish in lighted aquariums, occupy the Rainforest with other "family members": Tuki Makeeta the Baby Elephant, Nile the Crocodile, Bamba the Gorilla, Chai Chai the Tree Frog, and Iggy the Iguana. These stuffed family members are available for purchase in the Retail Village, which is located strategically between the reception desk and the food service.

The Rainforest Cafe is a "concept restaurant"; it attracts customers more for the entertainment than for the food. But what is it about the package of entertainment dished out here that assumes we will be reassured by the parrots' domesticity? Why does it help that they, too, are captives, zoo animals, raised to be readily available for our entertainment?

Perhaps the reassurance that real residents of the rainforest are not harmed is meant to release us, to act as a kind of cultural painkiller that allows us to give ourselves over to the entertainment. The reassurance of domesticity allows us to be transported, anxiety free, into the seamless dreamworld of advertising where everything is safe and for sale. The entertainment, we are told, is politically neutral; it comes guilt free in a politically complicated world. So just let your conscience go and enjoy it.

But, of course, the parrots, like Makeeta the Baby Elephant and Bamba the Gorilla, are property, not wild creatures of the Amazon. And does the Rainforest Cafe really benefit the rainforest? Not according to one spokesman, who told me that only the pennies customers toss into the wishing well are donated to environmental causes. Commitment to the environment doesn't reduce the Rainforest Cafe's bottom line.

Despite the advertised concern for rainforest animals, animals on the menu are similarly domesticated. Their domesticity makes them safe for consumption. The reality of their lives has no place in the adman's language.

Like the parrots and the food, there is no real adventure here either. The Cafe's insurance policy likely doesn't cover patrons who are struck by lightning, or who slip on wet, leafy trails of the rainforest. This is an experience of "the wild" strained through a concept, sold safe and domesticated to patrons who might just as well have gone out for a movie and popcorn. The Rainforest Cafe has as much to do with concern for the rainforest as Daffy Duck has to do with ducks. Entering the Rainforest Cafe is about sitting still in a three-dimensional fantasy; it's like imagining that you are Bob Hoskins in *Roger Rabbit*, or that you are Michael Jordan competing on the court with Porky Pig in *Space Jam*. This is a concept whose promises of domesticity are like those of game manufacturers who mollify parents by giving them the "choice" of controlling the level of squirting cartoon blood in the games their children play.

The Mall of America opened on August 11, 1992, at the site once occupied by an open-air ballpark. Its 4.2 million square feet of space and more than five hundred stores are surrounded by almost 20,000 parking spaces. Northwest Airlines, whose home base is across the 494 freeway, delivers shoppers from as far away as Japan for "Shop 'til you Drop" weekend packages. A small city in itself, the Mall has 11,000 year-round employees, and more than 13,000 at peak times around the Christmas holiday.

In a short time, the Mall has become the top tourist destination in the United States. Its more than 42 million visits a year eclipse Disney World's 29 million. The country's top natural destination, the Grand Canyon, draws only one visitor for every ten who visit the Mall of America.

The Mall is located in Bloomington, Minnesota, a suburban town of the 1960s, whose unruly sprawl seems organized only by endless rows of new car lots that line the freeway. In a town with no downtown, the Mall is incomparably more than a place to shop. It seeks to function as a center of the community: WCCO Radio, which bills itself as "The Good Neighbor," broadcasts live from the Mall. It sponsors "The World's Greatest Garage Sale" and has a room designated as the Community Center.

Need an education? The Metropolitan Learning Alliance is a campus for Minneapolis-area high school students based in the Mall. The National American University, billed as the "first-ever college campus in a mall," offers college courses on seventeen subjects. Like everything else here, knowledge is for sale. "The Store of Knowledge" offers kids "really neat instructional items."

Don't need entertainment or an education? How about love? At the Chapel of Love more than 1,200 couples have chosen to begin their married lives together.

The Mall is so vast and, for me at least, so disorienting that each of its four quadrants, anchored by Bloomingdale's, Nordstrom, Macy's, and Sears, is encoded by color. The vast northeast quadrant is green, the North Garden. It is designed to feel like a walk in the park. Benches line walkways lighted by natural skylights to give a "truly outdoors-like feel." Golf Mountain is an eighteen-hole "adventure-style golf course carved into a series of man-made mountains."

It was the color coding that guides shoppers around the miles of corridors that helped me see the Mall experience as an American pilgrimage, a Mount Kailas of American culture. Mount Kailas, in western Tibet, is a pilgrimage site for Tibetan Buddhist petitioners who circumnavigate the trail around the mountain prostrating themselves, moving ahead by the length of their body, and prostrating themselves again. The trail is studded with religiously significant sites, and the entire mountain functions as a great mandala, deep with religious significance.

Shoppers do not prostrate themselves as they rotate around this great dharmic wheel that flings out meaning, but it does appear to meet an almost spiritual need in the way it focuses life. Like a giant real-life mandala, the Mall is a great meaning-generator of American culture. Here, however, meaning is connected to fantasy, not to a higher spiritual order. It is a fantasy that freely invokes cultural, political, and ecological symbols, but it frees such symbols from their original attachments. If this place is a grand cultural fantasy, is it fair to ask what it allows us to escape from?

The Rainforest Cafe is far from the only store that enlists nature to sell its wares. The list of nature stores is Homeric in length:

Earth Ware	Into the Woods
Black Hills Gold Jewelers	The Nature Company
Abercrombie and Fitch	The Far Outside
Banana Republic	Underwater World
Colorado	Nature Food Centers
Northern Reflections	Cabin Fever

Destination Minnesota	The Eddie Bauer Home Store
Everything but Water	The Walking Company
Indigenous Handicrafts	Bighorn Sheep
Kiwi Beach	Dogs and Cats
Grassland Gallery	Mountain Zoo
Wild Wings Gallery	The Old Farmer's Almanac
The Wooden Bird	Southwestern Image
Wyland's Ocean Encounter Gallery	The Wild Bird Store
Golf Mountain	Pueblo Spirit
Northwood Stage	Natural Wonders
Gators	Recycle Now
Panda Express	Northern Getaway
Minnesota Picnic	Britches Great Outdoors
The Rainforest Cafe	American Eagle Outfitters
Animal Lover	Randy River
The Endangered Species	Big Dog Sportswear
Pacific Sunwear	Cuddly Critters
Aljohn's Beach Shop	Love from Minnesota
Living on Island Time	Peanuts
Snoopy's Boutique	A Snowman for All Seasons
Snow Stuff USA	The Sportsman's Wife
Knott's Camp Snoopy	Stampede Steakhouse
Wilderness Theater	Barnyard Cafe
Hooters	Tall Timber Grill
Caribou Coffee	Rocky Mountain Chocolate Factory
Natural Wonders	Garden Botanika
All about Horses	Bears 'N More
The Basic Brown Bear Factory	Butterflies and More
Colorado Pen Company	The Disney Store
Dogs and Cats	Dollar Tree

Any first-time visitor can tell that images of nature are powerful in this culture, but what do they mean? How do they work? Strolling randomly in and out of stores I took some notes:

- The Wild Bird Store sells Boundary Waters Oils, which "capture the fragrance of the wilderness." "[E]ach bottle" captures "the very essence of the Boundary Waters." The very essence of the wilderness! Right here in the Mall of America. No need to paddle hard.

- The Far Outside (Red 132). Inside the Mall of America.

- The Endangered Species Store is next to The Disney Store. To the right, Donald Duck entreats shoppers to enter the world of Daffy and Goofy. To the left, a life-sized stuffed gorilla stands guard over the wooden bridge that shoppers cross to enter the distant land beyond.

    Inside the Endangered Species Store there is a display of polished stones for sale from "The Iron Mountain Mine." A sign warns, "Caution: Rocks Will Get Your Hands Dirty. Please wear gloves."

- Recycle Now!, tucked away in an obscure location on the third floor, is run by BFI, "the world's largest processor of recycled materials." Inside, a class of seventh graders is watching a video of Dennis Weaver talking about Earthship, a house made out of cans and old tires. As the kids head off to the Mall's basement to see the daily production of real waste, I ask the clerk about the store. "We're closing on Monday," she tells me. BFI was required to open the store when the Mall opened because it is a Mall sponsor. But it's in a bad location. It used to sell all recycled items, but they were too expensive and no one bought them. The half-empty shelves now look like The Nature Company with a cash flow problem.

- Camp Snoopy, the entertainment center at the core of the Mall, wraps Snoopy in thick woolly blankets of cultural meaning. The Camp brings back memories of a Minnesota childhood. It is as if the Ma and Pa resort of the 1950s has been pumped up for a new generation that might find the original dull. I think back to summer vacations during the 1950s, before interstate freeways made long-distance vacations common. We visited Paul Bunyan Land in Brainerd. Beyond the stockade fence, next to Babe the Blue Ox, sat the lumbering giant himself, axe in hand. Somehow, he knew the name of every child who entered, and greeted each of them personally over the loudspeaker.

The rough-hewn lumber of Paul Bunyan's sawmill has been transported to Knott's Camp Snoopy. Rustic booths sell tickets to the rides. Log picnic tables await tired parents. Buildings are made from fiberboard log construction with plastic shake singles. There is even a flume that reminds me of old pictures of northern Minnesota logging mills. Logs carry screaming children over steep drops on their way to the lumber mill. Their photographs, mouths agape as they plunge over the edge, await them as they step off the ride. Does a photograph make the fantasy real?

Underwater World is an aquarium built into the basement of the Mall. Visitors first descend past cooling misters into the Boundary Waters ecosystem, an aquarium containing real smallmouth bass, walleyes, and bluegills. The Boundary Waters ecosystem reproduced in a fish tank! This is from Underwater World's advertising:

> Imagine traveling 14 feet underwater where sharks, stingrays and giant sea turtles swim so close, you'll feel like you can reach out and touch them! With over 1.2 million gallons of water, this aquarium features a 300 foot-long curved tunnel, complete with a moving walkway that simulates a scuba diving adventure—but without getting wet! (Underwater World)

What does this place tell you about American culture? First, the Mall is extremely popular with Americans. One doesn't need statistics from the Mall's publicity department to sense this. Just try to find a place to eat that doesn't have an hour-long wait, at midafternoon, on a weekday. We love this place.

What else? Americans love their material goods to be served up with a large portion of fantasy. This American ritual needs to be fun.

More than fun, many of life's important events are played out here: marriage, ministry, schooling. This is also the public space in which we connect to a larger community.

Perhaps more than anything else, there is also a deep need in this culture for connections to place: the lake cabin, the north woods, the far outside, distant lands with strange animals and indigenous peoples.

These aspirations are not odd or humorous. The need to be with others, and to have a place where one belongs, speaks deeply of what it means to be human. What seems odd, and sometimes humorous, is that this culture's means of generating a story about itself almost guarantee confusion. Community is important, but it occurs at a level so vast, and so ear-piercingly loud, that real engagement with others is impossible. No one goes to the Rainforest Cafe for good conversation or interesting food. The experience sold there relates most closely to the family that sits in front of their large-screen TV with theater sound, each eating in a separate world.

The names of stores, and many of the goods they sell, reveal a deep need for connection to place. But the Mall is a synthetic place that demands to be read as placeless. The cavernous interior is, quite literally, disorienting. It is like the hotel chain that advertises no surprises: every room is the same. Eating in its restaurants is like visiting Euro-Disney and dining on Big Macs. Don't bother with the local cuisine.

There also seems to be a longing for political commitment. From visiting the Mall we would guess that somewhere there are endangered species, and that the rainforest needs donations. But when the political really enters, the police show it to the door. Animal rights activists staged a protest of stores that sell fur coats. They were arrested for trespassing on private property. The protesters argued in court that they had a right to exercise free speech in a space that advertises itself as a public place that fosters community. The Mall countered that the protesters had no rights because they were on private property. The courts agreed with the Mall. The message is clear: those who threaten the Mall with a dose of reality are not welcome.

The Mall is littered with mixed meanings: It is a public space for community, but it is privately owned. It refers distantly to good politics, but bars the political at its doors. It speaks overwhelmingly of a need for nature, but it is a place where nothing is natural, where there are "ecosystems" in fish tanks, manmade mountains for golf, and tape-recorded weather. Mount Kailas becomes Golf Mountain. The Mall insists that we read it as culturally, politically, and ecologically neutral, though it cannot be, as anyone can witness in the hidden underbelly of the Mall where consumer waste is handled out of sight. We Americans have a deep longing for place, but the place we enjoy most is plastic.

I can imagine what you are thinking: we know that advertising is not about telling the truth. And what's wrong with fantasy? Life is hard enough. Just leave us alone if we want to "zone out" at the Mall!

OK, it is easy to take these observations too far. But I want to point out how unusual this advertising is: it is the opposite of what it announces itself to be. This is not a sleek come-on for urban sophistication: the elegantly dressed couple who leave the keys to their shiny black BMW with the valet as they are swept into a glittering cultural event. We may not be able to afford this lifestyle, or we may pay too dearly to achieve the appearance of wealth, but it is a fantasy that can be realized.

This is advertising that appears to celebrate the natural, but its underlying message is, "Nature will get your hands dirty. Please wear gloves." This is nature under control, nature that is clean and safe, and that can be owned and controlled by admen. It can't become real. Acting on conviction makes it disappear.

We are a culture that does not appear to be able to say what it means. We get meaning from what can be said through the language of the adman. Does the pervasiveness of nature themes throughout the Mall of America reveal a deep concern for nature, or does it represent the final silencing of nature, a culture in which images so thoroughly stand in for the real things that they no longer serve as markers or the way to real things? Real things resist neat classification. They are the adman's worst nightmare. Does meaning come for us, not through connections to people and place, but through a new sort of virtual reality? Are we domesticated by the Mall? Yes, let me say it: Is Saturday spent in the Mall a colonizing experience?

Before rejecting the idea, consider that this attitude toward ourselves did not happen accidentally. More than a half century ago, just as the "American century" geared up, retailing analyst Victor Lebow said, "Our enormously productive economy . . . demands that we make consumption our way of life, that we convert the buying and use of goods into rituals, that we seek our spiritual satisfaction, our ego satisfaction, in consumption. . . . We need things consumed, burned up, worn out, replaced, and discarded at an ever increasing rate" (Quoted in Durning 1992, 21–22).

Instead of demanding immediate answers, these questions are valuable if they stimulate reflection. Of course, there is nothing really dangerous about going to your local shopping mall. Unless *The Matrix* is reality rather than movie fantasy, we can generally distinguish the real world from virtual reality. We need not be colonized by a trip to the mall. The real question is what happens between "in here" and "out there." The question is whether an overload of such experiences thins out our self-conceptions until only the consumer remains. As with colonialism, commercial culture wins when it colonizes our minds. It wins when we no longer want to resist. A visit to the Mall leaves me pondering Ed Abbey: "Resist much; Obey little."

ALDO LEOPOLD'S VISION

In *A Sand County Almanac,* the great ecologist Aldo Leopold expressed his dismay with the level of environmental commitment he found among his fellow citizens in the late 1940s. Most people, he wrote, seemed to abide by the following rules: "obey the law, vote right, join some organizations, and practice what conservation is profitable on your own land; government will do the rest" (Leopold [1949] 1970, 243–44).

I take it that there is a familiar ring to Leopold's observations. We are still encouraged to care about what we own, and let the government take care of the rest—even if most of us seem to believe that government doesn't do a very good job with the leftovers. Fortunately, Leopold was not content just to criticize the limited ecological wisdom of his time. His real goal was to encourage a new sort of public commitment, what is now widely called ecological citizenship.

Leopold was one of the first to practice the new science of ecology. For years, he worked in New Mexico helping to mediate between private landowners and the public's interest in conserving open land. He spent the last years of his life at the University of Wisconsin, where he founded the university's ecology program.

Mainly on weekends, Leopold devoted a lifetime's worth of ecological wisdom to a farm he purchased in Sand County, Wisconsin. It had been ruined by disastrous farming techniques, and Leopold committed the remainder of his life to restoration of this damaged land. The property contained a dilapidated cabin. Many mornings, Leopold sat at an old table he placed near the cabin where he recorded his thoughts. His masterpiece, *A Sand County Almanac*, was published in 1949, a year after Leopold's death.

Leopold called on his readers to extend the circle of moral concern through human beings to the land community: "The land ethic simply enlarges the boundaries of the community to include soils, waters, plants, and animals, or collectively: the land." Although it was, in one way, an extension of moral principles we already accept—the moral significance of community—in another way, Leopold's proposal was radical. Previous ethical systems in Western culture had applied to *individuals*. Leopold called for recognition of the moral standing of whole *ecosystems*. This includes individuals within the ecosystem, human and other, but Leopold's emphasis was mainly on the ecological connections *among* individuals, rather than on the individuals themselves. Leopold's ethic is properly called an environmental ethic.

Of course, Leopold implicitly recognized the difference between having moral standing and being a moral agent. All of nature has moral standing for Leopold in the sense that it has an internal integrity that must be respected. Only humans, as far as we know, however, are moral agents; we can anticipate the consequences of our actions and thus be held responsible for them. So Leopold recognized that the human condition is unique in some ways, even though we are also parts of the broader land community.

Leopold's description of the change from a human-centered ethic to a land ethic is important, especially in terms of the issues addressed in this book:

> In short, a land ethic changes the role of *Homo sapiens* from conqueror of the land-community to plain member and citizen of it. It implies respect for his fellow-members, and also respect for the community as such.
>
> In human history, we have learned (I hope) that the conqueror role is eventually self-defeating. Why? Because it is implicit in such a role that the conqueror knows *ex cathedra*, just what makes the community clock tick, and just what and who is valuable, and what and who is worthless, in community life. It always turns out that he knows neither, and this is why his conquests eventually defeat themselves. ([1949] 1970, 240)

Leopold wrote these words shortly after the defeat of Adolf Hitler. Conquerors, he believed, are arrogant in their self-understandings. They imagine that they do not need anyone, or anything, else. This arrogance puts a distance between themselves and what they need to understand in order to survive. Conquerors carry within themselves the seeds of their own downfall.

It is remarkable how much of *A Sand County Almanac* remains relevant today. For example, Leopold contrasted the disastrous colonial development of the American Southwest with treatment by earlier occupants: "The Pueblo Indians settled the Southwest in pre-Columbian times, but they happened *not* to be equipped with range livestock. Their civilization expired, but not because their land expired" ([1949] 1970, 242–43).

Remarkably, this pioneer of the science of ecology was also willing to take his wisdom from those who were rarely thought of as having any expertise at all: "In India, regions devoid of any sod-forming grass have been settled, apparently without wrecking the land, by the simple expedient of carrying the grass to the cow, rather than vice versa" ([1949] 1970, 243).

Most of his ecology is also still up to date. Leopold described the Land Ethic in graphic terms through what he called the "Land Pyramid." He rejected the view that there is a "balance of nature." According to this view, nature reaches a state of perfection and stays there. Leopold preferred a much more dynamic depiction of nature: "Land, then, is not merely soil; it is a fountain of energy flowing through a circuit of soils, plants, and animals" ([1949] 1970, 253). At the bottom of the pyramid, and at the beginning of evolution, are soils and then plants. Plants absorb energy from the sun and the energy of the biotic circle begins. Then, an insect layer rests on top of the plants. Birds and rodents rest on insects. More and more complex forms of life evolve out of these, with large carnivores at the apex. Leopold's point is not that creatures at the apex are more important than the creatures that provide the foundation. His point is that the Land Pyramid is a fountain of energy in which energy from the top gets recycled at the bottom. The biotic community is interdependent.

Change is built into Leopold's dynamic depiction of nature. The pyramid itself changes as evolutionary changes occur. Leopold's account of human-induced change, therefore, resists the common Enlightenment idea that humans are outside of nature. On this idea all human activity is unnatural. Humans cannot help but corrupt nature because every human action changes what it is not: the natural order. For Leopold human-induced change is just as natural as the elephant that crushes everything in its way. Human beings are natural. The problem with human-induced change arises in the scope, the speed, and the violence of change.

Leopold also knew that the earth adapts to change differently in Europe or Japan than in the United States. He was interested in the health of European soils despite their heavy use since the Romans. Many changes have occurred there, including the loss of large carnivores. But the land remains fertile. "There is no visible stoppage or derangement of the circuit" ([1949] 1970, 256). The circuit of energy changed over time, but it remains open.

In the United States, some regions are more resilient than others: the Northeast and the Northwest. Damage is worse in the "Southwest, the Ozarks, and parts of the South" ([1949] 1970, 256). In these areas, the speed and violence of the changes have closed the biotic circuit. The principle Leopold derived from these observations is that "the less violent the man-made changes, the greater the probability of successful readjustment in the pyramid" ([1949] 1970, 257). "Health is the capacity of the land for self-renewal" ([1949] 1970, 258).

Leopold's final appeal was not to ignore economic considerations in dealing with the land, but to balance these against ethical and aesthetic considerations. His famous principle governing the Land Ethic is, "A thing is right when it tends to preserve the integrity, stability, and beauty of the biotic community. It is wrong when it tends otherwise" ([1949] 1970, 262). Leopold clearly decried the tendency to think that "The evidence had to be economic in order to be valid" ([1949] 1970, 247). He reminded us that when the language of money silences all other forms of public discourse we will no longer be able to say why the loss of songbirds would be tragic. But his history as a wildlife manager also taught him that economics couldn't be ignored. His bottom line was that economic activity that violates the Land Ethic does not even make good *economic* sense in the long run.

The half century that has passed since the publication of his book doesn't amount to much in the evolutionary terms that often framed Leopold's thinking. However, during this period we have witnessed changes on a scale that even the sage of Sand County would have had difficulty imagining. What might Leopold have said, for example, about a world in which the very DNA of the so-called "Harvard mouse" is corporate property?

Although Leopold was remarkably far-sighted, we cannot assume that his wisdom can guide us in a world of globalization. As this book reaches its conclusion, then, it is worth asking how we might move on from here. Keeping Leopold's inspiration in mind, we need to ask, "What might ecological citizenship look like today?"

I am concerned with ecological citizenship in the normative sense of the term. There is, of course, a sense in which citizenship is simply a legal concept: resident aliens are allowed to apply for citizenship if they meet certain requirements. Citizenship in the normative sense requires much more than this. This is what Leopold was getting at when he said it involves more than "obeying the law, voting right, and joining some organizations." Citizenship requires active participation in public life.

This idea—that a full human life includes a public dimension—traces back to the Greeks. In Athens, for example, at the edge of the public marketplace, the agora, there is a building called the Stoa. It is open on one side to the agora, and its purpose seems to have been to provide a public place where citizens could congregate to discuss public affairs. To be a citizen is to have a place in public life.

This idea of a public life was reawakened in the Renaissance. In Florence, Italy, for example, in order for a wealthy, self-made man to gain permission to demolish dozens of poor homes to secure enough land to build a private mansion, he had to agree to surround his home with stone benches where any citizen could sit. Private wealth needed to be balanced with the public good. Still, today if you ask Florentines the difference between Florence and Siena, a more aristocratic city, they will tell you with a clear note of disdain, "There's no place to sit in Siena." The normative concept of citizenship, then, assumes a public space for individuals within a largely democratic state. Subjects of a tyranny cannot practice citizenship.

As I have emphasized throughout this book, however, changes over the past half century show that citizenship can no longer be understood as a simple political relationship between the individual and one's city or state. Globalization has changed all that. Democratic governments must themselves now answer to unelected international institutions. People all over the globe now have common interests and share common challenges. Citizenship is now connected to issues of scale in ways that could not have been understood earlier.

The practice of citizenship today, almost everywhere in the world, is a practice of *resistance*. It is the attempt to establish and maintain a public space in which the common good can be fostered. One of the fundamental questions citizenship poses is how to maintain and shape one's identity in the face of a global homogenizing process. Identity itself has become a multidimensional project that must now respond to issues of scale.

I grant that citizenship today still carries with it the sense of local participation. Thomas Jefferson famously believed that citizenship occurred when gentleman farmers joined under the shade of a single tree to discuss their affairs. Today, there is still this sense of the local that gives shape and meaning to citizenship. When people attend local caucus meetings, or actively support urban public gardens, these are forms of local citizenship.

But it is clear from the very term "globalization" that not all issues an ecological citizen addresses today are local. Citizenship now operates at global and intermediate levels, for example, through the agency of NGOs that cross national borders and connect directly with local groups sharing common interests. Active support of and participation in environmental and social justice organizations can also be seen as expressions of citizenship. But, we might still ask, what distinguishes these activities from Leopold's concern to "join some organizations. . . ."?

Here, I think it's helpful to contrast two conceptions of citizenship. The first is based in the familiar concept of rights. It gives citizens the right to claim certain social goods, education and Social Security, for example. This minimal sense of citizenship need not affect the question of public identity. Rights to social goods on this conception of citizenship function as claims to the minimal conditions for a happy private life. Entitlements don't necessarily express who one *is*.

Put negatively, it is difficult to detect anything *ecological* in the rights conception of citizenship. Entitlements are based on traditional Enlightenment conceptions of the self that have been at the core of the exploitation of the environment as well as of those who are excluded from the moral core.

Often, this view of citizenship is defined in terms of satisfying "the interests of stakeholders," that is, those who will be affected by the outcomes of social and environmental decisions. We could write volumes about this idea, but I will be satisfied to leave the subject with one remark: the concepts of "interests" and "stakeholders" are deeply ambiguous. This minimal concept of citizenship based on rights could turn out to be profoundly conservative in its claims to traditional privilege. Recall the poll conducted by the Marymount University Center for Ethical Concerns that showed that respondents in the 18–34 age range were the least concerned about sweatshop labor of any age group. These people are certainly stakeholders. Without sweatshops their clothing would cost more. Given a certain sense of rationality, they are certainly expressing a rational interest to pay less rather than more. The problem is that, given the reading of sweatshops provided earlier, it is difficult not to see this expression of interests as morally obtuse. A truly environmental account of citizenship has to go deeper.

Citizenship as rights contrasts with a stronger conception of citizenship that includes a sense of one's *identity*. We are ultimately committed to social and environmental justice because of who we are, not just because of what we do.

The common conception of what it means to be human today is, to put it bluntly, antiquated. The seventeenth-century idea of humanness, according to which humans are, at least in part, unnatural beings whose essence is separate from nature, conflicts with the best of what science now tells us about humanness. Leopold was exactly right in his evolutionary view of ethics. The difference between humans and other primates is not a difference in *kind*, as we have been taught. Rather, it is merely a difference in degree of complexity.

Ecological citizenship then, in this more substantive sense, offers the promise of a conception of what it means to be fully human that is scientifically accurate and philosophically informed. It sees the public space in which humanness becomes fully possible as a large, plural set of intersecting spaces that are different from other natural spaces only in degree of complexity, not as a different *kind* of life on earth.

There are at least three clear benefits to be gained from this more substantive view of citizenship. First, it helps us understand the province of environmental ethics. Too often, debates in environmental ethics have broken down into questions of whether a position is anthropocentric or ecocentric. "Radical" environmental philosophers have often argued that a real environmental ethic, as opposed to a mere social justice ethic, needs to be ecocentric, not anthropocentric. Aldo Leopold has even been interpreted as the godfather of this position.

From the perspective of a substantive view of ecological citizenship, which includes a contemporary, scientifically informed view of humanness, this debate simply makes no sense. The debate assumes that people are different in kind from the rest of nature, not just different in degree. It assumes an antiquated conception of humanness, according to which humans are unnatural alien visitors to this planet.

Second, the reintegration of the cultural with the natural that the substantive concept of ecological citizenship offers shifts our very conception of what an environmental problem is. Ecocentric conceptions of environmental ethics have attempted to focus our attention on a real, but very narrow range of environmental problems: protecting wilderness from further human damage.

Critics have pointed out that this narrow conception of what an environmental problem is leaves out most third world environmental concerns, which usually have to do with the integration of people with place, not their separation. Urban ecology, as well as agriculture, is simply written out of the picture. More broadly, ecological issues that require understanding of their connections to social issues are pushed off to the side and discounted as not being the sort of issues an environmental ethic is designed to address.

This view literally deprives billions of the world's disenfranchised peoples from gaining a place in the conversation. Although this is perhaps not intentional, the effects of this narrow view of the environment appear to verge on a new form of intellectual colonialism.

Third, the substantive view of ecological citizenship has a shot at addressing our feeling of being alienated and disenchanted in a large, anonymous world. Even those who profess concern for social and environmental justice will often say, "It's nice to have moral ideals, but they don't count in the 'real world.' The real world runs on money."

I confess to deep feelings of frustration when the world's most privileged people cling to this sense of resignation and hopelessness as an excuse for inaction. However, I think one of the reasons for this bleak outlook is the outmoded conception of ethics that we have internalized. We think of ethics as a solitary enterprise. Ethics requires one to find a rule and apply it to one's life. Or, finding no rule, perhaps because of an awareness of cultural difference, one simply regards ethics as something humans make up.

What we lack is a public, cooperative sense of ethics that is not just a dreaded set of rules, but an evolutionary direction through which one can become fully human. Especially in a world of globalization, where it can seem, quite reasonably, that large, anonymous forces take control and make individual intention superfluous, we need the reassurance of working together in a public space, for the common good of a larger community.

The antidote to an anonymous world is not to retreat into the temporary refuge of consumerism, or even to send a check to the "right" organization. A role in the broader community is important to every individual because it is only through this public space that we can become fully human.

ANNOTATED LIST OF HELPFUL WEBSITES

Environment and Social Justice:

Centre for Science and the Environment: http://www.cseindia.org/. Centre for Science and Environment (CSE), based in New Delhi, India, is an independent public interest organization that works on issues of science, technology, the environment, and development. The Centre was started in 1980. Publisher of the environmental magazine *Down to Earth*.

The Ecologist: http://www.theecologist.org/. Published in London, the *Ecologist* reports on social and environmental issues.

Friends of the Earth: http://www.foe.co.uk. "The largest international network of environmental groups in the world, represented in 68 countries."

Global Witness: http://www.globalwitness.org/. Based in San Francisco, a good site for monitoring environmental issues such as oil, diamonds, and timber.

Rainforest Action Network: http://www.ran.org/. Activist organization dedicated to rainforest issues.

Sierra Club: http://www.sierraclub.org/. Political concerns include the environment and free trade.

Feminist Issues:

Manushi: A Journal about Women and Society: http://free.freespeech.org/manushi/. *Manushi* is an important Indian feminist magazine published in New Delhi.

Research Foundation for Science, Technology and Ecology: http://www
.vshiva.net/. Founded by Vandana Shiva, author of *Staying Alive*, devoted
to feminist and environmental issues. Based in Dehra Dun, India.

Food Security and Agriculture:

Food First: http://www.foodfirst.org/. A "peoples' think tank and educa-
tion-for-action center. Our work highlights root causes and value-
based solutions to hunger and poverty around the world, with a
commitment to establishing food as a fundamental human right."
Founded by Frances Moore Lappé and Joseph Collins.
The Institute for Agriculture and Trade Policy: http://www.iatp.org/. A
nongovernmental organization, based in Minneapolis, that monitors a
broad spectrum of issues: food safety, agriculture, trade, marine conservation, and forestry.
Pesticide Action Network: http://www.panna.org/.
The Rural Advancement Foundation (RAFI): http://www.rafiusa.org.
The American branch is located in Pittsboro, North Carolina. RAFI
is "dedicated to community, equity and diversity in agriculture."

Future-oriented Green Living:

Coop America: http://www.coopamerica.org/. Organization and website
offer information on "green" living.
People-Centered Development Forum: http://www.pcdf.org/. Founded
by David Korten, author of *When Corporations Rule the World*. A comprehensive site presenting a vision of a postglobalized world.

Indigenous Issues:

Center for World Indigenous Studies: http://www.cwis.org/. A nonprofit
organization based in Olympia, Washington, dedicated to increasing
understanding of indigenous issues worldwide.
Honor the Earth: http://www.honorearth.com/. Based in Minneapolis, a
site devoted to "environmental justice and indigenous knowledge."
Indigenous Environmental Network: http://www.ienearth.org/. "The Indigenous Environmental Network is an alliance of grassroots indige-

nous peoples whose mission is to protect the sacredness of Mother Earth from contamination and exploitation by strengthening maintaining and respecting the traditional teachings and the natural laws." Indigenous Women's Network: http://www.honorearth.com/. "The Indigenous Women's Network was created in 1985 to support the self-determination of Indigenous women, families, communities, and Nations in the Americas and the Pacific Basin."
Native Americans and the Environment: http://www.ncseonline.org/nae/ internet.html. A website maintained by Dr. Alx Dark, it contains information on treaty issues. Also provides links to many related websites.
The Seventh Generation Fund: http://www.7genfund.org/. Devoted to "rebuilding Native sustainable communities, promoting traditional economies, developing alternative energy, protecting sacred sites and traditional spiritual practices, pressuring the United Nations to recognize the rights of Indigenous peoples, and establishing national and international coalitions and linkages for social justice that span the globe."
Survival International: http://survival-international.org/. An international organization that works for the survival of tribal peoples.

Population Issues:

Population Connection: http://www.zpg.org/. The organization formerly known as Zero Population Growth.
The United Nations Population Information Network: http://www.un. org/popin/.
World Population Clock: http://www.census.gov/cgi-bin/ipc/popclockw. A website maintained by the U.S. Bureau of the Census that offers up-to-date information on population statistics.

Public Policy:

Maryknoll—Global Concerns: http://www.maryknoll.org/GLOBAL/ global.htm. The Maryknoll Sisters were the first American order to commit themselves to international service. Site provides ethical reflections on many international issues.

Public Citizen: http://www.citizen.org/. The organization founded by Ralph Nader devoted to "protecting health, safety and democracy."

The Worldwatch Institute: http://www.worldwatch.org. Important research organization based in Washington, D.C., "working for an environmentally sustainable and socially just society." Publishes *Vital Signs* and *State of the World*.

Sustainable Development:

Development Gateway: http://www.developmentgateway.org/. A website devoted to information on sustainable development and poverty reduction.

Development Zone: http://www.dev-zone.org. A clearinghouse for information of organizations concerned with globalization.

Great Plains Institute for Sustainable Development: http://www.gpisd. net/. Focuses on renewal of rural communities and alternate sources of energy.

Latin American Network Information Center: http://info.lanic.utexas. edu/. Information on Latin American issues, including sustainable development. Based at the University of Texas, Austin.

Sweatshops:

Clean Clothes Campaign: http://www.cleanclothes.org/. Activist organization committed to stopping sweatshops.

UNITE!: http://www.uniteunion.org/sweatshops/index.htm. Unit of the AFL-CIO that opposes sweatshops.

Trade and Economic Globalization:

50 Years Is Enough: http://www.50years.org/. Organization seeking to close the World Bank.

ARENA: http://www.arena.org.nz/. Based in New Zealand, this organization monitors trade and globalization issues.

Center for Economic Justice: http://www.econjustice.net/. Activist organization concerned with policies of the IMF and World Bank.

Centre for Research on Globalization: http://www.globalresearch.ca/. Site provides articles critical of globalization.

CorpWatch: http://www.corpwatch.org/. Exposes corporate misdeeds by companies such as Halliburton and Coca-Cola.

Third World Network: http://www.twnside.org.sg. Based in Malaysia, Third World Resurgence is a nongovernmental organization that focuses on trade and globalization. It publishes the magazine *Third World Resurgence*. The Third World Network, Africa, is a valuable site for development issues in Africa: http://twnafrica.org/.

REFERENCES

Africa Action. (1996). Nigeria Country Profile. http://www.africaaction.org/bp/
nigerall.html.
American Civil Liberties Union. Voter's Guide, Representative Jack Metcalf.
http://archive.aclu.org/vote-guide/Metcalf_J.html.
American Indian Policy Center. Treaty with the Chippewa. http://www.airpi
.org/pubs/1837.html.
American Lung Association. Fact Sheet: Minorities and Air Pollution.
http://www.lungusa.org/air/minority_factsheet.html.
Anderson, Gary Clayton, and Alan R. Woolworth, eds. (1988). *Through Dakota
Eyes: Narrative Accounts of the Minnesota Indian War of 1862*. St. Paul, MN:
Historical Society Press.
Anderson, Sarah, and John Cavanagh. (2000). *Field Guide to the Global Economy*.
New York: New Press.
Baby Milk Action. Nestlé Campaign. http://www.babymilkaction.org/.
Barthes, Roland. (1980). *Camera Lucida*. New York: Hill and Wang.
Berger, John. (1982). *Another Way of Telling*. New York: Pantheon Books.
———. ([1980] 1991). Why Look at Animals? In *About Looking*. New York: Vin-
tage International.
Bharatiya Janata Party. http://www.bjp.org/.
Blaut, J. M. (1993). *The Colonizer's Model of the World: Geographic Diffusionism and
Eurocentric History*. New York: Guilford Press.
Borlaug, Norman. (1971). The Green Revolution, Peace, and Humanity. In *Les
Prix Nobel en 1970*. n.a. Stockholm: Imprimerieal Royal P. A. Norstedt &
Söner, 226–45.

REFERENCES

Botz, Dan La. (2002). Loose Threads. Resource Center for the Americas. http://americas.org/News/Features/200206_Sweatshop_Movement/20020601_index.htm.
Brown, Lester R., Gary Gardner, et al. (1998). *Beyond Malthus: Sixteen Dimensions of the Population Problem.* Washington, D.C.: Worldwatch Institute, 1–45.
Burroughs, Edgar Rice (1990). *Tarzan of the Apes.* New York: Penguin Group.
Bush, George W. (2002). Remarks by the President at United Nations Financing for Development Conference. http://www.whitehouse.gov/news/releases/2002/03/20020322-1.html.
Césaire, Aimé. (1972). *Discourse on Colonialism.* New York: Monthly Review Press.
Chabousson, F. (1986). How Pesticides Increase Pests. *Ecologist* 16(1): 29–36.
Chadwick, Alex. Coltan Mining and Eastern Congo's Gorillas. Radio Expeditions, National Public Radio. http://www.npr.org/programs/re/archivesdate/2001/dec/20011220.coltan.html.
Chapela, Ignacio, and David Quist. (2001). Transgenic DNA Introgressed into Traditional Maize Landraces in Oaxaca, Mexico. *Nature* 414(6863): 541–43.
Churchill, Ward. (1997). *A Little Matter of Genocide.* San Francisco: City Lights Books.
Conrad, Joseph. (1988). Extracts from Correspondence, September 24, 1890. In *Heart of Darkness,* ed. Robert Kimbrough. New York: Norton.
Cronon, William. (1995a). Introduction: In Search of Nature. In *Uncommon Ground: Toward Reinventing Nature.* New York: Norton.
———. (1995b). The Trouble with Wilderness. In *Uncommon Ground: Toward Reinventing Nature.* New York: Norton.
Crosby, Alfred W. (1986). *Ecological Imperialism: The Biological Expansion of Europe, 900–1900.* Cambridge: Cambridge University Press.
Curtin, Deane. (1999). *Chinnagounder's Challenge: The Question of Ecological Citizenship.* Bloomington: Indiana University Press.
Curtin, Deane W., and Lisa Heldke, eds. (1992). *Cooking, Eating, Thinking: Transformative Philosophies of Food.* Bloomington: University of Indiana Press.
d'Errico, Peter. (1998). Sovereignty: A Brief History in the Context of U.S. "Indian Law." http://www.umass.edu/legal/derrico/sovereignty.html.
Daly, Herman. (1996). Sustainable Growth? No Thank You. In *The Case against the Global Economy,* ed. Jerry Mander and Edward Goldsmith, 193–96. San Francisco: Sierra Club Books.
Dark, Alx. (n.d.). The Makah Whaling Conflict: Background. http://www.ncseonline.org/nae/cases/makah/m1.html.
Durning, Alan. (1992). *How Much Is Enough?* New York: Norton.
Ehrlich, Paul R. ([1967] 1997). *The Population Bomb.* Cutchogue, NY: Buccaneer Books.

Ellwood, Wayne. (2001). *The No-Nonsense Guide to Globalization*. Oxford: New Internationalist Publications.

ETC Group. (2002). *Genetic Pollution in Mexico's Center of Maize Diversity*. Institute for Food and Development Policy. http://www.foodfirst.org/pubs/backgrdrs/2002/sp02v8n2.html#notes.

Fanon, Frantz. (1986). *The Wretched of the Earth*. New York: Grove Press.

50 Years Is Enough. http://www.50years.org/.

Flett, Chief Norman. (n.d.). *Our People, Our Land, Our Water, Our Future, Our Voice*. Split Lake, Manitoba: Split Lake Cree First Nation, 1–19.

Gaard, Greta. (2001). Tools for a Cross-Cultural Feminist Ethics: Exploring Ethical Contexts and Contents in the Makah Whale Hunt. *Hypatia* 16(1): 1–25.

Gadgil, Madhav, and M. D. Subash Chandran. (1998). Sacred Groves and Sacred Trees of Uttara Kannada. http://www.ignca.nic.in/cd_08008.htm.

Gandhi, Mahatma. (1996). *Selected Political Writings*. Indianapolis: Hackett Publishing Company.

Gedicks, Al. (1995). International Resistance to the New Resource Wars. In *Ecological Resistance Movements*, ed. Bron Raymond Taylor. Albany: State University of New York Press.

Global Exchange. China Campaign. U.S. Business Principles for Human Rights of Workers in China. http://www.globalexchange.org/campaigns/sweatshops/china/principles.html.

———. Saipan Campaign. GAP Campaign. http://www.globalexchange.org/campaigns/sweatshops/saipan/background.html.

Guha, Ramachandra. (1990). *The Unquiet Woods: Ecological Change and Peasant Resistance in the Himalaya*. Berkeley: University of California Press.

Haq, Mahbub ul. (n.d.). What is Human Development? United Nations Development Program. http://hdr.undp.org/hd/default.cfm.

Hardin, Garrett. (1968). The Tragedy of the Commons. *Science* 162: 1243–48.

———. ([1974] 1994). Lifeboat Ethics. In *Environmental Ethics: Readings in Theory and Application*, ed. Louis P. Pojman, 283–90. Boston: Jones and Bartlett Publishers.

———. ([1976] 1998). Carrying Capacity as an Ethical Concept. In *Applied Ethics: A Multicultural Approach*, ed. Larry May, Shari Collins-Chobanian, and Kai Wong. Upper Saddle River, NJ: Prentice Hall.

Hawken, Paul. (1994). *The Ecology of Commerce: A Declaration of Sustainability*. New York: HarperBusiness.

Hayden, Tom, and Charles Kernaghan. (2002). Pennies an Hour, and No Way Up. Global Exchange. http://www.marymount.edu/news/garmentstudy/overview.html.

Hochschield, Adam. (1998). *King Leopold's Ghost*. New York: Houghton Mifflin Company.

Human Rights Watch. The Price of Oil. http://www.hrw.org/reports/1999/nigeria. International Forum on Globalization. (2003). Globalization: Effects on Indigenous Peoples. http://www.ifg.org/programs/indig.htm#map.

Johnson, Keith. (1998). An Open Letter to the Public from the President of the Makah Whaling Conflict. http://www.ncseonline.org/NAE/docs/makaheditorial .html.

Kimball, Andrew. (1996). Biocolonization. In *The Case against the Global Economy*, ed. Jerry Mander and Edward Goldsmith. San Francisco: Sierra Club Books.

Kipling, Rudyard. (1961). Servants of the Queen. In *The Jungle Books*, 336. New York: Penguin Group.

Kloppenburg, Jack Ralph. (1988). *First the Seed: The Political Economy of Plant Biotechnology: 1492–2000*. Cambridge: Cambridge University Press.

Krotz, Larry. (1991). Dammed and Diverted. *Canadian Geographic*. February/ March: 36–44.

Lappé, Frances Moore, and Joseph Collins. (1978). *Food First: Beyond the Myth of Scarcity*. New York: Ballantine.

Leopold, Aldo. ([1949] 1970). *A Sand County Almanac*. New York: Ballantine Books.

Levins, Richard. (1986). Science and Progress: Seven Developmentalist Myths in Agriculture. *Monthly Review* 38(3): 13–20.

Lewontin, Richard. (1982). Agricultural Research and the Penetration of Capital. *Science for the People* 14(1): 12–17.

Locke, John. (1764). *Two Treatises of Government*. http://history.hanover.edu/ early/locke/j-l2-001.htm.

Lorentzen, Lois Ann. (1995). Bread and Soil of Our Dreams: Women, the Environment, and Sustainable Development—Case Studies from Central America. In *Ecological Resistance Movements*, ed. Bron Raymond Taylor. Albany: State University of New York Press.

Malthus, Thomas R. ([1798] 1970). *An Essay on the Principle of Population*. London: Penguin Books.

———. ([1798] 1965). *First Essay on Population*. New York: Augustus M. Kelley.

———. ([1815] 1969). *An Inquiry into the Nature and Progress of Rent and the Principles by Which It Is Regulated*. New York: Greenwood Press.

Marx, Karl, and Frederick Engels. (1968). Theses on Feuerbach. In *Selected Works*, 28–30. New York: International Publishers.

Marymount University Center for Ethical Concerns. (1999). The Consumer and Sweatshops. http://www.marymount.edu/news/garmentstudy/overview .html.

Memmi, Albert. (1967). *The Colonizer and the Colonized*. Boston: Beacon Press.

Mill, James. ([1817] 1858). *The History of British India.* London: James Madden, Piper, Stephenson and Spence.

Mill, J. S. ([1859] 1978). *On Liberty.* Indianapolis: Hackett Publishing Company.

———. (1965). *Principles of Political Economy.* Toronto: University of Toronto Press.

Minnesota v. Mille Lacs Band of Chippewa Indians. 000 U.S. 97–1337. http://www.oyez.org/oyez/resource/case/848/print.

Miswagon, John. (1999). *Remarks of the Pimicikamak Cree Nation/M.A.R.C. Inquiry into Northern Flood Situation.* Cross Lake, Manitoba: Pimicikamak Cree Nation, 1–8.

Mittal, Anuradha. (2001). Freedom to Trade?: Trading Away American Family Farms. Food First. http://www.foodfirst.org/pubs/backgrdrs/2001/f01v7n4.html.

Morse, Bradford, and Thomas Berger. (1992). *Sardar Sarovar: The Report of the Independent Review.* Ottawa: Resource Futures International, Inc.

Muir, John. ([1911] 1987). *My First Summer in the Sierra.* New York: Penguin Books.

Nader, Ralph, and Lori Wallach. (1996). GATT, NAFTA, and the Subversion of the Democratic Process. In *The Case against the Global Economy,* ed. Jerry Mander and Edward Goldsmith. San Francisco: Sierra Club Books.

Nussbaum, Martha. (1999). *Sex and Social Justice.* New York: Oxford University Press.

Perelman, Michael. (2000). *The Invention of Capitalism.* Durham, NC: Duke University Press.

Planned Parenthood. (2000). The Mexico City Policy and the Global Gag Rule. http://www.plannedparenthood.org/library/facts/030416_globalgag.html.

Rainforest Action Network. Fact Sheets. http://www.ran.org/info_center/fact sheets/.

———. (2003). "Facts About the Rainforest and Rates of Destruction." http://www.ran.org

Responsible Shopper. http://www.responsibleshopper.com/.

Roy, Arundhati. (1999). The Greater Common Good. In *The Cost of Living.* New York: Modern Library.

Rugmark. http://www.rugmark.org/.

Saro-Wiwa, Ken. (n.d.). Closing Statement to the Nigerian Military Appointed Tribunal. http://archive.greenpeace.org/~comms/ken/state.html.

———. (n.d.). Genocide in Nigeria. Niger Delta Congress. http://www.nigerdeltacongress.com/garticles/genocide_in_nigeria.htm.

———. (n.d.). The World Bank and Us. Industrial Worker. http://www.iww.org/~iw/jan/stories/worldban.html.

REFERENCES

Sen, Amartya. (1990). "More Than 100 Million Women Are Missing." *New York Review of Books* 37(20): 61–66.

———. ([1994] 1998). Population: Delusion and Reality. In *Applied Ethics: A Multicultural Approach*, ed. Larry May, Shari Collins-Chobanian, and Kai Wong. Upper Saddle River, NJ: Prentice Hall.

Sessions, George. (1993). Introduction (Deep Ecology) to *Environmental Philosophy: From Animal Rights to Radical Ecology*, ed. Michael E. Zimmerman, J. Baird Callicott, George Sessions, Karen J. Warren, and John Clark. Upper Saddle River, NJ: Prentice Hall.

Shelley, Mary. (1992). *Frankenstein*. New York: Penguin Group.

Shiva, Vandana. (1991). *The Violence of the Green Revolution: Third World Agriculture, Ecology and Politics*. London and Penang: Zed Books, Ltd. and Third World Network.

Slater, Candace. (1995). Amazonia as Edenic Narrative. In *Uncommon Ground: Toward Reinventing Nature*, ed. William Cronon. New York: Norton.

Sontag, Susan. (1973). *On Photography*. New York: Farrar, Straus and Giroux.

Stanley, Henry M. (1969). *Through the Dark Continent*. New York: Greenwood Press.

Stiglitz, Joseph. (2003). *Globalization and Its Discontents*. New York: Norton.

Sweatshop Watch. What Is a Sweatshop? http://www.sweatshopwatch .org/swatch/industry/.

SweatX. Clothes with a Conscience. http://www.sweatx.net/.

Third World Network. http://www.twnside.org.sg/.

Trachtenberg, Alan, ed. (1981). *Classic Essays on Photography*. Stony Creek, CT: Leete's Island Books.

Truman, Harry S. (1949). Inaugural Address. In *Inaugural Addresses of the Presidents*. Washington, D.C.: U.S. Congressional Budget Office.

Underwater World. http://www.underwaterworld.com/.

UNITE! *Stop Sweatshops Campaign*. http://www.uniteunion.org/sweatshops.

United Nations. (1948). Universal Declaration of Human Rights. http://www.un .org/Overview/rights.html.

———. (1990). United Nations Human Development Report 1990, chapter 1. http://hdr.undp.org/reports/global/1990/en/.

———. (2002). Human Development Report 2002, Human Development Indicators (PDF). http://hdr.undp.org/reports/global/2002/en/.

U.S. Congress. *Wilderness Act*. http://www.fs.fed.us/htnf/wildact.htm.

Williams, George Washington. (1988). An Open Letter to His Serene Majesty Leopold II, King of the Belgians and Sovereign of the Independent State of Congo. In *Heart of Darkness*, ed. Robert Kimbrough. New York: Norton.

Wolfensohn, James. (n.d.). Office of the President, Quotations. World Bank. http://web.worldbank.org/.

Working Assets. http://www.workingassets.com/.

World Conference against Racism. The Phantom of Racism: Racism and Indigenous Peoples. http://www.un.org/WCAR/e-kit/indigenous.htm.

World Resources Institute. (1994). *World Resources 1994–95: A Guide to the Global Environment*. New York: Oxford University Press.

INDEX

Godwin, William, xii, 77, 78, 80
Grace, W. R., 67
Green Mountain Coffee Roasters, 165
green revolution, 58–61, 82, 115, 117, 118
Greenpeace, 129, 139
Greystoke, Lord, vii, 27–28, 31
gross national product (GNP), 123. *See also* development
Guha, Ramachandra, 41–43
Gymboree, 162

Haileybury College, xii, 75–76
Haq, Mahbub ul, 123–24
Hardin, Garrett, xii, 6
Harvard mouse, 66, 192. *See also* private property
Hawkin, Paul, 168
health care, 125
Hegel, G. W. F., 55
herbicides, 21, 164
high yielding varieties of wheat, 58–59
Hilfiger, Tommy, 162
Himba people, 131. *See also* indigenous peoples
Hinduism, 101, 102, 117, 176
Hitler, Adolf, 190
Hopi people, 132. *See also* indigenous peoples
Huarani people, 13. *See also* indigenous peoples
Human Development Index (HDI), 123–26. *See also* development
human rights, 16. *See also* justice

identity, human. *See* colonialism
ideological superstructure (Marx), 103, 104

illegal workers, problem of, 65
Incas, 36. *See also* indigenous peoples
Indian Forest Act of 1878, 86
indigenous peoples, xiii, 7, 13, 14, 15, 16, 17, 20, 35–37, 41–42, 48, 60, 63, 65, 67, 69, 85, 99, 114, 115, 117, 118, 119–20, 131–32, 133, 135, 136, 185
Indira Gandhi National Park (India). *See* National Parks
Industrial Revolution, 27, 82, 95
intellectual property. *See* private property
International Forum on Globalization Indigenous Peoples' Project, 131
International Ladies' Garment Workers' Union, 160
International Monetary Fund (IMF), 21, 57, 62–63
International Nickel Company, 14
International Whaling Commission, 137
irrigation, 58
Islam, 85, 101, 102, 176

J. C. Penney, 162
J. Crew, 162
Jackson, Michael, 65
Jefferson, Thomas, 134, 194
Jim Crow laws, 39
Johnson, Keith, 138
Johnson, Lyndon, 59
Johnson vs. McIntosh, 135
justice: economic, 6, 7, 12, 49, 56–57, 70–73, 90–91, 93, 115–23, 156–73; environmental, x, 6, 7, 12, 13, 14, 16, 18, 25, 47, 73, 92, 97, 108, 114, 115–23, 130, 132, 140, 168, 170, 173; social, 6, 7, 12, 13, 14, 18, 25,

Nader, Ralph, 63
Narmada Bachao Andolan (NBA),
116, 119
Narmada Dam (India), 16, 115–19.
See also energy
National Charity Company, 44–45
National Coordinating Committee for
Salvadoran Women
(CONAMUS), 122
National Labor Committee, 162
National Parks, xii; Chitwan National
Park (Nepal), 8; Indira Gandhi
National Park (India), 9; Kanuzi
Biega National Park, 156; Yasuni
National Park, 121; Yosemite
National Park, 1, 3
nature: alienation from, 51, 55; vs.
culture, vii, 2, 12, 27–32, 37,
38–39, 51–55, 129, 130, 134
The Nature Company, 184
Nature Conservancy, 174
neem tree, 67
neocolonialism, 19, 25, 57, 72, 98, 159
Nestlé, 163, 164
Nicholas V (pope), 132
Nixon, Richard, 64
nonviolence, 101, 105–6
Nordstrom, 162, 182
Notestein, Frank, 94, 95

O'Connor, Justice Sandra Day, 135
Ogoni homeland (Nigeria), vii, 13,
70–71, 114. *See also* indigenous
peoples
oil production. *See* energy
Ojibwe, 135. *See also* indigenous
peoples
Old Navy, 162
ozone depletion, 168

pacifism, 45, 105
Panopticon (Bentham's prison), 44
Patagonia (clothing), 163, 170
Patent and Trademark Office (PTO), 66
patenting life. *See* private property
Patna Devi (goddess of the leaves), 42
PCBs (Polychlorinated Biphenyls), 132
per capita income, 56, 123. *See also*
development
Perelman, Michael, 43–44, 83
Perry, Admiral Matthew C., 59
pesticides, 21, 60, 68, 69, 164
Pizarro, Francisco, 36
Planned Parenthood, 128, 160
poaching, 44
poor laws, 78–79, 86
population, 6, 8, 13, 35–36, 40, 73,
74–97, 115; one child family
(China), 89–90
Porter, Jane, 29, 31
Potosí (mine in Bolivia), 36, 45
poverty (income vs. human), 125–26
primitive accumulation, 43–45, 83, 88
private property, 4, 84, 88, 133, 134,
186, 192; intellectual property, 21,
65–67, 69, 134, 192. *See also* terra
nullius
progress, 2, 9, 16, 33, 38, 40, 50, 55,
56, 68, 90, 94, 115, 140
Pueblo Indians, 191. *See also*
indigenous peoples

Quist, David, 149

racism, 23–24, 27–32, 100, 118, 132,
133, 144, 145, 146, 155, 171
Rainforest Action Network, 120, 160
Rainforest Café, 179–82, 186
rainforests, 7–8, 16, 67, 129

ABOUT THE AUTHOR

Deane Curtin is an environmental writer and a professor of philosophy. His interests focus on global environmental and social justice issues. Among his previous books is *Chinnagounder's Challenge: The Question of Ecological Citizenship*. Over the past three decades he has been a visiting professor in India, Japan, and England.

At Gustavus Adolphus College, Curtin served as the Raymond and Florence Sponberg Chair of Ethics. He teaches in the college's environmental studies program and founded the Community Development in India program, which sends American students to India each fall semester to study ethical community development.